THE POLITICS
OF THE

STUDIES IN SOCIAL
PHILOSOPHY & POLICY

THE POLITICS
OF THE PTA

Charlene K. Haar

transaction

Transaction Publishers
New Brunswick (USA) and London (UK)

Published by the Social Philosophy and Policy Center and Transaction Publishers 2002

Library of Congress Cataloging-in-Publication Data

Haar, Charlene K.
   The politics of the PTA / by Charlene K. Haar.
      p. cm. — (Studies in social philosophy and policy ; 22)
   Includes bibliographical references and index.
   ISBN 0-7658-0084-5 — ISBN 0-7658-0864-1 (pbk.)
   1. Parents' and teachers' associations — United States — History.   I. Title.
II. Studies in social philosophy and policy ; no. 22.

LC231 .H33 2001 2002
371.19′2′06 — dc21

                                                            2001020571

Cover Design: Lynne M. Newbound

Cover Image Credit: © Comstock Images

Series Editor: Ellen Frankel Paul
Series Managing Editor: Matthew Buckley

Contents

Acknowledgments

This book is the result of a series of unexpected events and associations. I extend sincere thanks to Victor Porlier for the initial suggestion to investigate one of America's icons. Thanks to all those along the journey who shared insights, documents, and data so that others may benefit from this study.

To my friend and colleague Myron Lieberman, for his encouragement, insight, and invaluable assistance throughout the project, I offer my deepest gratitude. His suggestions on how to organize the material—what to include and what to leave on the cutting-room floor—helped to bring this study to a conclusion. Also, I am especially indebted to Ellen Frankel Paul for her painstaking editing through numerous drafts.

Introduction

As a parent and high school teacher in Madison, South Dakota, I often worked closely with the parents of my students, especially the parents of gifted students. Each gifted student required an Individual Education Plan (IEP) that had to be reviewed with his or her parents. Regular progress reports and review sessions necessitated frequent conversations and periodic meetings with these parents. Routinely scheduled, district-wide parent-teacher conferences provided limited contact with the parents of other students, but I knew all my students well and most of their parents also.

On several occasions I worked closely with parents to help get something done. At various times, we fought the elimination of academic options, the reduction of curricular programs, or questionable changes in the school budget. Sometimes, parents simply sought unbiased information about proposed legislation concerning education, instead of the incomplete and often biased information available. Other situations required long-term parental sacrifice and commitment. Accepting the invitation for our award-winning band to march in the Macy's Thanksgiving Day Parade in New York City, for instance, involved a two-year commitment to raise adequate funds.

Each time my colleagues and I worked with parents, it was a rewarding experience. Most parents were eager to get involved. More often than not, however, parents did not have ready access to the information they wanted. The situation was very unsatisfactory, but I was not in a position to do anything about it.

After a career change in 1993, I hoped to launch a national organization for parents. Because the National PTA was not a presence in my district, my motivation did not derive from any strong feelings about this organization. My purpose was to enable parents to obtain information about proposed federal legislation; to provide reviews of education-related books and materials; and to encourage research, studies, and surveys. Communication to interested parents

1

would be through the Internet and timely newsletters. Ultimately, I hoped to host a weekly television program that would be of help to parents.

But I didn't do these things. Instead, I accepted an invitation to coauthor *The NEA and AFT: Teacher Unions in Power and Politics*.[1] In addition, a writing assignment in mid-1994 for Capital Research Center, a Washington, D.C. research organization, took me to the headquarters of the National PTA, located in downtown Chicago. For the better part of two days, the staff let me review documents, take notes, and even copy a few items. The research I did there was revealing, giving me important insights into the PTA's goals and strategies. My continued work on education issues led me to write this book.

While pursuing this project I have met hundreds of devoted, caring PTA members who deserve nothing but praise for their efforts to improve the education of our young people. This book is intended to help them succeed in this vital task. Regrettably, there are negative dimensions to the PTA that need to be discussed in a fair and objective way. In the following pages, I have tried to do this. Of course, readers will have to decide for themselves whether or not I have succeeded in this effort.

The Plan of This Book

There is no ideal way to organize a study of a large organization that has existed for over a century. The plan that I have adopted is a compromise between a historical approach to the organization as a whole and an effort to follow key issues over long periods of time. Chapter 1 is an overview of the organization. Chapter 2 is devoted to the founding era, and Chapter 3 traces the historical development of the organization up to 1924, when it adopted its present title. Chapter 4 explains how the PTA responded to World War I and its aftermath; peace, security, health, and nutrition issues were among the myriad of noneducational concerns tackled by the PTA during this time period. Chapter 5 analyzes the PTA's close relationship with the National Education Association before and after its conversion to a union, and how this relationship impacts the PTA's educational policies and operations. Chapters 6 and 7 are devoted to discussion of the PTA's political agenda and an examination of its involvement in Goals 2000 and other contemporary political issues. Chapter 8 examines the disconnect between parents' roles in fundraising at the local level and the National PTA's urging that they become advocates instead. Because the PTA treats parental involvement as an important reason to join the PTA, Chapter 9 is a critical analysis of the concept of parental involvement, including how parents can help their children learn more. Chapter 10 includes a brief discussion of other parent organizations and my thoughts about the future of the PTA.*

---

*A note on nomenclature: Technically, the subject of this book is the "National Congress of Parents and Teachers," but this is a cumbersome title to use repeatedly. Furthermore, in 1897, the organization was founded as the National Congress of Mothers; from 1908 to 1924 the organization was entitled the National Congress of Parent-Teacher Associations; and since 1924, the National Congress of Parents and Teachers has been the name of the organization. It is widely known as the PTA.

The organization has registered "National PTA" and "PTA" with the U.S. Patent and Trademark Office, as well as several other trademarks and service marks that include "PTA." Common usage often fails to distinguish between the local, state, and national levels of the organization, or all the levels combined. In this book, "the Mothers' Congress" refers to activities and programs during the period from 1897 to 1908; "the National Congress" refers to activities between 1908 and 1924. The "PTA" refers either to the national office only, or to the national, state, and local affiliates combined. The intended meaning is specified or should be clear from the context.

A word also about parent involvement. In some of its publications, the National PTA refers to diverse activities by parents as "parent involvement." A more grammatically correct presentation is "parental involvement," the phrase most often used in this text. Nevertheless, "parent involvement" is cited sometimes in a quotation or the ensuing discussion. The intended meaning is the same for both phrases.

In its publications, the U.S. Department of Education uses the more encompassing term "family" to mean the most significant adults in the lives of children, including grandparents, aunts and uncles, brothers and sisters, or even neighbors who provide child care. This inclusive definition is intended here, but the context may indicate that the conventional definition is intended.

1

About the PTA

At a time when our country is as stable financially as it has ever been, when our people are employed and we are at peace, we somehow can still not address the most basic needs of our children.

I speak not to cast blame, it is not about blame or to engage in hand-ringing [sic] despair, but to give us the motivation that we simply must change the country . . . . I believe we can do that because we are PTA.[1]

— Ginny Markell, president, National PTA, 2000

I. Introduction

The National Congress of Parents and Teachers, commonly referred to as "The PTA," is the fifth-largest voluntary organization in the United States. If past as well as present members are counted, it may have enrolled over its lifetime more members than any other existing organization.[2] Since at least as early as the 1920s, the PTA has been widely perceived as the primary representative of most public school parents and teachers. However, the PTA is now actually a minority player after almost four decades of decreasing membership.[3] This is not widely recognized because the term "PTA" is often applied to any school association of parents and teachers, including those not affiliated with the National PTA. In fact, most schools, public and private, have a parent or parent-faculty organization. These organizations may be limited in function, such as a booster club for athletics, debate, or band, a parent group that raises funds for

5

scholarships, or an advocacy group for the support of students with special needs. The scope of the function of such organizations notwithstanding, most parents are members of parent organizations not affiliated with the National PTA, or are not members of any parent organization.

II. The PTA's Mission

All organizational levels of the PTA—national, state, and local—exist to enhance the PTA's mission, which is, as stated in the National PTA's *PTA Handbook:*

- To support and speak on behalf of children and youth in the schools, in the community and before governmental bodies and other organizations that make decisions affecting children; and
- To assist parents in developing the skills they need to raise and protect their children; and
- To encourage parent and public involvement in the public schools of this nation.[4]

As a blueprint to fulfill its mission statement, the PTA developed the "Objects of the PTA." These are goals incorporated into the organization's bylaws, which establish the basic rules and procedures and management structure of the organization. The National PTA requires that the specific bylaws critical to maintaining organizational unity be identical at the national, state, and local levels. For example, the "Objects of the PTA" must be included in the bylaws of each state affiliate, as well as in the bylaws of each local PTA.

The "Objects of the PTA" are:

1. To promote the welfare of children and youth in home, school, community, and place of worship.
2. To raise the standards of home life.
3. To secure adequate laws for the care and protection of children and youth.
4. To bring into closer relation the home and the school, that parents and teachers may cooperate intelligently in the education of children and youth.
5. To develop between educators and the general public such united efforts as will secure for all children and youth the highest advantages in physical, mental, social, and spiritual education.[5]

The PTA's publications, conferences, conventions, committees, and activities are intended to support its legislative program. In addition to its advocacy concerning contemporary political issues, the National PTA determines its remaining advocacy agenda based on its "Statement of PTA Principles," resolutions, and board policy statements. Only two of the twelve "Principles" deal specifically with education: vocational-technical competence and educational opportunity. The other "Principles" are human values, spiritual faith, good homes, sound health, safety, conservation of natural resources, constructive leisure, human relations, civic responsibility, and international understanding. The PTA seeks to achieve these objectives through its lobbying efforts in the state legislatures and in Washington, D.C.

As organizations exempt from federal income tax under Section 501(c)(3) of the Internal Revenue Code, PTA affiliates must comply with the IRS rules governing tax-exempt organizations. In addition, PTA rules require that all organizational levels operate in a noncommercial, nonsectarian, and nonpartisan way. The National PTA also restricts the manner in which state and local PTAs can cooperate with other organizations. Of course, in a multimillion-member organization, these restrictions are sometimes overlooked.

III. Membership and Dues

Despite sketchy membership data, a picture of today's PTA emerges from PTA documents, polling data, interviews, and education statistics. At the start of the 2000–2001 school year, 53 million students in kindergarten through twelfth grade were enrolled in over 118,000 public and private elementary and secondary schools in the United States; of this student population, about 11 percent were enrolled in private schools and 89 percent were enrolled in public schools.[6]

The PTA claims approximately 6.5 million members. If all were parents, the PTA would enroll members of about 22 percent of all families with school-age children. Using only very rough figures, however, I estimate that the PTA enrolls members from only 10 percent of such families. The PTA's figure of 6.5 million members does not take into account several factors: the discrepancy between the membership claimed in publications and the amount of dues collected; the double (or triple) counting of parents with more than one child in different schools; the number of members who join because they are teachers or administrators, not because they are parents; the fact that many of these members are in special classes of membership that do not have voting rights; and the fact that many of these members are school students.[7]

Local affiliates, or units, of the National PTA operate in approximately 25,000 of the 118,276 public and private elementary and secondary schools that enrolled students during the 1997–98 school year.[8] This is probably an overestimate, since some PTA publications refer to 24,000 local affiliates and an April 1995 internal PTA document referred to "21,849 PTA schools."[9]

When local units drop their affiliation with the National PTA, their individual members depart from the national organization as well. This attrition, coupled with the fact that over two hundred child-advocacy organizations compete with the PTA for members, renders it more difficult than ever to increase PTA membership.[10] In fact, PTA membership has continued to decline after reaching a peak of 12,131,318 in 1962–63. Furthermore, there are over 2.8 million teachers in the nation's public schools, but no one knows how many are counted as dues-paying members of the PTA. Because the National PTA relies on summaries submitted by state PTAs compiled from local PTA data, the national office cannot identify its members, nor does it maintain a membership list by names. Conversely, many members are not even aware of the existence of the National PTA or their membership in it.[11]

Local PTAs submit summaries of total membership to their respective state PTA office, which combines them in reports to the national office. Even without any national membership database, the total amount the National PTA collects in member dues should correspond to the product of annual dues times national members; it rarely does, however. The PTA's 1997–98 annual report states that the organization collected $6,201,805 in membership dues in 1998, when dues were $1.00 per year. This figure, however, is significantly lower than what one would expect given the PTA's claims of 6.5 million members. The *National PTA Annual Reports* indicate that 245,244 members dropped their PTA membership from school year 1993–94 to 1996–97, and 209,509 more left the PTA from 1996–97 to 1997–98. National PTA internal documents show total membership of slightly over 6.5 million members; however, no corresponding paid-membership dues were included in the documents.[12]

The PTA's board of directors in 1998 implemented a pilot program to collect demographic data on PTA members in selected locals. This data-collection effort arose more from its potential use in attracting advertisers than from the PTA's interest in an accurate membership count. Also in 1998, new membership categories were added to solicit contributions from those who do not fit the standard membership categories of parents and teachers. In an on-line appeal, the PTA website suggests that visitors choose "to make a difference in the lives of children and youth" by contributing in one of four categories, each carrying recognition and subscription rights, but not voting or representation rights at state and national conventions. National PTA contribution categories now include: Supporter, $25–$99; Contributor, $100–$999; Patron, $1,000–$4,999; and Benefactor, $5,000.

Members whose dues are current are entitled to voting rights and are eligible to seek elected or appointed positions within the organization. Depending upon local provisions, some Parent-Teacher-Student Associations (PTSAs) also accept dues-paying student members. An Honorary National Life Membership carries no voting rights unless the unified dues (local, state, and national) have been paid to a local PTA. The PTA bestows such memberships upon people who have distinguished themselves in service to children and youth. The PTA bylaws stipulate that the sponsor of the person proposed for honorary life membership in the National PTA "shall make a contribution . . . in recognition of the selection of the nominee."[13] Life-membership contributions, often $100 per life member, must be deposited into the National PTA Endowment Fund, a special fund established in 1915. The PTA reported life-membership revenue of $39,950 during 1999, up from $4,575 during 1998. According to an audit report, as of December 31, 1999, the endowment fund of the National PTA had a balance of $3,394,108.[14]

About 75 percent of local PTAs operate in conjunction with a public elementary school; in fact, the name of the local PTA typically includes the name of the school with which it is affiliated. There are considerably fewer PTAs in junior high schools, and fewer still at the high school level. In short, parents are less involved in the PTA as their children progress through school. Young mothers (eighteen to thirty-nine), and those who are separated or divorced, with a high school or less education, are slightly more likely than college graduates to be active members of a local PTA. Of approximately 25,000 local affiliates, about one-fourth operate in midsized cities (in schools that enroll 300 to 1,000 students), 36 percent operate in schools in large cities, 14 percent operate in large and small towns, 12 percent serve urban schools, and 12 percent operate in rural areas. Local PTAs seldom exist in schools that enroll 200 or fewer students.[15] Parents in the Midwest are the least likely to be PTA members. California is the only state in which PTA membership exceeds one million, followed by Texas with over three-quarters of a million. At the other extreme, Maine, Vermont, and Wyoming have fewer than 3,000 members each.

The PTA has divided its membership into eight geographic regions to facilitate management of the association. Regional directors conduct regional meetings convened during the annual National PTA convention. For organizational purposes, some regional PTAs divide their territory into districts or councils as well.

Although membership is not formally restricted to parents of children in public schools, the PTA's rules, messages, and positions in effect discourage membership by parents and teachers of children in private schools. Furthermore, public school parents are often dismayed to find that they must pay dues in order to participate in discussions and decisions at PTA meetings; dues requirements, therefore, may serve to discourage PTA membership of public school parents.

With a few exceptions, such as preschools, kindergartens, Head Start programs, and a recently chartered gay/lesbian chapter in Greater Puget Sound, local PTAs operate through public schools and typically sponsor programs intended to benefit particular public schools. PTA meetings are held in schools, and PTAs frequently use the school mail system and school facilities. Students carry PTA messages home from school. Despite the National PTA's bylaws that prohibit the practice, teachers sometimes utilize pupils to carry home political messages approved by PTA leaders.[16]

Each local PTA determines its own fundraising agenda and activities, while depending upon school facilities for its base of operations. Even if a local PTA affiliate were to meet elsewhere and take no interest in a school or in educational affairs, it could still be a local affiliate in good standing with the National PTA. Practically speaking, however, if school administrators did not allow PTAs to meet in the schools, the entire PTA structure would probably collapse quickly. For this reason, the National PTA urges local PTA leaders to include school principals in their meetings, but not necessarily in PTA planning sessions. Local affiliates are urged to maintain a distinct identity from the school that they serve, including separate goals, bank accounts, and agendas, in order to avoid the appearance of either being in lockstep with the school's administration or antagonistic toward it. Despite these school-PTA relationships, the National PTA insists that local PTAs are autonomous bodies not affiliated with any school board or school.

The National PTA's legal position is that it is not legally affiliated with schools at any level. This issue emerged in an interesting way. The Governmental Accounting Standards Board (GASB) is a nonprofit organization that seeks to clarify and improve accounting standards for state and local governments. The GASB standards are widely accepted by state and local governments, and are generally considered authoritative in state and local government financial accounting. According to GASB Statement No. 14, approved in 1992, "primary governments" (here, state and local governments) are required to include in their financial statements "information about the component units [nonprofit organizations, like the PTA, that operate within a school district to raise funds for district schools] and their relationships with the primary government."[17] As originally proposed, Statement No. 14 would have required the disclosure, in school financial reports, of fundraising revenue earned, and expenditures made, by the National PTA on behalf of a school or school district. The National PTA strongly objected to the proposed standard. Legal counsel for the National PTA pointed out that

> each local PTA is a part of NPTA [the National PTA], a 99 year-old national organization dedicated to a variety of purposes relating to the welfare of all children and youth in the home, school, community, and place of worship. Although PTAs are organized on a national, state and local level, no state or local PTA is affiliated with any primary government. Any reference to a particular school, local school system or state educational system made in organizational documents or an Application for Recognition of Exemption under Internal Revenue Code ("IRC") section 501(c)(3) would be incidental to these various purposes and only to locate the given PTA unit within the broader national structure.[18]

After additional considerations, the PTA and other organizations succeeded in changing the designation of their relationships with primary governments. Such organizations are now referred to within Statement No. 14 as "nonaffiliated organizations." After discussion of disclosure options, the GASB announced that it would issue a revised Exposure Draft in mid-2001 regarding Statement No. 14. As in the past, therefore, school district financial reports do not yet include financial data in a separate column of the financial statement disclosing local PTA revenues, even if local PTAs are completely devoted to school activities—and most are. The National PTA's opposition to the originally proposed Statement No. 14 standard is not surprising given the PTA's legislative agenda. Although public schools are the National PTA's organizing base, school affairs are not its primary interest, as will become evident.

Local PTA dues vary, but are often less than $10.00 per person each year. In addition, most local PTAs engage in several annual fundraising activities. Each local PTA collects and forwards the mandatory $1.75 (as of April 1, 2002) annual per capita dues to the state affiliate for transmittal to the National PTA. The local PTA is obligated to follow the same procedure for state PTA dues, which range from $.50 to nearly $5.00 per member each year.

IV. Sources of Revenue

Although per capita dues are the primary source of funds for the state PTAs and the National PTA, both of these organizational levels supplement dues income with revenue generated from investments, training programs, legislative conferences, convention exhibits, merchandise sales, and government grants.

Dues

Dues constitute 80 percent of the National PTA's revenue. National membership dues from 1992–94 were $.75 per member. As the debate to increase dues moved through the state PTA conventions in 1994 and 1995, Arnold Fege, then director of the PTA's governmental relations office in Washington, suggested that national dues should be $25.00 or more per year even though some members would drop out as a result. Fege argued that those who remained would be committed to the PTA agenda. The incumbent National PTA leaders argued against the increase in dues and also against a proposal to allow one membership fee to cover two or more children in different schools. Although their rhetoric emphasized membership availability for low-income parents, PTA leaders may have preferred $1.00 dues because most parents would not be concerned about an organization to which they pay such a minimal amount. In contrast, dues of $25.00 might encourage members to scrutinize the association's operations and policies more closely.

In 1995, delegates to the national convention raised National PTA dues to $1.00 per member, per year; delegates in 2000 raised this figure to $1.25, and delegates in 2001 raised it to $1.75 (effective April 2002). Prior to the convention vote in 2000, most PTA leaders urged delegates to approve a 100 percent dues increase—from $1.00 to $2.00.[19] Ultimately, only a $.25 increase in dues was approved that year, but PTA leaders are certain to propose subsequent increases along the lines of that approved in 2001 as they move toward implementing a new long-term, expensive public relations and advocacy program for the organization. In 2000, reacting to delegates' concerns over the likely membership losses if the $1.00 increase were approved, the PTA's director of public relations said, "We want people who are committed to this agenda, and if they're not, that's fine. Go be a PTO and have a nice life."[20] (Independent, parent-teacher organizations [PTOs] are not affiliated with the PTA hierarchy.) This attitude signifies a departure from the National PTA's legacy of keeping dues very low to attract all parent groups.

Other Revenue

The Headquarters Building Fund includes proceeds from the sale of the property used as the National PTA headquarters from 1954 to 1993. On November 7, 1996, the government of Thailand bought the PTA's Chicago property for $3.1 million. After depreciation and other expenses, the PTA reported proceeds of $2,595,357 from the sale. With the sale of its headquarters building and land, the PTA has greatly increased its income from investments. Investment gains, interest, and dividends generated more than $2 million for the PTA in 1998, and $1.4 million in 1999.

Additionally, according to the aforementioned auditors' report, the National PTA derived 6 percent ($564,333) of its total 1999 revenue of $9 million from convention fees. Subscriptions to the PTA newsletter, "What's Happening in Washington," *Our Children* magazine, and the PTA's pay-for-view website accounted for about $383,000.[21]

Corporate Sponsors

Tax-deductible contributions are also often a major source of income for not-for-profit organizations, such as the PTA, that are classified by the IRS as 501(c)(3)s. However, at no time during 1992–99 did such contributions comprise more than 8.5 percent of the National PTA's annual income. Usually, contributions were less than 5 percent. In fact, in 1996–97, corporations and non-member individuals contributed only 1.5 percent of the National PTA's total annual revenue. Outside consultants have advised the PTA that its current revenue base of 80 percent dues and only 20 percent from other sources is a dangerous risk to the organization's survival. These consultants recommend a revenue base that relies on 50 percent from dues, 25 percent from grants, investments, and services, and 25 percent from sponsors.[22]

To achieve membership approval of corporate sponsorships, the National PTA hosted a workshop on the topic at the 1998 national convention. PTA leaders had negotiated corporate sponsorships with five companies, including Office Depot. Discussion materials, prepared in consultation with the National PTA parliamentarian and legal counsel, assured doubting PTA members that sponsorship was not an endorsement of a company or company product; endorsement of either is prohibited by the National PTA bylaws. "Corporate sponsorship," on the other hand, "is a funding mechanism in which a commercial concern provides cash, products, or know-how to a charitable or educational organization in return for an acknowledgment of thanks. The acknowledgment of thanks generally takes the form of public recognition for the sponsor's support."[23]

The workshop handout also declared that for decades, corporate sponsorship agreements had "enhanced" PTA programs and projects. The handout cited sponsorship by the National Broadcasting Company (NBC) in 1942 of *Family in War,* a PTA radio program which focused on family activities in wartime. When the program continued beyond its scheduled thirteen-week run, other advertisers helped sponsor the program. In recent years, some PTA publications and videos have acknowledged corporate sponsors. Corporate sponsors have made their mark at past National PTA conventions as well. Bottled water by Dannon has been included in Target tote bags distributed to conventioneers. Microsoft and Family Education Network representatives have made presentations during general sessions, and the Schering-Plough Corporation has conducted a program session and distributed a survey about its asthma products to delegates.

Two months after the 1998 convention, newspaper headlines read: "PTA under Fire for Letting Advertiser Use Its Name."[24] The issue arose because Office Depot had used the PTA name and logo in back-to-school advertisements in its stores, in print, and on television. PTA leaders had agreed to the arrangement for an undisclosed fee, laptop computers for every state and National PTA office, teacher appreciation breakfasts, discounts for PTA members, and a back-to-school sweepstakes for teachers.

When corporate sponsorship came up for discussion again at the 1999 convention, a delegate asked if the PTA's membership had increased because of Office Depot sponsorship. The answer was "No." Office Depot representatives, however, acknowledged significantly increased sales as a result of the partnership.[25] In 1999, Office Depot literature included coupons to be presented by customers at the time of their next Office Depot purchase indicating that Office Depot would donate as much as $50,000 to the National PTA.[26] In return for purchasing $100.00 of merchandise, Office Depot would contribute up to $5.00 to the National PTA. In addition to renewing its arrangement with Office Depot, the PTA in 1999 adopted guidelines for corporate sponsorship. It also reported that for the first time, corporate sponsors had "more than fully funded" a National PTA convention.[27]

At its convention in June 2000, the National PTA included two sessions on corporate sponsorships, including instructions on how PTAs could enter into and evaluate corporate sponsorship agreements. Paula Cozzi Goedert, the legal counsel for the National PTA who conducted the convention sessions, advised PTA delegates to "get as much as we can for as little as we can." She urged local PTAs not to underestimate the positive image of PTA in negotiating with potential sponsors for cash contributions.

Some local PTAs reported complications when potential corporate sponsors at the local level were preempted by National PTA corporate sponsorship agreements. For example, a competitor to Dannon Natural Spring Water refused to help sponsor a local PTA event because Dannon is a corporate sponsor of the National PTA. Similarly, schools that have also jumped onto the corporate sponsorship bandwagon can cause problems for the PTA. If a school has agreed to an exclusive provider provision, and the local PTA is holding an event at the school, the exclusive provider (for instance, Coca-Cola) may refuse to allow Pepsi products to be available at the PTA event. With willing corporate sponsors and eager PTAs, these complications are likely to continue.[28]

Despite its recommendation that local PTAs disclose corporate sponsorship revenue, the National PTA considers its corporate sponsorship revenue information to be off-limits to PTA members; no detailed information on the subject is included in the National PTA's audited financial statements.

Federal Grants

Federal agencies fund or cosponsor several PTA projects. In fiscal year (FY) 1997–98, the National PTA received a $30,000 grant from the U.S. Department of Education Star School program to assist the PTA in implementing its parent involvement standards in schools, and a $100,000 supplemental grant from the Centers for Disease Control (CDC) through the American School Health Association for a nationwide study of PTA affiliates' health program needs. Previously, the CDC had provided funds for the production and distribution of HIV-AIDS brochures.

In June 1995, the PTA entered into a cooperative agreement with the Environmental Protection Agency (EPA). This initial three-year project included publications, environmental awareness training workshops, and minigrants to state affiliates. The EPA contributed approximately $250,000 (95 percent of the cost of the project) per year for each of the three years; in 1998, the agreement was extended for another three years. The PTA uses the funds to promote environmental policies on which it has position statements or resolutions, such as policies on testing for radon and lead, pesticide uses, and indoor air quality. Along with the EPA, several other government agencies pay the PTA for exhibit space at the National PTA's annual convention.

V. Annual Convention and Officers

The PTA's largest deliberative and voting body is the annual national convention. In addition to the state PTA president, one delegate for each one thousand active members (or major fraction thereof) is elected or selected according to the bylaws of each state's PTA. Under this formula, approximately 6,500 members could qualify as delegates to the national convention; typically, however, only about 1,500–2,000 delegates attend the convention. (Interestingly, fewer delegates and guests attended the 1996 centennial convention than attended the first convention in 1897, when there was no organization.) Of the 1,921 convention delegates in 1998, 37.5 percent were first-time delegates. All convention delegates have the right to introduce motions, participate in debate, and vote at the business meetings; however, the rules governing the introduction of new issues at the convention ensure leadership control. Delegates serving in the odd-numbered years elect the national officers.

With the exception of the California PTA convention, which usually hosts more delegates (5,000 in 1998) than the national convention, only a few hundred delegates attend PTA state conventions.

Delegates to the 2001 National PTA convention adopted a complete revision of the National PTA bylaws. Significant changes included: reducing the number of executive officers from seven to three—president, president-elect, and secretary-treasurer; reducing the National PTA board of directors from eighty-seven members to twenty-eight; broadening the National PTA's seven committees (bylaws and policy, finance, resource development, field service, membership, legislation, and board development and nominating) to include appointments by the National PTA president from the PTA membership at large; and creating the sixty-six-member National Council of States. Each of the three executive officers now serve one two-year term.

Candidates for national office, PTA officers and regional directors, are selected by a seven-member nominating committee. However, additional nominations may be made from the floor if proper qualifications are submitted in writing to the National PTA president thirty days prior to the beginning of the national convention. In 1999 and in several previous years, some nominees from the convention floor waged successful challenges to the PTA's slate of candidates, despite the fact that the rules governing nominations from the floor had been tightened.

Kathryn Whitfill served as National PTA president from 1993–95. Independent, quick with a quip, and a straight-talkin' Texan, Whitfill oversaw significant changes during her term—most of which tightened control from the top.

In 1994, Whitfill had cited data from focus groups and PTA polls as the rationale for proposing extensive amendments to the National PTA bylaws. These changes took effect at the 1995 convention.

Several changes related to PTA officers. After 1995, all elections for national officers are held in odd years only. Another bylaw change requires that one serve on the national board of directors if one wishes to be eligible for nomination or election to national office. This change prevents rank-and-file members from unexpectedly challenging a slate candidate for national office by nomination from the floor. Challengers can still come from within the ranks of those who serve or have served on the national board. Organizational continuity was cited as the main reason for the changes.

Some rank-and-file members had a different view of the motivation behind the changes. They declared that the bylaw changes were made to thwart any sudden takeover of the PTA by the Christian Right or other organizations deemed to be "radical right" or "right-wing extremists" by the PTA leadership. To tighten top-down control even further, particularly in local affiliates, the PTA amended its bylaws in 1996 to allow only dues-paying PTA members to attend PTA meetings. To avoid takeovers by small groups, additional requirements passed in 1997 included a provision that the "[b]ylaws of each constituent organization shall include a provision establishing a quorum."[29]

Floor nominations at the 1995 National PTA convention gave rise to some additional bylaw changes passed later. In 1995, delegates nominated seven contenders to oppose the slate nominees. Two such challengers won handily in their respective regions, defeating the slate nominees; however, a floor challenger failed in her preplanned strike against Joan Dykstra, the slate nominee for president. In surviving the challenge, Dykstra was the last incumbent vice president to become president. Following Dykstra's election, bylaw changes eliminated the direct election of the National PTA president. Instead, delegates must now elect as the president-elect an individual who has served for at least four years on the national board of directors. After two years, the president-elect automatically ascends to the position of National PTA president for a two-year term.

In their campaigns for office, both slate and floor nominees refer almost exclusively to their PTA credentials. Each résumé cites an extensive list of national, state, district, regional, council, and local PTA activities and honors; business and professional experience receives only limited attention, if any. In recent contests for national office, only candidates for treasurer—a post whose occupant oversees $8–12 million in annual national revenue—cited their professional experience as important. Of the twenty-three candidates in 1995, nine were grandparents, and ten were public school teachers, administrators, or school district employees. Affiliation with the teacher unions or other unions of school district employees is seldom mentioned. Candidates realize that since the

PTA is widely regarded as a parents' organization, teacher union membership might have a negative effect on their candidacy. Given the length of service required before becoming eligible to hold a national office, many candidates are grandmothers who became PTA members when their children were in school.

To become acquainted with the candidates, delegates are invited to mingle with them during an evening reception at the national convention. As delegates sip iced tea or fruit punch, campaign workers hand out buttons, candy with slogans attached, and candidate biographies to persuade delegates. Voting is a formal affair, requiring delegate documentation, polling rules, and electronic balloting. As in the past, however, these elections continue to be a shuffling of the chairs, not a significant change in leadership or policies.

Amidst the personality parade in 1995, only treasurer candidate Bill Austin campaigned about serious issues. He pointed out that while the former PTA headquarters building in Chicago had been vacant since 1993, the PTA was spending $34,000 per month for spacious leased offices on the twenty-first floor of the IBM building three blocks away. The PTA board had put the property on the market after investigating the costs of upgrading electrical capabilities to allow for the installation of computers. Renovation was further complicated by the presence of asbestos in the 1954 structure.

Austin expressed concern about the drain on the national treasury and the continued cost to PTA members as the former headquarters remained vacant and the PTA paid monthly rent for nearby offices. Most members were completely unaware that this situation existed because PTA leaders never mentioned the problem to convention delegates. Furthermore, most delegates were not aware that the dues increase to $1.00 per member, per year that was adopted in 1995 would generate more than enough funding to cover the "dual headquarters problem." Only a handful of delegates heard Austin's message at the candidates' reception, and even Austin did not mention his concerns in his speech before the delegates. He lost to the slate nominee by 311 votes out of 1,183 votes cast.

In 1997, under the previously adopted bylaw changes, all officers were up for election. Lois Jean White, the 1995 president-elect, automatically ascended to the presidency. The nominating committee presented its slate, which included Catherine Belter, a public librarian in Fairfax County, Virginia and PTA volunteer lobbyist who worked closely with the PTA's governmental relations staff. Belter had waged an unsuccessful floor challenge to Dykstra in 1995, when Belter received slightly more than one-third of the votes.

Belter, a long-time PTA activist, now the nominating committee's candidate, lost again in 1997. In her speech to the delegates, she urged them to "get on board as we take the PTA train forward into the twenty-first century." Her candidacy was derailed by Ginny Markell, a floor nominee from Clackamas, Oregon. Markell sprinkled her campaign literature with pictures of herself with

President Bill Clinton and Vice President Al Gore. Without any specifics, she pledged to "continue to collaborate and form stronger coalitions with both new and existing partners."[30] Markell, a public school teacher and registered nurse, was one of the few candidates who included her membership in the National Education Association (NEA) as part of her current activities. Of three candidates nominated from the floor, Markell was the only winner. She defeated slate candidate Belter to become the 1997–99 president-elect. After another defeat, Belter turned to politics at home; with Democrats backing her, she was elected to the Fairfax, Virginia school board in 1999.

New business in 1998 included the adoption of another bylaw amendment to curtail unexpected nominations from the floor. The condition it establishes was mentioned above: "Nominees running from the floor must give thirty (30) days notification before the beginning of the national convention of their intent to run."[31] Although some convention delegates dissented, most accepted the proponents' arguments that this was a fairness issue for both the slate candidate and the floor-nominated candidate. The delegates were told that in the absence of the amendment, a slate candidate with no known opposition might not invest in campaign materials; a floor-nominated candidate, on the other hand, could come prepared to launch a surprise challenge, thereby gaining an unfair advantage over the slate candidate.

Despite restrictive bylaws, the uprising against the nominating committee slate reached unprecedented levels in the 1999 National PTA convention; seven of eight floor-nominated candidates defeated slate nominees for the positions of officer and region director. With so many unfilled delegate slots, it is possible for a few state PTAs to collaborate in order to get their candidates elected to national office. Candidates who meet the requirements of nomination from the floor can be successful when strategies are coordinated in advance. One of the seven winners in 1999, Shirley Igo of Texas, defeated the slate nominee for president-elect and will serve as president for the 2001–2003 term.

The 2001 bylaw changes constitute severe restrictions on who is eligible for the National PTA office. For example, the president-elect must make at least an eight-year commitment to head the national organization. She must serve at least four years on the National PTA board, another two years as president-elect, then two years as president. She is also expected to be a PTA leader in a local or state affiliate. Needless to say, the implication that delegates must not be allowed to elect officers who do not meet these onerous requirements is not a compliment to their ability to choose their leaders. Obviously, single parents and young couples who must support their families cannot attend all of the state and national conventions that one must attend to be a viable candidate for national office. All of the PTA's officers and other members of its board of directors are volunteers who serve without compensation, although they are reimbursed for any expenses incurred in connection with their PTA duties and responsibilities. Inevitably, full-time grandmothers and a few grandfathers will continue to control the National PTA.

VI. The National PTA Board of Directors

The National PTA's twenty-eight-member board of directors consists of the three national officers, seven National Council of States (NCS) representatives chosen by the NCS, ten PTA members elected by convention delegates, and eight individuals (six PTA members and two students) appointed by the PTA president. This twenty-eight-member board, which resulted from the bylaw changes adopted in 2001, is smaller than the PTA's previous board of eighty-seven members; regional PTA directors and state PTA presidents no longer serve on the board. The board meets four times each year to manage the affairs of the National PTA, act on recommendations by the NCS, approve the PTA budget, and establish PTA policies and legislative agendas. In addition, board members frequently attend state meetings and participate in training sessions at state and national conferences.

At the national convention, national officers and board members serve as workshop speakers, moderators, and hosts for the numerous sessions. For example, in 2000 (when there were seven PTA executive officers rather than the current three), a vice president presented a session on "Supervising Volunteers"; another explained how to "Build Successful Partnerships"; and the treasurer conducted a session on "Tips for Treasurers" that covered identifying local PTA financial problems, developing a basic financial disaster recovery plan, and taking precautions when fundraising.

VII. PTA Staff

As we might expect, the PTA staff carries out the day-to-day operations of the organization. As in other organizations with volunteer officers and transient membership, the staff remains a permanent and stabilizing force. Indeed, some PTA employees have been with the organization for twenty-five years. Needless to say, although the staff is formally subordinate to the elected officers, it exercises a major role in shaping the PTA's policies and programs.

Approximately fifty-six full-time employees work at the PTA's headquarters in downtown Chicago; another four employees handle lobbying activities from its Washington office. As listed in the 2000 convention program, the National PTA's departments and the number of staff assigned to each are as shown in Table 1.

Usually, staff dominate organizations with transient membership, especially if the leadership positions are subject to term limits. In the case of the PTA,

Table 1. 2000 National PTA Staff and Assignments

PTA Department	Number of Staff Assigned
Executive Director's Office	4
Human Resources	2
Meetings	3
Public Relations	2
Development	2
Accounting	6
Office Services	5
Information Systems	8
Program	6
Communications	9
Field Service	3
Membership	2
Customer Service	3
Legislative—Washington, D.C.	4

Source: 104th Annual National PTA Convention and Exhibition program, June 24–26, 2000, 49.

however, the top national officers hold office for several years. Even though there is some shuffling of positions, the elected officers are more influential than one might expect from the governance structure.

PTA public relations staff and lobbyists led ten of sixty workshop sessions at the 1999 PTA convention in Portland, Oregon, and six of forty-six sessions at the 2000 convention in Chicago, Illinois. By design, the PTA staff is not prominent at the national conventions; in fact, the absence of staff recognition at the annual conventions is remarkable. An exception occurred in 2000 when the convention was held a few blocks from National PTA headquarters; Markell, the PTA president, introduced each staff member who joined her on stage.

VIII. Employee Salaries and Benefits

Internal Revenue Service Form 990, which must be filed yearly by all tax-exempt organizations, requires information about such organizations' staff compensation. In 2000, the National PTA paid $3,357,891 for salaries, pension plan contributions, benefits, and payroll taxes for PTA employees. Table 2 shows the compensation of the PTA's five highest-paid employees as of December 31, 2000. In addition, the PTA paid $25,815 for accounting fees in 2000, and $14,466 for legal fees.

National PTA staff compensation appears to be considerably lower than in the other major national education organizations. An estimate indicates that in

Table 2. Compensation of National PTA Staff, January 1–December 31, 2000

Title	Compensation ($)	Contributions to Employee Benefit Plans and Deferred Compensation ($)	Expenses
Executive Director	115,832	4,419	0
Director, Development	82,000	9,973	0
Information Systems Director	76,875	4,311	0
Legislative Director	70,840	8,102	0
Public Relations Director	70,156	4,279	0

Source: IRS Form 990, Return of Organization Exempt from Income Tax, National Congress of Parents and Teachers.

1996, the NEA and the American Federation of Teachers (AFT) (with combined memberships of 3 million educational and support staff) employed over 6,000 people, with more than half earning over $100,000 annually in salaries and fringe benefits.[32] Although PTA staff compensation is rather modest compared to compensation in other large national associations, it may be generous in terms of the qualifications of its managerial personnel. Like its officers, very few PTA staff have graduate degrees or impressive managerial or professional experience outside the PTA.

IX. PTA Services and Materials

According to its literature, the National PTA's "services, materials and resources enable each PTA in the network and the millions of individual members to be more effective."[33] Unfortunately, it is difficult to identify any services that an individual receives as a result of National PTA membership. Meetings often require a registration fee in addition to out-of-pocket transportation and housing expenses. Access to the PTA website is also available to nonmembers.

Despite advancements in technology, the National PTA is unable to contact individual members, and there is no immediate plan to remedy this weakness. In her remarks at the Region 8 meeting of delegates at the 2000 convention, Ginny Markell said that the PTA's new strategic plan calls for state PTAs to be the National PTA's primary customer.[34] Along with increased advocacy efforts, a new focus of the National PTA will be to train state PTA leaders, who will in turn develop strong regional, council, and unit PTAs into effective advocates for public education.

National PTA services consist largely of inexpensive publications, access to PTA programs, such as its successful arts competition for students, and advocacy training and leadership development.

Publications

Most PTA publications are available to nonmembers as well as members for a nominal fee, hence membership per se does not provide any unique benefits in this regard. The PTA sends its magazine, *Our Children,* to local PTA presidents and other leaders. The magazine, and the PTA's legislative newsletter, "What's Happening in Washington," are also posted on the National PTA website.[35] In 1999, the PTA reported magazine subscription sales of fewer than 31,000 copies. In addition, the National PTA produces materials, kits, brochures, videos, and posters to assist in developing membership, raising pupil self-esteem, working with teachers and school administration, team-building, and promoting the arts. All materials are available for a nominal charge through catalog sales, at the national convention, or from the PTA's website.

Some PTA publications are developed with corporate or government grants. With assistance provided by J.C. Penney and the Mexican American Legal Defense and Educational Fund, the PTA reworked a booklet entitled *The Busy Parent's Guide to Involvement in Education* into a Spanish video on how to encourage children to enjoy school and work with their teachers. The Getty Center for Education in the Arts funded several brochures that explain why arts education should be part of every school curriculum. In cooperation with the NEA, the PTA offers advice on how to improve homework skills and utilize parent-teacher conferences effectively. Funded by the Centers for Disease Control and Prevention, the PTA developed "How to Talk to Your Teens and Children about AIDS," also available in Spanish. *Our World* is the PTA's environmental newsletter, funded by the U.S. Environmental Protection Agency. Sprint, Allstate, and Kellogg supported the "Ebony/National PTA Guide to Student Excellence" video, in conjunction with the Yale Child Study Center, Johnson Publishing Inc., and Conrad Productions. Though these materials might be helpful to PTA members, several commercial and nonprofit publications cover the same topics.

The National PTA also sells logo jewelry, T-shirts, sweatshirts, cups, note cards, tote bags, ties, and other items. PTA officials no longer report the number of items sold, but the National PTA reported revenues of $321,382 from all publications and fundraising items during FY 1996–97.

The Reflections Program

Reflections is the only program sponsored by the National PTA that appears to involve children directly. Reflections is an arts program for pupils from kindergarten through grade twelve. Each year, more than a dozen experts in the arts judge student work in four categories: literature, musical composition, photography, and the visual arts. In 1999, 11,783 local PTAs participated in the competition, averaging fifty-eight entrants each, for a total of 684,436 entrants. The experts grant three awards of excellence and five awards of merit to winning students in each of four grade divisions. Each year, several hundred thousand students respond with their interpretation of a child-suggested theme such as "Wouldn't it be great if . . . ," "Suddenly you turn around and . . . ," or "Love is . . . ." Corporate sponsors for the 1997–98 competition were Binney & Smith, Inc., Microsoft Home, and QSP, Inc., a fundraising subsidiary of the Reader's Digest Association, Inc.[36]

The Reflections program to celebrate the arts was initiated in 1968 when Mary Lou Anderson, a member of the National PTA board of directors, broached the idea with her cousin, John Allen, an executive of *Reader's Digest*. *Reader's Digest*, through QSP/Reader's Digest, became an early sponsor of the program, and in 1984, Anderson provided a generous gift to the National PTA to establish the Reflections Scholarship Program.

Advocacy Training and Leadership Development

One of the PTA's goals is "[t]o secure adequate laws for the care and protection of children and youth."[37] From its inception in 1897, PTA leaders have emphasized that the organization must concern itself with the legislative process—and it has. Throughout its existence, the National PTA has cooperated with other organizations to lobby for and against legislation that affects children. These efforts are ongoing despite the PTA's recognition that its emphasis on national legislative issues often overshadows parent concerns.[38]

While the National PTA claims that its lobbying efforts help children, it summed up its program services and commission reports in 1997 as "indirectly" serving the entire membership. No details were provided, except that the three National PTA commissions (standing committees) on health and welfare, education, and membership development spent $2,367,425. Participants in the PTA's program services included 87 board members, approximately 2,000 rank-and-file members who attended the national convention, and approximately 700 who participated in leadership training programs.[39] In addition, a few local leaders participate in programs and training sessions sponsored by state PTAs. As a result, very few PTA members have first-hand experience with state and national operations. Local schools usually benefit from local PTA fundraising activities, but state and National PTA programs are not designed to help parents help their children in school. Instead, the PTA lobbies for legislation such as government-funded programs before and after school, and for federal mandates for parental involvement.

With such limited direct participation in National PTA programs, it should come as no surprise that most PTA members are not familiar with National PTA operations or the operations of their state organizations. These are important topics to be discussed in upcoming chapters, but first, we shall step back in time to meet the founders of this century-old organization.

2

The Founding Mothers and Their World

*It is universally admitted that feminine influence has been a mighty fac-
tor for good in all ages, and therefore, incalculable benefit may be expected from the assembling of many women for the interchange of views,
and the study of home problems which can be solved by woman alone.*

*It is proposed to have the Congress consider subjects bearing upon the
better and broader spiritual and physical, as well as mental training of
the young, such as the value of kindergarten work and the extension of
its principles to more advanced studies, a love of humanity and of country, the physical and mental evils resulting from some of the present methods of our schools, and the advantages to follow from a closer relation
between the influence of the home and that of the school. . . .*[1]

— From invitation to attend the first National Congress of Mothers,
held in Washington, D.C., February 17–19, 1897

I. The Historical Context

Our story begins in the late nineteenth century. In the 1870s, about 75 percent
of America's 40 million inhabitants lived in the country or in rural villages and
towns of fewer than 2,500 residents. It was the age of dirt roads, of carriages and
wagons, and of covered bridges with wooden sides plastered with circus posters
and notices of county fairs. It was the age of oil lamps, wood stoves, the hand
pump, and the Saturday evening bath in a washtub in the center of the kitchen

25

floor. The latter part of the 1870s was also the age of sewing circles and the country store with its tubs of butter and pickles, its cracker barrel, and its clutter of groceries, clothing, and household articles hanging from the ceiling.

On weekdays, rural children attended a one-room elementary school which, like the flag, had become a symbol of patriotism. Boys and girls often walked two or three miles each way along the country roads to get to school. School terms were only four or five months because children were needed to help with spring planting and fall harvesting. The teachers, usually single young women, taught all grades and emphasized the three Rs: reading, writing, and arithmetic. During the school term, teachers often lived in the homes of the pupils, staying a month in one home, then a month in another. The school was also a center for community events, such as spelling bees for parents as for well as for their children. The school, the church, and the nearest town were the centers of social activity for most farm families, except for those who lived near a growing city or a large town.

Economically, farmers were becoming more dependent upon forces they could not control, such as the railroads that carried their goods to market, prices fixed in distant markets, tariffs that sometimes raised the cost of manufactured goods, and fluctuations in the supply of currency made available by the federal government. Throughout America, millions of farmers and workers were drawn to cities from small towns; by 1890 about a dozen American cities had populations of more than 100,000.

By the turn of the twentieth century, the United States was rapidly becoming the leading industrial nation in the world. New sources of power, new inventions and industrial processes, and the enormous expansion of the nation's transportation and communication networks stimulated urbanization at a remarkable pace. In cities, opportunities to climb the economic ladder far surpassed those in the Old World. Immigrants came seeking these new opportunities, and they played an indispensable role in U.S. industrial development.

From 1870 to 1899, more than 11 million men, women, and children entered the United States, swelling America's population to 76 million. Chicago had a million citizens in 1889; almost three-quarters had been born outside the United States.[2] The changing origins of immigration, as well as the population swell, alarmed many Americans. Until the early 1880s, most immigrants came from Great Britain, Ireland, the Scandinavian countries, Germany, and the Netherlands. After 1890, an increasingly large number came from southern and eastern Europe. The languages and cultures of these immigrants were quite different from those of immigrants from northwestern Europe, and the newcomers were often greeted with distrust and suspicion. As we shall see, of all the demographic and social changes that led to the establishment of the PTA, none was more important than the changes in immigration.[3] These changes gave rise to the idea that it was essential to Americanize the immigrants and their children — an objective that clearly appealed to the affluent founders of the PTA.

By the turn of the twentieth century, almost two-thirds of Americans no longer labored on farms. Instead, they worked on railroads or construction sites; in factories or trades; in shops, offices, or banks; in hospitals, schools, or libraries; or in government offices.[4] Seven out of ten industrial workers earned no more than ten cents an hour, but there was always the hope for any child to do as Andrew Carnegie did; starting as a bobbin boy in a textile mill at age thirteen, Carnegie eventually became the richest steel producer on earth.

Women also were taking advantage of opportunities to be gainfully employed. The 1890 census indicated that almost 4 million women were in the labor force. Of that number, over 1 million were servants or waitresses, nearly 500,000 were hired farm workers, 300,000 were dressmakers, and the rest were employed as saleswomen, teachers, or in other domestic and personal service occupations. In addition, female participation in the labor force included 7,500 doctors, 3,000 ministers, and 1,000 lawyers. About 1.75 million children worked, some in tobacco fields for as little as twenty-five cents a day. Many deemed child labor to be appropriate; a popular slogan of the times proclaimed, "The factories need the children and the children need the factories."[5]

Businessmen and financiers presided over the new world of throbbing machines, noisy factories, and crowded cities. Business leaders also dominated local, state, and national politics. Between 1789 and 1860, thirteen presidents had been elected — seven from the South, six from the North. Between 1860 and 1900 each of the seven presidents elected was from the industrial regions of the Northeast or from the Middle West. Business leaders of this period, like the settlers, prospectors, and frontier farmers, were pioneers — and many were enormously successful. A new class of millionaires arose: self-made men with social and cultural aspirations. Their wives were often strong personalities as well. Women who became leaders of society because of their husbands' money, their family connections, their intelligence, their energy, and their appeal to the press could not be shrugged off as "suffrage women." Interestingly enough, many of the era's influential women did not regard voting rights for women as essential to raising the status of women. In their voluntary associations, these women emphasized changes in home and family life, just as they had done for decades. In their ornate parlors, their voices were soft, their demands were tactfully phrased, and they were always well mannered.[6]

Other women were not as genteel. Henrietta Rodman, a schoolteacher who bobbed her hair — a heresy in her day — led a fight against the New York City school system for its policy of dismissing women teachers if they got married. Women labor leaders led strikes and mass demonstrations. Women of this more assertive stripe, as well as their more traditional sisters, both came to exercise a great deal of influence through grassroots organizing for political action.

II. The Nineteenth-Century "Woman Movement"

One social historian identifies three distinct emphases within the nineteenth-century women's movement: a benevolent role toward the poor, equal rights for women, and emancipation from tradition.[7] The first emphasis became obvious early in the century, when the women's movement was characterized by neighborly concern for the less fortunate. These efforts to help the poor eventually brought women together to discuss religious and literary reforms; however, such women addressed other issues from time to time. As early as 1834, "in the name of virtue, women in New York and New England who were enraged about moral decay set up Moral Reform Societies to abolish prostitution."[8] Three decades later, during the Civil War, thousands of women participated in the Sanitary Commission, a voluntary association that raised millions of dollars for the Union army. Women sold donated gifts and refreshments at huge fairs in every big northern city, and organized free lodging for soldiers. The money they gained by these sales purchased food, uniforms, and medical supplies for the Union soldiers. Many women took special pride in their contributions toward the war effort.

Some women's organizations were established as a result of discrimination against women. After journalist Jane Croly was refused admission to a New York Press Club dinner for Charles Dickens in March 1868, she created Sorosis, a woman's organization that challenged the restrictions on women. The professional women of this club, whose membership was by invitation only, met twice a month at Delmonico's restaurant. As Hester M. Poole, a journalist and member of Sorosis, wrote, "Prior to [the creation of Sorosis], no woman, even in daylight, when unattended, could procure a meal at a first-class restaurant in New York. Neither could she get a room in a reputable hotel. Grievous restrictions hedged about evening amusements, lectures, and concerts. The greater liberty of action heartily enjoyed by women today [1893] is primarily due to women's clubs."[9]

After the Civil War, hundreds of thousands of women expanded their interests beyond narrow domestic issues; they began to grapple with education, employment, legal and civic rights, and social reform. They created and supported women's institutions: homes for widows and orphans, normal schools and colleges, health institutes and medical schools, mothers' organizations, wage earners' protective leagues, and settlement houses. Tirelessly, they made speeches and published books and pamphlets, petitioned and lobbied state authorities, brought cases before courts, and occasionally even resorted to direct-action techniques and civil disobedience.

Legal, political, and economic equality was another nineteenth-century emphasis for women. Lucretia Mott and Elizabeth Cady Stanton had called for equal rights at the first women's rights convention, held at Seneca Falls, New York, in July 1848. Political equality for women was a controversial issue because it challenged the idea that a woman's place is in the home. In fact, when the first National Congress of Mothers convened in 1897, only Wyoming and Utah had given women the right to vote. In addition, a few other states provided women with limited voting rights; women in these states could take part in local elections and serve as elected school board members. Gradually, opposition to women's participation in public affairs began to yield to the champions of women's rights. As individuals and in collaborative efforts, these champions sought rights and prerogatives then available only to men, and a reevaluation of women's nature and abilities. Dedicated suffragettes hoped that their efforts would eventually lead elite and middle-class women (many of whom were not convinced before the early 1900s) to advocate full female enfranchisement. Although suffragettes participated in the 1897 National Congress of Mothers, that body avoided taking a stand on voting rights for women.[10]

The third emphasis in the nineteenth-century women's movement was emancipation from customs and traditions that disadvantaged women. Of course, equal rights for women was part of this effort. Most women believed that as one woman helped herself, all women would benefit. Nineteenth-century feminists argued for equal opportunity in education and employment, and for equal rights in property, law, and political representation, while also maintaining that women per se would bring special benefits to public life.[11] In order to produce those special benefits for the public, women created organizations to establish collective voices for change, despite the aforementioned popular belief that women should stay in the home.

III. The Founding Mothers

As we shall see, the founders of the National Congress of Mothers agreed with the axiom that women's place is in the home, but they also believed that they could communicate the ideals of family life to less fortunate women. No one better illustrates this point than Alice McLellan White Birney, the first president of the National Congress of Mothers. Born in October 1858 to a genteel southern family in Marietta, Georgia, Birney attended private schools, unaware that her legacy would be an organization devoted to public schools. After her first husband died when Birney was a pregnant nineteen-year-old, she moved to Washington, D.C. to live with her mother.

A career in advertising and marriage to a prominent Washington lawyer followed soon thereafter. After the birth of her third daughter in early 1895, Birney became enthralled with the idea of a national organization of mothers. Later, recalling how her idea developed, Birney wrote in her personal journal:

> I was impressed . . . with the great number of conventions and assemblages of all kinds and for all purposes held at the national capital. . . . I asked

myself . . . [h]ow can the mothers be educated and the *nation* made to recognize the supreme importance of the child? Congress was in session at
this time, and I knew how its doings were telegraphed to all parts of the
earth and how eagerly such messages were read . . . and then like a flash
came the thought: Why not have a National Congress of Mothers . . . ?[12]

In the summer of 1895, Birney proposed the idea at the annual Chautauqua
summer school. The Chautauqua movement was an educational enterprise established in 1874 on the shores of Chautauqua Lake in upper New York. In Birney's day, thousands of Americans from all over the United States traveled to
Chautauqua Lake to enjoy a summer vacation and to benefit intellectually and
spiritually from the programs available there. Discussions about education,
children, and mothers were routinely held in the Mothers' Building. After meeting Birney, two prominent proponents of kindergarten, Mary Louisa Butler and
Frances E. Newton, invited her to address a mothers' meeting in August 1895.
Birney accepted the invitation to promote her idea for "better trained mothers";
her view was that mothers needed their own organization, just like the organizations of other vocations.

The men as well as the women at Chautauqua reacted positively to Birney's
message. Several pastors among the ten thousand people in attendance at the
Chautauqua summer session subsequently asked Birney to speak at their churches.
While men frowned upon some women's activities, such as advocacy of women's
rights, they were favorably disposed to female activism involving churches and
issues that concerned children. Encouraged by her husband and other family
members, Birney devoted most of her time to promoting a "national Congress of
Mothers."[13] Eventually, Birney met Phoebe Apperson Hearst, who became the
main source of financial support for the first national mothers' congress.

Clearly, Hearst had more than enough resources to bring Birney's vision to
fruition. At the age of sixteen, she was a teacher in Missouri before marrying
George Hearst of California, a legendary gold-mine owner. Their only child,
William Randolph Hearst, was born in 1863 in San Francisco; he became a
leader in the publishing world at the time that his mother was promoting the
idea of a mothers' congress. From 1887 on, Hearst and her husband, who had
become a U.S. Senator, lived in Washington, D.C. Their son built the fabled
Hearst Castle in California and was the real-life counterpart of the protagonist
of "Citizen Kane," Orson Welles's classic movie about a wealthy, power-dri-
ven publisher who thought that money could buy the presidency for himself and
fame for a mistress with no musical talent.

Widowed in 1891 and left with a legendary fortune, Phoebe Hearst became
involved in philanthropic activities. By 1895, she had sponsored seven kindergartens in San Francisco, South Dakota, and Washington, D.C. The Hearst Elementary School in the District of Columbia was dedicated to the education of

black children and is still part of the public school system there. Located across the street from the Sidwell Friends Quaker school that enrolled President Clinton's daughter, Chelsea, the Hearst school serves kindergarten through third grade students and includes a PTA that charged $10.00 dues and a $180.00 assessment in 2000—not exactly what Hearst had in mind for poor beneficiaries over one hundred years ago.

IV. The Mothers' Congress of 1897

In 1896, with financial support from Hearst and the power of the Hearst publishing empire behind her, Birney and her colleagues invited state and local leaders of all leading women's clubs in the country to participate in the first Mothers' Congress, to be held in Washington, D.C. in 1897.[14] An introductory letter indicated that the Mothers' Congress would focus on the need to educate mothers so that children might benefit. Specifically, the invitational letter requested the name "of one woman of position in your community with whom we may correspond concerning the organization of mothers' clubs." Showing an awareness of public relations, the letter stressed that "[t]he press is literally clamoring for matter for publication bearing upon our work, . . . will you not, therefore, endeavor to enthuse the editors with whom you have influence?"[15]

Many women invited to attend the Congress were members of the nationally organized and prestigious General Federation of Women's Clubs (GFWC), an extensive network of women's clubs established throughout the United States. Hearst had been the GFWC's first national treasurer in 1890, and had nearly a decade of club experience in her San Francisco Century Club before the 1897 meeting of the Mothers' Congress.

Although the GFWC publicly welcomed the emergence of the Congress, GFWC President Ellen M. Henrotin privately expressed doubts about its desirability to Hearst. In a letter to Hearst, Henrotin reported that many thoughtful women "have said to me that they should not go to the National Congress of Mothers because they so strongly disapproved of a new organization being formed and pressed upon an over-burdened world . . . they feel that another National organization distinct in itself and not related to other associations is against the tendency of the age and to be deplored." Tactfully, Henrotin suggested that "whether the Executive Committee [of the National Congress decides to] form a separate organization or not, it might consider having the new Congress formulate programs of study [and] traveling libraries on this subject and use the great organizations already in existence like the National Association of Teachers [and] existing State Federations of Women's Clubs of which there are now twenty-three."[16]

Although Henrotin's suggestion was not accepted, the GFWC and the Mothers' Congress cooperated on various projects, and their memberships often overlapped. Despite her reservations, Henrotin presented two papers at the first Congress, on the "Need of Organization" and on "How to Organize."

In the invitation to the Mothers' Congress—the "Official Call"—Birney explained that Washington was "the most fitting place for such an assemblage because the movement is one of national importance." Of course, the nation's capitol did offer more concrete advantages as well, such as access to national leaders.

On Monday, February 15, 1897, two days before the opening session, the *Washington Post* announced the upcoming meeting of the National Congress of Mothers in a headline that read: "Rulers of the World: Mothers to Meet in Congress at the American Capital [*sic*]." A front page sketch on February 17, 1897 greeted the delegates and guests. (See Figure 1.)

Referred to by *Post* writers as the "origin of the movement for the education of mothers," the founders expected the conference to lead to a fuller understanding of mothers' "duties and responsibilities." As with the Chautauqua programs, a number of celebrated women would read papers or deliver addresses about childhood, motherhood, and the social concerns of the 1890s.

For nearly a week that followed, the *Post*—amid advertisements of $5.00 men's suits, new-style summer corsets for $.68, and chiropodists' guarantees to fix aching toes and remove corns and bunions for $.25 each—recounted the

Figure 1. Announcement of Mothers' Congress

Source: *Washington Post,* February 17, 1897, 1. (© 1897, *The Washington Post.* Reprinted with permission.)

high points of the Congress and described the speakers with details vivid enough to engage a reader a century later.

Like Birney and Hearst, most of the delegates to the first Congress were white, upper-middle-class wives of socially prominent men. As they arrived from all parts of the country, committee members met the delegates and guests at the railroad depots and escorted them to the Arlington Hotel. Registration was chaotic. By midmorning of the first day, almost 1,000 delegates and guests had signed in, overwhelming the corresponding secretary and her helpers. The founders had anticipated that 60 to 100 delegates would attend; lured by the prospect of a reception at the White House, over 2,000 delegates and guests arrived. Of those in attendance, 300 were delegates; all others were guests.[17] Delegates housed in the Arlington paid the special rate of $4 or $5 per night. Many, including children who accompanied their mothers, stayed elsewhere for $1 or $2 per night. Although women's organizations generally excluded blacks, one delegate was a black woman from the District of Columbia.

The first day's session opened promptly at 10:00 A.M., only to be adjourned at 11:30 A.M. so that delegates could attend a White House reception hosted by Frances Cleveland, the thirty-two-year-old wife of President Grover Cleveland. Frances Folsom had become the nation's youngest First Lady, at twenty-one, when she married Grover Cleveland during his first term in the White House (1885–89). Cleveland, reelected to a second term after an interruption of four years, was completing his second term (1893–97) when the Mothers' Congress convened. The *Post* described the First Lady's reception the day after it took place:

> The crush at the hall was nothing, compared with that at the White House. The moment Chaplain Milburn announced that every one [*sic*] present was invited to Mrs. Cleveland's reception there was a grand rush for the street; and the mothers from the different States entered a race, and when they reached the Executive Mansion it was a decided contest to make the entrance first. Col. Crook stood at one of the windows and gallantly helped those in over [window] sills who would attempt the climb, and the corridor was packed until the state of the proverbial sardine box was reached, and the ladies who had on their heavy wraps gasped for breath. The crowd was certainly a surprise to Mrs. Cleveland. She had been notified that probably two or three hundred would call, but in place of that there were nearly 2,000. She had an engagement at 12 o'clock, but with her usual good nature, she stood and shook hands until all had passed her.
>
> She looked very lovely in a simple morning gown of dark red cloth, the waist in bolero effect, with black braiding and a wide girdle of black satin. Mrs. Theodore Birney, President of the congress, stood at Mrs. Cleveland's left and introduced each [attendant] by name, and those who had never seen the first lady of the land were as delighted with her as those who have

become familiar with her gracious smile. Many turned back for a second look at her, and there is no doubt that every mother will carry home with her a pleasant recollection of the reception at the White House.[18]

But there was work to be done. Afternoon sessions were scheduled for 2:30 P.M. each day, following luncheons provided at the First Advent Church by the Ladies' Aid Society. These luncheons were to be "a great convenience to delegates" and would "afford opportunities for them to become better acquainted during the noon recesses of the congress."

In addition to the sessions at the Arlington Hotel, two additional sessions were held simultaneously in the First Baptist Church to accommodate the crowds. One was held in the auditorium, with the overflow in the large Sabbath-school room. After a speaker had finished in one room, she repeated her address in the other. Evening sessions began at 8:00 P.M. and were held on the upper floor of the Center Market Hall, remodeled as the city's convention center a few years earlier.

From newspaper accounts, we learn that dozens of women from the 300,000-member Women's Christian Temperance Union (WCTU) responded to the call to attend the Mothers' Congress. Of the sixteen delegates from Illinois, six gave their address simply as "The Temple, Chicago." The Temple was the Woman's Temple, headquarters of the WCTU in Chicago.

One speaker discussed "Heredity," a concern many women shared as a reaction to the uneducated immigrants arriving in the United States. Another speaker discussed her efforts in the Philadelphia public schools to instruct irresponsible mothers in the proper care of children. A well-known editor at *Harper's Bazaar* and several other speakers emphasized the need for the education of mothers, who could in turn instill a love of learning in their children.

Several supporters of the kindergarten movement were on the program. The idea and value of kindergarten had been introduced to the United States at the Centennial Exhibition in Philadelphia in 1876. Kindergarten was described as the science of motherhood and emphasized the importance of mother-child interactions and instructive play with very young children. In support of the idea, various publications, such as the *Mother Play Book*, had been developed and used in kindergartens. During the Congress, mothers were encouraged to try fifty specially designed games and play activities with preschool children.[19] In addition to the sessions on kindergartens, a model nursery, equipped with the "latest scientific-made clothes" and several games—not only to amuse, but "to instruct the youthful mind"—were on display. G. Stanley Hall, a prominent psychologist at Clark University, addressed the Congress about the different stages of child development. Hall's studies had shown how children's problems differed from those of adults, and changed during childhood. The mothers were told that special parental skills were required to cope with this newly discovered complexity of childhood.

There were a few lighter moments amid the serious discussions. The appearance by a designer of a very controversial women's ensemble caused a furor. Her design, publicized as "The American," was praised by some as a fashionable and practical design for working women: it featured "hems at least one foot and in some cases eighteen inches from the floor. To cover the intervening length of leg, the dress reformers wore gaiters, a covering for the instep, ankle and lower leg which often encased the shoe, and was made of leather or cloth."[20] The design was so controversial that women's groups formed Dress Reform Committees to consider it as an alternative to the strict dress code of the day. The dress code required large hats—top-heavy with ribbons, feathers, and flowers—and veils. Shoes were high and buttoned, barely visible below full, ankle-length skirts. The idealized "Gibson Girl," the work of Charles Dana Gibson, depicted the perfect American woman: slim, small-waisted, feminine, and frivolous.

While no self-respecting woman would go hatless to a meeting, hats were a problem at the Congress. Indeed, Hearst pleaded with the mothers to remove their bonnets. She publicly acknowledged at one session that the "mothers did a little better during the afternoon, for in the central block at the First Baptist Church there was a very fair sprinkling of bonnetless heads, and those who sat toward the back devoutly wished that everybody in front of them had been as considerate."[21]

By the final day, Birney received a card which requested, "Please remove your hat. We who are behind you cannot see. Ask the lady in front of you to remove hers also." This card had been passed all around the church from hand to hand and had created great amusement. Birney thought the idea was a good one. When she removed her own hat, her example was quickly followed, and a "flutter passed through the audience as hat pins were withdrawn and hundreds of hats removed."[22]

The delegates to the Congress proposed several resolutions which "were adopted by a Chautauqua salute. Every delegate waved her handkerchief high in [the] air, and the scene was a pretty one."[23] Not surprisingly, their fifteen resolutions reflected the attitudes of the founders and the speakers. For example:

> Whereas this is the first great National Congress of Women ever crystallized about the single idea of maternity and the improvement of the relation of mother and child; and
>
> Whereas we desire that the influence of this meeting shall be as far reaching as possible, therefore,
>
> Resolved, That we endorse the work of the Universal Peace Union, an international organization that promoted peace and justice at home and abroad.
>
> Resolved, That the National Congress of Mothers heartily approve the founding of a national training school for mothers—that the women of

America may be taught the method for making hygienic homes and for becoming intelligent mothers—in a word, that they may be taught the laws of health and heredity.

It is resolved that we use our influence to encourage legislation in our various States and Territories to secure a kindergarten department in our public schools.

Furthermore, it is recommended that every woman's organization in every State in our Union be invited to cooperate in the establishment of adequate training schools for kindergartens.

Resolved, That we will endeavor to exclude from our homes those papers which do not educate or inspire to noble thought and deed . . .

Resolved, That we hereby petition both houses of Congress to raise the age of protection for girls to eighteen years at least, in the District of Columbia and the Territories . . . .[24]

About half of the delegates' resolutions were related to the future of the Mothers' Congress. The women voted to keep the same national executive board, to establish a press committee to send out monthly articles, and to prepare and sell circulars. No formal plan to establish state or local affiliates was adopted; however, delegates agreed to "strive toward the formation of mothers' or home sections in the local organizations" that already existed. The intent of the Congress was to establish a mothers' section within local chapters of the GFWC or WCTU to advance the goals of the Congress. In addition, these arrangements presented leadership opportunities for many delegates who were already discussing the next Congress. The delegates also voted to hold annual meetings, including a meeting every other year in Washington.

Finally, the Congress extended high praise and thanks to the press, the organizers, the speakers, those who attended, and especially to Frances Cleveland for the White House reception. At adjournment, Birney urged the delegates and guests to "take into their homes the spirit of co-operation in the cause suggested in the call for Congress," which was "to carry the mother-love and mother-thought into all that concerns or touches childhood . . . ."[25]

Obviously, carrying out the directives of the Congress would be very time-consuming. Birney, however, noted a special reason to be hopeful.

Now that reform is being effected in domestic science by the establishment of schools where servants can be properly trained and by the lifting of household and kitchen work from the realm of drudgery to that of science, there is a fair prospect of more bodily rest for mothers, more time for study for and with their children, and for outside recreation of a sort helpful to both mind and body.[26]

Needless to say, the mention of "schools where servants can be properly trained" reflects the upper-class origins of the founders, and would not evoke much enthusiasm today, at least not much overt enthusiasm. In historical context, the emphasis placed on retraining mothers, attention to child development, and the welfare of children reflected a sea change in attitudes toward children. Prior to the Industrial Revolution, large families and high child mortality rates were the norm. The death of a child was unfortunate but too common to be a shattering event. Early in the nineteenth century, however, a dramatic revolution in attitudes toward children emerged among upper- and middle-class families in Western Europe and the United States. The death of a young child became the most painful and least tolerable of all deaths. By the latter part of the nineteenth century, the high mortality rate among poor urban children in the United States had become a visible and embarrassing anachronism in a society newly committed to the welfare of its children. As a consequence, the reduction of infant and child mortality rates emerged as a national priority. Pediatrics was established as a separate medical specialty in the 1880s. At the same time, specialized institutions were being created to treat childhood diseases and preserve the health of children. By the mid-1890s, most large cities had at least one children's hospital. Health, like education, became a community concern, not solely an individual or family matter.[27]

The increasing value of children inevitably heightened the importance of motherhood. "Exalting the child went hand in hand with exalting the domestic role of woman; each reinforced the other while together they raised domesticity within the family to a new and higher level of respectability."[28] Properly loved children belonged in a domesticated and shielded world of lessons, games, and play money. Proper mothering was considered a key element in the conservation of child life and health. While lower-class mothers were to be instructed in proper child care, middle-class mothers would be active in organizations devoted to the health and welfare of all children. The National Congress of Mothers assumed the task of educating the nation and women in particular "to recognize the supreme importance of the child."[29]

At home in their respective communities, the members of the National Congress of Mothers viewed their commitment in a very broad way. In making the transition to a child-centered culture, they did not abandon the concept of a woman's special domestic sphere. Instead, they extended their sphere into what came to be called "municipal housekeeping." In the words of a 1910 book about clubwomen in politics:

> Woman's place is in the home. This is a platitude which no woman will ever dissent from . . . . But Home is not contained within the four walls of an individual home. Home is the community. The city full of people

is the Family. The public school is the Nursery. And badly do the Home
and the Family and the Nursery need their mother.[30]

As civic housekeepers in their communities, many clubwomen devoted
themselves to improving libraries and schools and cultural activities for children. With their new directive from the National Congress of Mothers, they
promoted their view of effective motherhood and the proper instruction of children. Understandably, municipal housekeeping and educating mothers led inevitably to a broad social reform agenda. Mothers were to lead in campaigns
against illiteracy, intemperance, divorce, child labor, juvenile crime, tubercu-
losis, malnutrition—whatever the problem, effective motherhood was the solution. After dramatizing the problems, the next step for the mothers was to
seek public and political support from the larger community.

Looking back, we can see that the National Congress of Mothers was founded
by two groups of women. For the most part, one of these groups accepted the
prevailing ideology about the role of women; their objective was to perfect the
role women should play in a world that assigned very different roles to men and
women. The other group sought to eliminate or reduce the barriers to women's
equal participation in our political, social, and economic systems. Clearly, the
first group dominated the formation and early years of the National Congress of
Mothers, the forerunner of the PTA.

From our perspective at the beginning of the twenty-first century, however,
the PTA is an anomaly. It was founded upon an ideology that appeals less and
less to upper-middle-class women, despite the social status of its early leaders
and activists. The steep decline in birth rates among upper-middle-class women,
the huge increases in cohabitation and children born out of wedlock, the expansion of educational and occupational opportunities for women, and the declining prestige of homemaking suggest that the founding rationale for the PTA no
longer holds much appeal for upper-middle-class mothers. As we shall see, the
PTA survived these dramatic social changes by gradually replacing its focus on
motherhood with a welfare-state agenda. But for the National Congress of Mothers, approaching the dawn of the twentieth century, these problems lay well in
the future. The immediate challenge was membership expansion. Although several women from the nation's elite strata founded the organization, thousands of
members were necessary to sustain it. Thousands more were necessary to
achieve national and international recognition. Building the National Congress
of Mothers into an influential national organization was the principal objective.

3

From Mothers Only to Parents and Teachers

We are stateswomen. Any woman interested in social problems and anx-
ious to unravel them, any woman who feels that around her there are con-
ditions that she wishes to improve is a stateswoman. . . . [O]ur government
should be maternal, some may prefer to call it paternal, there is no differ-
ence. The state is a parent, and, as a wise and gentle and kind and loving
parent, should beam down on each child alike. . . . We, the mothers of the
land, should go in a body and make the appeal for what we wish. . . .[1]

— Mrs. G. H. Robertson, president, Tennessee Congress of Mothers, 1911

I. Introduction

Even before the close of the first National Congress of Mothers, a group of
women from New York discussed the possibility of setting up state branches
of the organization. That autumn, they formed the New York Assembly of
Mothers, the first state branch of the organization.[2]

With the exception of New York, however, the growth of the organization at
that time remained largely in the hands of the national officers. In 1898, Birney
outlined the strategy by which the early leaders intended to carry out their platform and policies: "by the formation of mothers' clubs throughout the country; by
parents and teachers meeting twice a month if practicable; by concerted, by individual, by continuous effort on the part of such clubs to obtain the cooperation of

all other existing organizations, in whatever concerns the welfare and development of the child."[3]

The Mothers' Committee on Education prepared study guides as one of the first projects of the Congress. These guides were an organizing tool as well as a venture aimed at promoting education. To coordinate the effort, the Executive Committee authorized a selected group of state and territorial organizers to promote educational activities in designated regions. Often, the nationally appointed organizer was subsequently elected as the first state president when a state affiliate was organized. These presidents then became members of the managing board of the national organization.

II. Growth and Development

Such was the case with Mrs. Roger B. McMullen, the organizer for Illinois. A young mother herself, prior to becoming affiliated with the National Congress of Mothers, McMullen had worked ceaselessly to establish a child-and-home department in the Evanston Woman's Club. In her view, training for motherhood was as necessary as training for any profession.

Promptly after the first National Congress, McMullen began to organize the Illinois Congress of Mothers. Throughout her travels, she had the support of her husband, who often sent telegrams of encouragement when audiences criticized her for leaving him and her children "helplessly at home." Elsewhere, regional organizers and officers traveled throughout the country to organize state and local affiliates. The Congress's national vice president, Hannah Schoff, organized Pennsylvania in 1899; appointed organizers successfully created state branches a year later in Connecticut, Illinois, Iowa, and New Jersey. During her first term as president, Birney also traveled throughout the country to promote the new organization. In addition to visiting women's clubs, Birney visited all the child welfare institutions she could find—free kindergartens, day nurseries, social settlements, newsboys' clubs, and whatever other institutions might be brought into the fold. To her astonishment, new affiliates were quickly established, greatly exceeding her expectations.

In February 1899, the Mothers' Congress met again in Washington, D.C. A crippling blizzard delayed arrivals from twelve to twenty-four hours while their trains were dug out. When delegates finally reached Washington, ten-foot walls of snow on both sides of the streets covered the lower windows of the houses. Many streets were impassable; coal and gas were giving out; food was scarce. All speakers and delegates from twenty-four states managed to arrive, but the convention was delayed one day. Undaunted, Birney continued to urge parent education through mothers' clubs in every community and the "close union of parents and teachers." In addition to emphasizing character building in the young and the cooperation of fathers, Birney "begged women not to seek employment outside the home unless forced to do so by necessity."[4] Although "necessity" can be defined in many different ways, Birney's message is not one that would appeal to college-educated, career-oriented mothers one hundred years later.

In 1900, Birney attended her first state-affiliate meeting, sponsored by the New York Assembly of Mothers and held in the state capitol in Albany. Edith Roosevelt, wife of then Governor Theodore Roosevelt, hosted a reception at the governor's mansion. At the reception, Birney, Mary Mears (the president of the New York State affiliate), and Schoff invited Theodore Roosevelt to serve on the proposed advisory council of the National Congress. Roosevelt quickly agreed and held the chairmanship of the all-male Advisory Council from its establishment in 1900 until his death in January 1919. Just as women had established auxiliaries to men's organizations, the men's Advisory Council became a way for husbands and fathers to be supportive of the work of the Mothers' Congress.

In 1901, the fifth National Congress in Columbus, Ohio featured discussions on the practical methods of cooperation between home and school. Tensions had already surfaced between parents and teachers. Charles R. Skinner, New York superintendent of public instruction and a staunch supporter of the Congress, presided at the meetings. Discussions included how a mothers' committee could promote cleanliness and beauty in the schools as well as help overburdened teachers. Skinner believed that the Mothers' Congress could bring parents and teachers closer together at a time when a visit—even a friendly visit—from a mother to a teacher was a rare event. To carry out the idea, the president of the New York affiliate outlined a plan to establish organizations of mothers and teachers in New York. Although cooperative activities were encouraged, the majority of the delegates and the leadership still declined to allow single women working as teachers to become members, despite the fact that practically every working woman was single in the early 1900s.

As indicated by the initial exclusion of teachers from membership, in its early years the National Congress of Mothers did not focus primarily on formal schooling; education was important to the organization, but only as one of several major areas of interest. In retrospect, it is easy to see how and why the fifth Congress devoted more attention to formal schooling than had its predecessors. When the organization was founded in 1897, formal schooling played a much smaller role in the lives of children than it did even five years later. Only a handful of states had enacted compulsory education laws since the first such law passed in 1852, and the laws that were enacted mandated only a few years of schooling. Both the school year and the school day were much shorter than they are today; agriculture was still the largest industry and children were needed on farms.

A growing emphasis on education and schools, and on assistance to overburdened teachers, was evident at the 1902 National Congress in Washington. Mothers at the meeting, for example, reported on the projects they promoted in their own communities: vacation schools, public playgrounds, better school sanitation, and cooperation between home and school.

After more than five years as president of the National Congress of Mothers, Birney resigned in 1902 because of poor health. She was immediately elected honorary president, and in 1905 her title was changed to Founder. At the time of her resignation, the National Congress of Mothers included eight state Congresses. In addition, the organization had awakened interest in child welfare in Canada, England, Brazil, India, Japan, and Australia. As a result, the National Congress of Mothers established an International Congress Committee. In 1908, the National Congress sponsored an international conference, and the National Congress's president represented the Congress at similar conferences around the globe. At home, the group changed its name to become the National Congress of Parent-Teacher Associations, although it continued its involvement in noneducational matters.

Despite criticisms that the Congress "was composed of lay members and had no professional leadership, the leaders worked diligently to organize affiliates and get their messages out."[5] Through extensive correspondence with other women's clubs, public child welfare conferences, and a speaker's bureau, speakers from the Congress often appeared on the programs of well-established organizations. In rural areas, speakers frequently urged farm organizations to establish mothers' clubs and raised such controversial subjects as teachers' salaries and the consolidation of small rural school districts. Sometimes the leaders of the Congress offered to send speakers to address these organizations as long as the newly formed clubs deemed them useful.

At the time, thousands of women's organizations existed throughout the United States—women's clubs, mothers' clubs, mothers' roundtables, mothers' councils, women's aid societies, Progressive Culture clubs, the Women's Christian Temperance Union, home and school organizations, and kindergarten associations. For the most part, these groups were organized locally but not nationally, and it was to them that the National Congress appealed. Working as a coordinating body, the National Congress drew these scattered groups into a more cohesive organization that placed growing emphasis on reform through legislation.

The effort was financed haphazardly. In the first few years, the board of managers relied almost entirely on cash or in-kind donations from both its own members and affluent supporters outside the organization. As a founder, Phoebe Apperson Hearst donated the office building and most of the operating costs for several years. The husbands of national and state officers frequently covered the costs of printing and distributing leaflets. At first, there were no individual memberships, but local affiliates were assessed $5.00 for every fifty members. After state branches were formed, one-half of their revenue was sent to the national office.

The revenue of state affiliates frequently reflected grassroots commitment to the organization. The Illinois Congress of Parents and Teachers reported that "three rummage sales in 1910 and 1911 raised a total of $180."[6] The Illinois finance chairman collected club recipes and published a cookbook; sales were brisk at the Illinois Congress's annual convention, at which 638 copies sold in a ten-minute period. Mothers' buttons sold for five cents each in quantities of 100. Amateur talent events at members' homes, with admission at ten cents per person, were popular and successful fundraising ventures. Money raised from such activities funded the Illinois Congress's legislative agenda.

During this expansionist era of the PTA, its leaders worked with legislators to establish juvenile courts, kindergartens, libraries, better training for teachers, teacher tenure, detention homes, and schools for delinquent children. In doing so, the national organization encountered internal and external opposition to its agenda. In 1910, when the chairman of the Illinois Congress advocated a $5.00 a week minimum wage for women and a state colony for epileptics, the state board of the Illinois Congress instructed the chairman "to deal only with laws concerning mothers and children."[7] In the cause of international peace, the national board urged all branch associations to work for the elimination of military toys and the abolition of capital punishment. These recommendations were frequently ignored by affiliates. In 1911, the National Congress created a Marriage Sanctity Committee, and encouraged its state and local affiliates to do likewise. Its avowed purpose was to "work with national groups for national uniform divorce laws." At the time, the national chairman was a resident of Salt Lake City, Utah. Although Utah, virtually a Mormon theocracy, had officially abandoned polygamy in 1890, this new committee was probably an anti-Mormon initiative.[8] In any event, few state affiliates organized the requested committee.

A Family Planning Committee met with similar resistance, particularly after some newspaper headlines asserted that the National Congress advocated birth control. The Congress published only one pamphlet on the subject—*Medical, Social, Economic, and Religious Aspects of Birth Control*. Although it did not endorse the use of contraceptives, or any specific method of birth control, the Family Planning Committee was discontinued. The social and economic aspects of family planning were incorporated into the regular work of the social hygiene committees, which favored sex education classes as part of the school curriculum. The sex education curriculum was supposed to be "those principles and methods which best train children and youth to fine habits and attitudes and ideals concerning love, the home partnership and parenthood."[9] We can surmise that even the most ardent advocates of sex education in these early days would have been horrified by condom distribution and AIDS education in our public schools today.

The National Congress was undaunted by criticism that it was advocating more government control over the lives of American families. Critics charged that many of the social spending reform programs of the Congress would invite political corruption and escalate government spending beyond women's benefits.[10] Other critics accused the National Congress of promoting state planning and control that would weaken individual freedom.

Nevertheless, the National Congress and other women's groups continued their efforts to remedy the problems of urban industrialization. Through their organizations, women discussed issues, developed leadership skills, honed their organizational talents, and learned to focus their lobbying energies. In its advocacy of government benefits and services, the Mothers' Congress was helping to lay the foundation for the welfare state that would emerge in the late 1930s. At a time when legislative affairs still revolved around the state capitals rather than Washington, D.C., there were countless opportunities close to home for women to be activists for welfare legislation of one kind or another.

III. Mothers' Pensions

Of course, self-interest was not completely absent from the legislative objectives of the National Congress. Early in 1911, the Congress formally endorsed state legislation to promote "mothers' pensions." At the time, juvenile court judges frequently removed the delinquent children of impoverished working widows from their homes and placed them in orphanages. To remedy this situation for both the mother and the child, juvenile court judges proposed that an award of government funds be given to proper, moral women. Eventually funded by state governments, these pensions covered at least part of the cost of maintaining children at home, thus reducing the need for foster homes or orphanages. Local affiliates and the twenty-two state affiliates of the National Congress took up the cause, as did the forty-eight state affiliates of the General Federation of Women's Clubs (GFWC) and other reform groups. The persistence of the National Congress was responsible for the passage of mothers' pensions in many states. As one social historian writes, "[T]his association of elite and middle-class married ladies deserves much of the credit for transforming an idea initially sponsored by a few juvenile court judges into a national social movement and legislative reality."[11]

The Illinois legislature passed a mothers' pension law late in 1911. In reporting this success to *Child-Welfare Magazine*, the Illinois Congress of Mothers explained that "[the] pension removes the mother and her children from the disgrace of charity relief and places her in the class of public servants similar to army officers and school teachers."[12]

In a three-year span, the National Congress sent out over 700,000 pieces of literature to its state and local branches urging their members to support mothers' pensions. The nationwide Hearst newspaper chain editorialized on behalf of mothers' pensions, as did *The Delineator*, the third-largest women's magazine (with a mail circulation of about one million readers). *The Delineator*'s emotional editorial in the 1912 Christmas issue inspired advocates. It read, "Our Christmas Wish for Women: That Every Decent Mother in America

Could Have Her Babies With Her." Over a period of several years, other national magazines published articles endorsing mothers' pensions. Throughout
the campaign, *Child-Welfare Magazine* included updates on the efforts of state
affiliates of the National Congress to enact such legislation. The president of
the Oregon Congress reported:

> Some idea of the work done may be realized when I say that over one thou
> sand letters and over 2,500 pages of typewritten matter were sent out over
> the State . . . at a total cost of less than $100 to the Congress, . . . and that
> the bill has passed both houses *just as presented* with only one dissenting
> vote, and today, February 8, 1913, was signed by Governor West.[13]

Recipients of mothers' pensions were discouraged from working full-time.
Each was supposed to be "a proper person, physically, mentally, and morally
fit to bring up her children." Recipients also had to provide proof of poverty and
the dependent children were not to be over fourteen or sixteen years of age, depending on the state. Some communities required mothers to attend parent education classes to maintain eligibility. In retrospect, the program can be criticized for several reasons, but many would probably prefer it to the federal Aid
to Families with Dependent Children (AFDC) program that existed from 1935
until August 1996, when it was replaced by the Temporary Assistance to Needy
Families program. Throughout much of its long existence, AFDC was a "chronically underfunded public assistance program of last resort. Its clients became
very impoverished families in which mothers were divorced, or not married, or
widows of men without histories of wage earning. . . . "[14]

Nineteen state legislatures enacted mothers' pension laws between 1911 and
1913; twenty-one more did so by 1920, followed by six others before 1932.
Georgia and South Carolina were the only holdouts. In 1935, the program was
folded into the AFDC provisions of the federal Social Security Act. States with
stricter prohibitions against child labor tended to pass mothers' pension laws
earlier than other states; states with relatively high proportions of females over
the age of ten in the labor market, on the other hand, were slower to enact such
legislation. Anticipating the problems of implementing the law, the National
Congress urged its affiliates to appoint local committees to assist mothers "in
getting their share of this State aid."[15] Eligible applicants were frequently not
aware of the benefits; to facilitate identification of those in need, school nurses
were asked to report such cases. Quite often, the allowances were not sufficient
to enable mothers to remain at home with their children. As is often the case,
the proponents of these programs were not able to secure what they deemed to
be adequate funding. As the initial flurry of activism died down, the National
Congress, the GFWC, and other support groups tended to lose interest in the
less dramatic yearly funding campaigns.

Critics characterized the distribution of benefits under mothers' pension programs "as a social-control strategy," "welfare," "state socialism," "charity," and "poor relief." Many were concerned that the aid-giving practices might lead to pauperism among their beneficiaries by undermining the work ethic. Furthermore, the critics insisted that aid to the poor would do nothing to effectuate needed character reform. They argued that public benefits would disadvantage widowed women by advocating a children-first strategy that identified children's interests as separate from and of higher priority than those of their mothers. In some cases, women were encouraged to leave good salaried jobs for a government payment. Some professional women who were employed as social workers were clear beneficiaries, perhaps more so than poor mothers. Still other critics of the program warned that "the increasing powers of the state to intervene in parent-child relations also weakened paternal power, but since mothers were held responsible for children's welfare, the state's policies impinged on them more directly."[16]

IV. The Children's Bureau and Welfare Funds

Also in 1911, the National Congress endorsed the establishment of a federal Children's Bureau to gather data about infants and mothers throughout the United States. The National Consumers' League, a female-dominated reform association within the labor movement, supported the establishment of the Bureau, as did the GFWC, which had offered even earlier and stronger support for it. After several years of lobbying, supporters succeeded in convincing members of Congress and President William Howard Taft to establish and fund the Children's Bureau in 1912. Nevertheless, the vote in the U.S. House of Representatives foreshadowed the appropriations difficulties the Bureau would encounter; more representatives failed to vote at all on the establishment of the Children's Bureau than voted for or against establishing it.

In any event, the Children's Bureau was created as a federal agency in the Department of Labor. It was charged to "investigate and report . . . upon all matters pertaining to the welfare of children and child life among all classes of people."[17] Over time, the Children's Bureau became involved in labor and social-insurance issues, neither of which focused primarily on children. Employment issues tended to ignore women wage earners, focusing instead on the need to supplement the male family wage to reduce poverty. Social-insurance advocates ignored children almost entirely, advocating instead programs to aid workers as soon as they suffered a loss of earnings.

Despite its self-styled role as the national champion of children, the National Congress was not the driving force in the establishment of the Children's Bureau. The credit or blame, as the case might be, goes to the women active in the social-settlement movement. Jane Addams, the founder of Hull House in

Chicago, was the leading figure in this movement. In a commune-like setting, Addams had helped to educate young immigrants in American ways and protect them from abuse. The National Child Labor Committee and the GFWC also played important roles in the establishment of the Children's Bureau. Of course, the National Congress was supportive; as a prominent educational historian pointed out, "the National Congress of Mothers and Parent-Teacher Associations did not spawn the Children's Bureau, but it might well have."[18]

The Children's Bureau led the campaign for the first federal program to educate mothers about their own and their babies' health needs. First introduced in 1918 by Jeanette Rankin of Montana, the nation's first female member of Congress, the Act for the Promotion of the Welfare and Hygiene of Maternity and Infancy did not receive serious attention until 1921. During the hearings on the bill, it received the support of Senator Morris Sheppard of Texas and Representative Horace Mann Towner of Iowa; it was widely known as "Sheppard-Towner."

As with the campaign for mothers' pensions, the expanded membership of the National Congress—now organized in thirty-seven states—worked for the enactment of Sheppard-Towner. The million-member GFWC also strongly supported the measure, as did the Young Women's Christian Association, the Daughters of the American Revolution, the Women's Christian Temperance Union, the Council of Jewish Women, the National Education Association, the women's committees of the Democratic and Republican parties, and other organizations. Many passed resolutions endorsing the legislation and generated favorable publicity in the press. The National Congress sponsored a contest to determine which state could submit the most signatures in support of the bill to the U.S. Senate. To facilitate the effort, petitions were printed in *Child-Welfare Magazine,* which also carried advertisements which cried out, "Babies have a right to live. Mothers have a right to such instruction as will save infant lives. The country needs every life. It will take several generations to make up for the losses of human life in the war [World War I]. Never has there been greater need for saving life."[19]

Coordinated lobbying by the largest women's organizations was implemented through the Women's Joint Congressional Committee, a lobbying clearinghouse for women's organizations, including the National Congress. The Sheppard-Towner Act passed overwhelmingly in late 1921; it was the first allocation of federal funds for welfare purposes "supporting public-health nursing for mothers and infants."[20] Congress voted for it just *after* American women were fully enfranchised by the Nineteenth Amendment in 1920, but *before* actual patterns of female voting in national elections had become clear. Politicians feared that suffragists who had promised to clean house when they got the vote might do just that. It took a few more years before politicians realized that women were not going to vote as a bloc; the "gender gap" was still far in the future.

Sheppard-Towner expanded the responsibility and resources of states and of the federal government in educating mothers in hygienic and health practices. Difficult as it was, getting the law passed was only the first hurdle. Obtaining federal appropriations was an ongoing struggle; federal funding for the act was appropriated only until 1927, although it remained in operation until 1929. Public-health nurses were the mainstay of the program; they staffed nearly 3,000 prenatal centers. Sheppard-Towner funded other programs that encouraged state and local services for homeless, dependent, and neglected children, and provided means-tested mothers' pensions to needy women. Women physicians, who typically faced gender obstacles in building private practices, were also highly supportive of Sheppard-Towner programs.

Buoyed by the initial legislative success of getting federal funding for Sheppard-Towner, the National Congress developed plans for a program to be administered through the schools. As a result of the organization's growing involvement in the schools, in 1924 it changed its name to the National Congress of Parents and Teachers, commonly known today as the National PTA.

V. Summer Round-Up

In 1925, the National PTA joined the U.S. Bureau of Education (forerunner of the U.S. Department of Education) in a campaign to identify health defects that could interfere with a child's education. At the time, the incidence of communicable diseases, such as diphtheria, measles, mumps, and whooping cough, especially among the rural and urban poor, was a major health problem. Through its alliance with the Children's Bureau, the National PTA launched "The Summer Round-Up of the Children" to ameliorate the situation. In cooperation with local health officials, teachers and parents identified remediable defects in children entering the first grade.

At participating sites, white and, occasionally, black children received a medical and dental examination in May, then were scheduled to have any defects corrected during June, July, and August. The PTA's intent was to have the children mentally and physically ready for school in September, at which time there would be a reexamination.[21] In the mid-1920s, however, many parents did not believe that medical examinations or diphtheria prevention and other immunizations were useful if children were not sick at the time. Parents were also skeptical that dental examinations were useful; few parents associated the condition of baby teeth with later dental problems in permanent teeth.

The Summer Round-Up was precisely the kind of early childhood preventive program that Julia Lathrop had promoted through the Children's Bureau, the federal agency that the Mothers' Congress had enthusiastically supported years earlier as well as in 1925. To encourage participation in the Summer

Round-Up by local PTA affiliates, the editor of the *Delineator* offered $500 in cash prizes to the association with the best results. Prizes in the 1925 competition were won by the Barrow School of Columbus, Mississippi, the Putnam-Washington School of Marietta, Ohio, and the Baker School of Austin, Texas. A similar contest was held in 1926 and for several years thereafter.

Acknowledging praise of the Summer Round-Up project that she had initiated, National PTA President Margaretta Willis Reeve reported to the 1926 convention that "[t]he U.S. Bureau of Education, the Children's Bureau, the National Education Association, and the American Medical Association have publicly recognized the value of this movement and have lent valuable and active assistance."[22] Mary C. Baker, the president of the American Federation of Teachers, asserted that the National PTA was "the most wonderful invention in the school world in the last quarter century. . . . The ideas that underlie the program of the AFT chime beautifully with those that have built up your own organization."[23] At the time, the AFT was a struggling teacher union that enrolled only 3,497 members nationwide. The NEA was not much larger, with 9,000 members.

Despite effusive praise from some quarters, Sheppard-Towner did not survive. In 1926, when Sheppard-Towner came up before the U.S. Congress for renewed appropriations, the American Medical Association opposed renewing appropriations for the act, partly because doctors had to deal with competition from government services funded by Sheppard-Towner. Antisuffrage groups, defenders of states' rights, and citizens trying to protect the Public Health Service also lobbied heavily against Sheppard-Towner. Representative Frank L. Greene, an opponent of the act, repeated the arguments against it that he had made when it was first proposed:

> [Behind this] unpretentious, simple looking bill today are the agencies that for a long time have been persistently and insidiously working to incorporate into our American system of public policy . . . Government supervision of mothers; Government care and maintenance of infants; Government control of education; Government control of training for vocations; Government regulation of employment, the hours, holidays, wages, accident insurance and all; Government insurance against unemployment; [and] Government old-age pension.[24]

After considerable negotiation, the U.S. Congress extended funding for Sheppard-Towner just one more year. The act expired on June 30, 1928, leaving a greatly weakened Children's Bureau in its wake. The stock market crash of 1929 and the depression that followed slowed down the program, but in some areas—particularly in the South—the program lasted more than twenty years before it was taken over by local health agencies.[25]

VI. The National Congress of Colored Parents and Teachers

In Atlanta, Georgia, Selena Sloan Butler closely followed the expansion and activities of the National Congress. Educated by missionaries throughout her elementary school years, Sloan graduated at age sixteen from Spelman Seminary in Atlanta. She taught English and elocution for several years in Florida and Georgia and married Dr. Henry Rutherford Butler. After his graduation from Harvard, the Butlers returned to Atlanta, where Dr. Butler became one of the city's foremost black doctors. After the birth of Henry Jr., Selena Butler set up an at-home kindergarten, and when Henry Jr. entered public school, she established the first black parent-teacher association in the country at the Yonge Street School. By 1919, the other local mothers' clubs that Butler had organized throughout the state became the Georgia Congress of Colored Parents and Teachers. On May 7, 1926 she issued the call for the first national convention of black PTAs. Delegates from four states responded, and the group became the National Congress of Colored Parents and Teachers (NCCPT) and elected Butler as its first president. Once the NCCPT was established, Butler made every effort to coordinate its policies and programs with those of the National PTA. In a program comparable to the Summer Round-Up, black women provided mobile health vans in black churches, the only black-controlled public spaces for sharecroppers. In addition, medical clinics immunized children and provided dental and medical services to several thousand black children each summer. Local black parent-teacher associations grew rapidly, and reached 18,000 members in a thousand local associations in sixteen states by 1930, the year before Butler completed her term as president.[26]

The NCCPT operated primarily in the southern states, where there were large concentrations of racially segregated schools. Black parents and teachers formed local associations wherever segregated school systems existed, but these local associations did not ordinarily try to affiliate with the National PTA. When black parents and teachers applied to join the National PTA, the National PTA suggested that state affiliates encourage "colored people to have independent organizations as a Branch of the National Congress of Parents and Teachers, with an advisory board of whites, since they want to use the same name." The president of the National Congress urged the establishment of black organizations "wherever practical, so that they may advance in education and learn to work for themselves."[27]

In states that had no segregated state or local branches, blacks and whites participated together. However, a member who traveled frequently and often visited integrated meetings and state conventions observed that "[where] there were Negroes in membership, at no time did I see a Negro participating."[28] The member concluded that although blacks did not take leadership roles in integrated PTAs, segregated PTAs at least provided leadership opportunities.[29] For many years before the merger in 1970 of PTAs that had exclusively either black or white members, the National PTA and several state associations did refuse to hold their conventions in hotels that had not adopted a policy of equal treatment for all delegates.[30]

During the same week in May 1926 that Butler was establishing the NCCPT, the National PTA met for its thirtieth annual convention in Atlanta, Georgia. Margaretta Reeve included no reference to Butler's work in her president's convention report. Other documents, including an early history of the NCCPT, reveal that Reeve had encouraged Butler to persuade the local and state affiliates of black parents and teachers to join a national organization of black parents and teachers. Midway through the National PTA's convention, on May 6, 1926, Reeve announced to the delegates the formation of the NCCPT. The delegates were also informed that for the first time, the PTA enrolled nearly one million members; twenty-two state organizations had established a state office, and the organization was becoming more unified and influential.

Even without the right to vote, women and their organizations exerted considerable influence on the men in government who did vote on legislation. But in "putting children first" and seeking welfare and charity for others, the women (and men) of the upper and middle classes were also concerned about the threat to the social order created by the new immigrant urban masses. The socialization of poor immigrant children became a major interest for the growing PTA and its expanding agenda. As the next chapter makes clear, its agenda expanded dramatically as a result of that concern.

4

The PTA's Extensive Agenda

Ours is a curious organization . . . . [W]e go in and out among the great family of educators . . . [to] serve only as torches to make still clearer to us our opportunities and consequent responsibilities . . . .

In every activity we promote, in every policy we adopt, let us be ever mindful of our responsibility for the physical and mental health and happiness, the moral rightness and the spiritual significance in the lives, not only of the children, but because of them, of the parents and teachers, of America.[1]

— Margaretta Willis Reeve, president, National Congress
of Parents and Teachers, 1926

I. Introduction

Although it failed in its goal to establish a "PTA in every school," the PTA continued to expand by starting new PTA chapters, merging with local affiliates of the NEA, and absorbing mothers' clubs. For example, in 1919, the Maryland State Board of Education set forth its standards for one- and two-room schools. In doing so, the board of education requested that a separate entity, such as a parent or community group, make annual progress reports.[2] At the time, nearly four hundred such independent associations, mothers' clubs, and parent-teacher groups existed in Maryland. The PTA made every attempt to absorb these organizations as local affiliates and to adopt the 1919 standards as local-affiliate goals.

In addition, it promoted membership among organized but nonaffiliated women's clubs. The PTA's broad agenda appealed to thousands of mothers who eagerly engaged in activities to correct social ills. Even as the National PTA grew into a multimillion-member organization, its noneducational programs reflected concern for such diverse issues as the value of thrift, combating disease, outlawing war, and promoting disarmament. The fact that some of these programs have continued to the present time is reason to review their development in the PTA.

II. Noneducational Programs

Up to 1920, the state PTA affiliates exercised considerable discretion in determining their state program activities and legislative agendas. Along with the projects encouraged by the national organization, state leaders supported dozens of different projects and committees, some only slightly related to the general themes and mission of the organization. During her tenure as National PTA president from 1920–23, Katharine Chapin Higgins consolidated the national committees into departments encompassing many of the state project committees. To streamline the business of the organization, she grouped the state affiliates into geographic regions. Her successor, Margaretta Reeve, continued to bring the local and state affiliates into the unified—albeit still expansive—programs of the National PTA during its continued growth.

Each national vice president directed a department and supervised the activities of the committee chairmen within that department. In turn, each national committee chairman urged each state PTA to identify a state committee chairman who would enlist a cadre of volunteers at local-level PTAs. This organizational structure encouraged thousands of women to become involved in a program important to them and greatly helped the expansion of the organization. The responsibilities of the vice presidents were:

> VP and Director of the Department of Organization and Efficiency
> > Founders' Day
> > *Child-Welfare Magazine*
> > Literature
> > Membership
> VP and Director of the Department of Public Welfare
> > American Citizenship
> > Juvenile Protection
> > Legislation
> > Motion Pictures
> > Recreation
> > Safety

VP and Director of the Department of Education
  Humane Education
  Illiteracy
  Music
  Art
  School Education
VP and Director of the Department of Home Service
  Children's Reading
  Home Education
  Thrift
  Standards in Literature
  Home Economics
VP and Director of the Department of Health
  Child Hygiene
  Mental Hygiene
  Physical Education
  Social Hygiene

Each vice president, along with the committee chairmen, proposed resolutions that were considered for passage by the delegates to the national convention. If adopted, these resolutions became the basis for state and national legislative agendas. At times, the PTA formed coalitions with other organizations to support legislation that eventually became law. For instance, a federal hot-lunch program was a PTA priority, and such a program was enacted by Congress in 1946.

In 1926, the National PTA endorsed an extensive list of resolutions and vowed to enlist support to:

- Enforce prohibition
- Secure a uniform marriage and divorce law
- Educate on child labor
- Protect children from hazardous occupations
- Reaffirm its endorsement of a program for world peace
- Endorse the creation of a federal department of education
- Extend educational activities in the Bureau of Education
- Support continuation of the Sheppard-Towner Act
- Approve narcotics education
- Eliminate cigarette use by minors
- Bar national cigarette advertisements
- Enforce compulsory school attendance laws
- Wipe out illiteracy among five million illiterates
- Protect minors from the sale of salacious magazines and periodicals

- Protest the commercialized rodeo as a form of recreation
- Urge state affiliates to form committees for spiritual education
- Use "kindly interest in the amalgamation and adjustment" of immigrants
- Recognize the role of "Home-maker" on the national census
- Encourage programs on safety education to reduce child accidents
- Discourage extravagance by teaching thrift
- Express approval or disapproval of motion pictures
- Urge a constructive plan in each community for diversified recreation
- Promote community "Hymn Festivals"[3]

Although this agenda appears to be overly ambitious for any single organization, the PTA has been remarkably persistent in pursuing some of these objectives throughout its history.

Cigarette Smoking by Minors

As early as 1926, the National PTA had pointed out harmful consequences of cigarette smoking, and it continues to do so today.[4] Interestingly, the 1926 resolution referred to cigarette smoking as "pernicious" and "detrimental to character building," but it did not refer to the medical effects of cigarette smoking. After years of conducting antismoking campaigns among its membership, in 1964 the PTA received funding from the U.S. Department of Health, Education, and Welfare for a program to support the U.S. surgeon general's report that pointed out the health hazards of smoking. Through public service announcements, news releases, and the pamphlet "His First Cigarette May Be a Matter of Life and Death," the PTA waged a nationwide campaign to inspire young people to become the nation's first "smokeless generation." In 1982, Surgeon General C. Everett Koop also released a government report that included medical evidence on the damaging effects of smoking. Since then, the PTA has published additional brochures, sponsored workshops, developed a public relations campaign, and urged its members to encourage minors to quit smoking.

Antismoking resolutions were adopted annually by the National PTA convention delegates throughout the 1980s. From 1984 to 1993, the PTA adopted eleven different resolutions on various aspects of cigarette smoking. Several resolutions called for legislation requiring warning labels stating that tobacco is addictive and causes cancer, heart damage, and other diseases. Others called for legislation to prohibit smoking in establishments that allow the presence of children. To lobby against "the tobacco industry's deadly lies," the PTA joined the Campaign for Tobacco-Free Kids in 1996.[5] Along with 130 other organizations, the PTA continues to seek to prohibit the sale and marketing of tobacco products to children. To encourage local PTAs to implement their own antismoking programs, the

1997 national convention included a workshop on how local PTAs could use resources from the Centers for Disease Control in planning their own programs.

Although most of the PTA's statements of fact about cigarette smoking are justified, a few are not. A 1993 resolution relied upon EPA publications alleging that "secondhand tobacco smoke" was among the "most serious cancer threats" and that it "causes lung ailments in thousands of non-smokers every year."[6] In 1998, medical research disputed the findings of the EPA report, which exaggerated the harmful consequences of secondhand smoke.[7]

The Leisure Time of Children

How children and families spend their leisure time has concerned the PTA throughout its history. During the early 1920s, the National Congress tried to eliminate radio programs its leaders deemed harmful to children; subsequently its focus turned to shielding children from harmful movies. By 1929, motion picture theaters averaged eighty million paying customers each week, with affordable ticket prices from ten to seventy-five cents. The PTA's efforts were largely unsuccessful, but in 1942 the PTA began to preview and rate movies in its *National Parent-Teacher* magazine. Brief reviews indicated whether the language and performance were appropriate for children, youth, or adults.

The huge increase in television viewers in the 1950s presented the PTA with a new challenge: how to live with television. To heighten awareness of families' television viewing habits, the PTA developed a self-audit worksheet for each family member to complete each week. The worksheets were intended to be the basis for family discussions of the amount of time each member spent watching television, reading, attending the movies, and listening to records or the radio. By the late 1950s, the PTA magazine evaluated television programs as well as movies. Throughout the 1960s and 1970s, the PTA appealed to the mass media to act responsibly in their advertisements and programming, and in the early 1980s, the PTA initiated an awards program to encourage television producers to follow PTA guidelines.

The National PTA adopted different tactics in the 1990s. In 1995, the PTA announced its support for legislation requiring a "V-chip" in new television sets. The V-chip can be programmed to block whole channels, programs, and possibly even segments of programs that carry a rating code. In 1997, along with other organizations, the National PTA was involved in negotiations with the television industry that led to letter ratings specifying the type of content in television programs. The cable stations and networks—except NBC and Black Entertainment Television (BET)—accepted the rating system that became effective in October 1997. Networks and producers assign ratings to each show. (S) means that the television program contains sexual situations, (V) indicates violence, (L) signals coarse language, and (D) conveys the presence of suggestive dialogue. A rating icon appears in the upper corner of the TV screen for fifteen seconds at the start of each program. News and sports shows remain unrated. In addition, the PTA urges newspapers to publish the ratings. Children's programs are rated as suitable for children of all ages, or for children older than seven years of age.

Reactions to the PTA's efforts "to clean up" television have split along historically predictable lines. On the one hand, networks and stations have criticized efforts to restrict their freedom as "censorship" or interference with freedom of speech. In their view, PTA pressure should be exerted on parents, not on television producers. In any event, it appears that efforts to restrict the content of television shows watched by children are not likely to be successful.

Technology, however, may enable parents to monitor children's viewing habits more effectively than in the past. More recently, the National PTA joined the National Urban League in support of the "Parents' Guide to the Information Superhighway: Rules and Tools for Families," a publication discussing "parenting in a world of computers and new forms of media."[8]

Health and Nutrition Issues

The National PTA has been active on health and nutrition issues throughout its existence. As demonstrated by its Summer Round-Up program, the PTA was an early proponent of preventive health measures. In 1954, thousands of PTA volunteers assisted in the mass vaccination against polio of 1.8 million children with the Salk vaccine, developed by Jonas Salk in 1953. On a more contemporary note, the National PTA governmental relations staff continues to monitor health care legislation, as it has since 1977. In addition to its support for programs directed at specific health problems, the PTA was an enthusiastic supporter of the Clinton administration's universal health care proposal in 1994. It continues to support comprehensive health care plans for all children, an issue likely to be prominent for years to come.

Spirituality and Ethical Character

The PTA's founding mothers not only openly acknowledged the significance of spiritual training in character development, they practiced it. A vesper or prayer service was often the opening event at annual state and national conventions; Jewish, Catholic, and Protestant ministers participated. State conferences often met in churches, and local PTA meetings opened and closed in prayer as well.

In 1929, the National PTA discontinued the Department of Parent-Teacher Associations in Churches. Mothers' clubs, kindergarten clubs, and parent-teacher study clubs that met regularly in churches were encouraged instead to focus on the school community and to meet in school buildings. This effort to unite these disparate groups and to bring them into the state and national PTA networks disappointed some religious leaders, who deplored the loss of the opportunity to work with the PTA on parent education in denominational facilities.[9]

By 1947, PTA publications emphasized the importance of holding PTA meetings regularly in schools, including private schools. Before the Catholic Church began to organize its own parent-teacher organizations in the early 1980s, many Catholic schools had a PTA; almost all Catholic schools, however, dropped their affiliation with the National PTA after 1978. That year, the National PTA president led the National Coalition to Save Public Education, a coalition which convinced Congress to reject tax deductions for private school tuition.

In 1963, the U.S. Supreme Court held Bible reading without comment and school-sponsored prayers in the public schools to be unconstitutional. In 1981, the PTA adopted a resolution encouraging its state and local affiliates to "develop programs designed to promote understanding of Supreme Court decisions regarding religion in public schools."[10] In 1987, citing its "long-established PTA policy of cooperation with the public schools," the National PTA announced that "PTAs will avoid bringing pressure to continue any practices that the constituted authorities find unlawful." Nevertheless, it suggested that "PTAs may continue their own inspirational exercises within their own meetings. Whether or not they meet in school buildings, PTA's [sic] are voluntary and private associations, and determine for themselves the observances that will meet their needs."[11] As a result of these policy statements and resolutions, the National PTA has opposed all proposed federal legislation to permit voluntary prayer in the public schools. To provide guidance on religious issues and character development in public schools, the PTA disseminates "A Parent's Guide to Religion in the Public Schools." This guide was prepared by the Freedom Forum First Amendment Center at Vanderbilt University and includes brief discussions of such topics as prayers at high school baccalaureate services, the wearing of religious garb by students at school, and student religious clubs in public schools.[12]

Peace and National Security

From its inception in 1897, the Mothers' Congress had put international peace prominently on its agenda; peace, national security, and international relations have always been PTA concerns. Closer to home, state and local PTA members focused on the public schools to foster the ideals of American citizenship. The PTA also promoted "a well-educated citizenship for the security of the country" as a critical component of the curriculum.

Of course, there was no objection when the National Congress put aside most of its normal activities to aid the war effort during World War I. One of its first actions was to establish the Mothers' Army and Navy Camp Committee of the National Congress of Mothers and Parent-Teacher Associations. Under the committee's leadership, the National Congress transformed its headquarters building on Massachusetts Avenue in Washington into a service club for military personnel. State affiliates were urged to provide centers for servicemen, and some did so. The largest service club in the country sponsored by an affiliate was in Philadelphia, the hometown of the chairman of the Mothers' Army and Navy Camp Committee.

The second-largest service club was in Baltimore, a pass-through for large numbers of transient servicemen. Utilizing buildings in downtown Baltimore, the Maryland Congress joined other groups in staffing and furnishing recreation rooms, dormitories, canteens, libraries, a pool, and a dining room. A 'melting pot' in the window of a business on a busy street was the receptacle for public contributions of gold, silver, tinfoil, copper, and brass to be sold to defray war expenses. The Maryland Congress began the service club with fifteen dollars in its treasury, and received donations amounting to thirty thousand dollars. From the initial fifteen beds, the facility could eventually accommodate seven hundred overnight guests for twenty-five cents each.[13]

According to the records of the Illinois PTA, "the most outstanding World War service of the Illinois Congress was The Jolly Tar, a unique servicemen's center operated in Waukegan, Illinois."[14] A report by the Illinois State War Recreation Board described the Jolly Tar center as "unique among all army and navy camp clubs in that it retained absolutely the feeling and atmosphere of home."[15] Operated by women, the Jolly Tar provided a home atmosphere with motherly attention for young servicemen far from their own homes.

The club opened in September 1917 in a sixty-year-old mansion prepared for service under a newly employed housemother. In addition to plentiful free snacks and a moderate-cost cafeteria, the Jolly Tar also provided dormitory cots for twenty-five cents per night. On Sundays, hostesses from the Illinois Congress took turns providing cakes and cookies. Affiliates too far away to render personal service sent jams and jellies, nuts, popping corn, apples, and other foods. During the influenza epidemic of 1918, parents of ill sailors stayed at the Jolly Tar to visit their sons more easily. By the time the Illinois Congress closed the Jolly Tar in September 1921, the service club had become a much larger enterprise than the Congress itself.[16]

Elsewhere, Red Cross work and other war-related activities superseded the normal activities of the National Congress. Local groups participated in sewing projects, victory gardens, canning demonstrations, and various fundraisers for relief activities. Members of the Congress often stretched the meaning of "child welfare" to show that their activities were consistent with the purpose of the Congress, but it is doubtful whether anyone really cared about the discrepancy.

Despite its support of the war effort, the Congress was caught up in the anti-radical hysteria that followed World War I. After the war, a renewed spirit of patriotism tended to demonize liberal economic and social policies as "un-American." During 1919, more than four million workers went out on strike. In response, industrial management launched a widely publicized campaign to identify labor unions as hotbeds of socialism and communism. Many Americans feared that radicals might try to instigate a communist revolution in the United States. Federal and state governments conducted a vigorous drive against anarchists, communists, and socialists. Several hundred immigrants were arrested and deported as suspected revolutionaries.

Caught up in the wave of nationalism, women founded a host of new patriotic organizations, such as the American War Mothers, the Service Star Legion, and the American Legion Auxiliary. Advocating military preparedness and anticommunism, these groups positioned themselves opposite women's peace organizations, such as the National Congress of Parent-Teacher Associations.

In 1920, the National Congress led the American Association of University Women, the Women's Christian Temperance Union, the National Federation of Business and Professional Women, and the League of Women Voters in a lobbying effort to promote international peace. In addition, the National Congress vigorously expressed the view that public schools should educate the next generation to prevent war. Through the Women's Joint Congressional Committee (the women's lobby on Capitol Hill), the president of the National Congress participated in the National Council for Prevention of War as well as the Women's Committee for World Disarmament. An antiwar group that favored national disarmament, the Women's Committee for World Disarmament protested postwar increases in the U.S. military budget. In 1921, the committee sponsored mass "Disarmament Day" meetings in sixteen states and Washington, D.C. Its supporters were responsible for waves of speeches, meetings, petitions, telegrams, and resolutions sent to President Warren G. Harding and members of Congress. The major women's organizations with peace departments claimed to speak for five million women—more than one out of every five in the United States. Partly because of the public sentiment they created, President Harding called for the Washington Disarmament Conference in midsummer 1921. As might be expected, some formidable opponents were also aroused.

In 1922, Brigadier General Amos A. Fries of the Chemical Warfare Service, assigned to the military intelligence unit that monitored domestic subversion, accused the National Council for Prevention of War (NCPW) of being a front "to establish Communism in America." Fries also attacked Florence Watkins, executive secretary of the National Congress of Parent-Teacher Associations, who was an NCPW executive board member. Feeling the pressure generated by Fries's accusations, the National Congress withdrew its affiliation from NCPW in December 1922, as did the General Federation of Women's Clubs (GFWC).[17] The National Congress, however, continued to sponsor activities intended to foster world peace.

Patriotism, feminism, socialism, communism, internationalism—each "ism" spawned new women's organizations with profound effects on existing women's organizations. In many situations, women were on opposite sides of issues; there was a notable absence of gender solidarity. Some groups delegated decisions on controversial issues to their local affiliates, while others implemented new procedures to protect their organizations from criticism. For a time, the National Congress avoided controversial issues, but it continued many of its existing relationships with organizations under attack. The president of the Illinois Congress explicitly urged her state convention to follow this strategy: "Don't ever get so wedded to your own organization that you think it the panacea for all the ills of the world, but be willing to join hands with other groups in promoting work that is for the general welfare."[18]

Although it had curbed its post–World War I peace activities, the PTA joined the call for "the outlawry of war" at its 1927 annual convention in Oakland, California. A resolution adopted at that convention and renewed in subsequent years read: "We believe that war between nations as a settlement of international disputes is a crime against civilization, and heartily endorse the outlawry of war."[19]

The PTA and the United Nations

In 1944, the world was again at war. At the PTA convention that year, the delegates welcomed First Lady Eleanor Roosevelt, who addressed the national gathering. For the first time in the PTA's history, the president of the National Congress of Colored Parents and Teachers also spoke to the delegates.[20] Under the convention theme banner, "All Children are Our Children," the National PTA board adopted another policy regarding international disputes:

> To safeguard our children and ourselves from a third world war . . . we agree that this nation should join with other peace-loving nations in the creation of an international organization to enforce a just and peaceful settlement of all disputes.[21]

Needless to say, this was a highly controversial position, but it foreshadowed PTA activities on national security for many years to come.

At the Dumbarton Oaks Conference in Washington, D.C. in the autumn of 1944, China, Great Britain, the United States, and the USSR drafted the outline for a charter for the United Nations (UN). In early 1945, at the Yalta Conference, President Franklin D. Roosevelt's last war conference, Roosevelt, along with Prime Minister Winston Churchill and Premier Joseph Stalin, agreed to hold a founding conference before the year's end to draw up a charter for a permanent organization. Delegates from fifty nations took part in the conference, held in San Francisco from April 25 through June 26, 1945. As an experiment in citizen-government relations, the U.S. State Department invited forty-two organizations to serve as consultants to the official U.S. delegation. Although the 1945 National PTA convention was cancelled because of World War II, the PTA's national president, Minetta A. Hastings, and Mrs. J. W. Bingham, a member of the PTA's board of managers, represented the PTA. Hastings described her experience:

> These organizations represent the various major interests of our country—labor, industry, religion, patriotic services, women's interests, and education. The National Congress of Parents and Teachers was one of the three educational organizations, the other two being the American Council on Education and the National Education Association. Here at San Francisco the representative of the American Association of University Women is working closely with us, since that group too, is chiefly interested in education. . . .
>
> We who are consultants are pioneers under a new policy of the Department of State. It is the belief of the Department that responsible national organizations having definite policies on matters of international interest should have an opportunity to be heard and also that they should serve as a liaison between the Department of State and the citizens of this country included in their membership.[22]

According to the PTA representatives, these four groups were determined to promote "an International Office of Education through which education could be used as a means of keeping the peace."[23] Hastings recorded her dismay at the delegation's response:

> But before very long we noticed something rather curious. It appeared that some members of the American delegation were allergic to the word *education*. They would have nothing to do with it—a fact that seemed rather strange to us in a country where education has been almost a religion. They would take the word *cultural,* but *education?*—absolutely no! We finally learned that if provisions were made for an International Office of Education or if any specific statement was made about education, certain people believed that somehow or other Russian propaganda would get into American schools. I am still not quite sure whether or not the word *education* will find its way into the final document![24]

As was feared, the American delegation rejected the idea of including an international office of education because they feared that communists or other extremists might take over American schools. Undeterred, the educational consultants campaigned among foreign delegations and interest groups throughout the nation to garner support for an international office of education. Although their efforts were unsuccessful, the setback was not a total loss, since the United Nations Educational, Scientific, and Cultural Organization (UNESCO) was created early in 1946 as one of eleven specialized agencies of the UN.

Soon after the UN Charter was signed, the National PTA adopted a new Four-Point Program. For each of the four points — world understanding, formal education, health, and parent and family life education — four specific objectives were identified, and for each objective, four action projects were planned. To provide the framework for carrying out these objectives, the PTA published a list of responsibilities for its officers and leaders at every organizational level. As always, compliance with the national organization's agenda was a high priority.[25]

The PTA's faith in the efficacy of international organizations was not borne out by subsequent events. In 1984, the United States formally withdrew from membership in UNESCO, charging that mismanagement and politicization had rendered the organization unable to carry out the mandates of its charter.

The United Nations International Children's Emergency Fund (UNICEF)

On December 11, 1946, the UN General Assembly established UNICEF as an affiliated agency of the UN to deal with children's health needs as a result of World War II. Although UNICEF was supposed to be short-lived, the UN General Assembly voted on October 5, 1953 to support the organization indefinitely.[26] At the same time, the UN General Assembly shortened its name to the United Nations Children's Fund, but kept the initials UNICEF.

Thirty-seven national committees have been set up around the world to raise money for, and thereby to carry out the work of, the UN Children's Fund.[27] Among other programs, the U.S. Fund for UNICEF encourages children to "Trick-or-Treat" for UNICEF during October, which is National UNICEF month.

Although it has approved most UNICEF programs, the National PTA Executive Committee rejected the "Trick or Treat" UNICEF project in which children are supposed to collect funds for UNICEF instead of asking for treats on Halloween. Although the National PTA disapproves of any project that requires children to collect money, some local PTAs participate in the "Trick or Treat" UNICEF project. Begun as a UNICEF fundraiser in 1953, the "Trick or Treat" project continues to be a popular program. To teachers who request it, UNICEF provides a curriculum guide that features issues of international concern and culminates in the "Trick or Treat" fundraising project. Although the National PTA does not promote this particular event, it frequently cites UNICEF publications and supports programs very similar to those sponsored by UNICEF.

To show its support, the National PTA presents an annual statement at Congressional committee hearings to urge adequate appropriations for UNICEF programs. For fiscal year 2001, the Clinton administration requested a $110 million contribution for UNICEF from the 106th Congress as part of the foreign operations appropriations.

In 1989, the UN mobilized international support to update its 1959 Declaration of the Rights of the Child, first adopted by the UN General Assembly in 1948. For children's rights to carry the weight of international law, a United Nations 'Covenant' or 'Convention' was required. In 1978, when the United Nations sponsored the International Year of the Child, work began on the development of the forty-one substantive articles of the Convention on the Rights of the Child. On February 16, 1995, then UN Ambassador Madeleine Albright signed the Convention on the Rights of the Child on behalf of the United States. However, because the Convention on the Rights of the Child is an international treaty, the U.S. Constitution mandates that it be approved by the U.S. Senate, which has resisted approval because of intense opposition from many conservative pro-family groups.

Through its policies and practices since 1964, the National PTA has continued to support the UN and UNICEF.[28] Somewhat surprisingly, however, the PTA has not formally endorsed the UN's Convention on the Rights of the Child. In June 1997, the PTA did not respond when the U.S. Fund for UNICEF invited the National PTA to sign the letter of appeal for ratification that it sent to U.S. senators. The letter, signed by 170 organizations, dramatically stated its appeal: "The Convention is the most rapidly and widely adopted human rights treaty in history with 191 States Parties. As of June 11, 1997, only two countries have not ratified this celebrated agreement—Somalia, which is unable to ratify an international treaty, and the United States." Elsewhere, the letter stated that "we have studied the claims made by opponents of the Convention and have found them spurious."[29] Neither the "spurious claims" nor the responses were provided. As of September 2000, the U.S. Fund for UNICEF had not planned any subsequent appeal for ratification.

The PTA's activities on international affairs and national security illustrate a problem that surfaces in many organizations. On the one hand, virtually any activity or policy can be justified by its (hoped for) effects on children. On the other hand, the PTA cannot become involved in every policy or activity that impinges or might impinge on its mission in some way. The problem is where and how to draw the line between the noneducational matters that the PTA should support and the matters that should be left to other groups.

III. From "Mothers" to "Parents": An Era Ends, Another Begins

Looking back, we can see that as membership in the National PTA increased rapidly after 1924, more diverse points of view emerged within the organization. The fact is, however, that the growing diversity within the PTA did not lead to major conflict within the organization until the 1960s and 1970s. Remarkably, the PTA experienced huge increases in membership while other leading women's organizations declined and even went out of existence. For example, the Women's Christian Temperance Union (WCTU), founded in 1873 by Frances Willard, was the first women's mass organization. The WCTU's primary goal was prohibition of the manufacture, sale, and transportation of alcoholic beverages, but it also ran day nurseries for working mothers, supported labor reforms, and fought against prostitution. When the Eighteenth Amendment, the prohibition amendment, was ratified in 1919, the WCTU lost its main raison d'être and faded into semiobscurity.

Another example is the GFWC. At the height of its influence during the early 1900s, the Federation was active in art, civil service reform, education, forestry, home economics, industrial and child labor, legislation, library extension, public health, pure food, and other domestic concerns. In 1919, the Senate passed the suffrage amendment and in August 1920, the thirty-sixth state ratified it as the Nineteenth Amendment to the United States Constitution. The GFWC seemed to lose its momentum as its principal issue, women's suffrage, gained in the legislatures.

Prior to 1924, the National Congress of Mothers, ostensibly devoted to the welfare of children, had considerable appeal and was less controversial than some other organizations with social goals. State and local affiliates of the National Congress worked for reforms intended to help women and children, but the reforms did not severely threaten business or labor interests. Indeed, the National Congress was an early advocate of child labor legislation that restricted the employment of children, an objective long sought by labor unions. Eventually, the states enacted compulsory education laws that served the objectives of the National Congress and the labor unions.

Criticisms and competition from the women's clubs exerted strong pressure on the National Congress to de-emphasize its broad social agenda. At the same time, public education was expanding rapidly, and hence the National Congress devoted more and more of its energies to organizing chapters in urban and rural schools. Because there were still thousands of local women's clubs not affiliated with any national movement, the National Congress was able to expand by incorporating nonaffiliated women's organizations as well.

Despite its forays into other fields, the National PTA was also increasingly active in education. As we shall see in Chapter 5, PTA educational activities have been guided by the NEA since the early 1920s. Careful consideration of the relationship between these organizations is, therefore, the key to understanding the PTA's positions and objectives on educational issues.

5

The PTA, the NEA, and Education

Teachers' unions, federal agencies, special interest groups—when we talk about the power structure of our educational system, we sometimes forget to include parents. At the National PTA, we are committed to putting parents back into the educational power equation, and we've been taking some steps to do so.[1]

— Grace Baisinger, president, National Congress
of Parents and Teachers, 1979

I. Introduction

As an adjunct of the public schools since the 1920s, the National PTA adopted an agenda shaped by school administrators at the local level and by the NEA at the federal level. This framework prevailed until the 1960s, when unionization of the NEA led to the expulsion of administrators from the association. Changes in the NEA resulted in basic changes in the PTA that have continued to this day, but have not been widely recognized. Although the formal relationship between the two organizations has remained constant, virtually every aspect of the PTA has been and is deeply affected by the unionization of the NEA.

II. PTA/NEA Relationships: Phase I

In 1919, the steadfast financial support for the National Congress provided by Phoebe Apperson Hearst ended with her death. Without her support, the National Congress could not raise enough money to keep the thirty-two-room mansion on Massachusetts Avenue in Washington, D.C. as a permanent headquarters. The building, which had been used as a service club for enlisted men during World War I, was sold in the summer of 1920. After the sale, the National Congress of Parent-Teacher Associations, already closely allied with the NEA, moved its offices into the NEA's Washington headquarters. Despite membership of over 180,000, the executive secretary was the only employee of the National Congress.

As more Americans moved away from farms to towns and cities, secondary-school enrollment rose from 1,115,000 in 1910 to 2,500,000 in 1920, and to 4,812,000 in 1930.[2] These increases resulted jointly from immigration, increases in the native population, the enactment of compulsory education laws, and more vigorous enforcement of such laws. The increases also resulted in a major policy dilemma. During the early 1900s, high schools were primarily college preparatory institutions. As their enrollments increased, high schools were enrolling increasing numbers of students who did not plan to enroll in college and were not interested in a college preparatory curriculum. To resolve the dilemmas over the objectives of secondary education, the National Congress accepted the NEA's lead.

The *Cardinal Principles of Secondary Education*

The NEA was founded in 1857 as a national organization of college presidents and school superintendents, almost all of whom were men. Women teachers were not allowed to become NEA members until 1866. Unlike the National Congress, the early NEA had only three appointed committees; their tasks were to recommend a course of study for high schools, prepare an ideal program for the education of youth, and provide annual reports of staff qualifications and compensation, student enrollment, and library resources.[3] By the 1890s, the NEA was creating a national agenda via its issuance of reports, through which the NEA impacted public opinion on educational issues.

In 1918, in response to the tremendous increases in secondary-school attendance, an NEA committee issued a report which contrasted sharply with an 1893 study that had recommended that all secondary students study English, foreign languages, mathematics, history, and science. That study, chaired by Harvard University President Charles Eliot, was promptly criticized for allegedly assuming that secondary schools should be primarily college preparatory institutions. In contrast, the new report, *Cardinal Principles of Secondary Education,* recommended a much more diversified curriculum emphasizing the importance of educating "the whole student," thus departing from the previous emphasis on academics.[4] According to *Cardinal Principles,* the goals of U.S. education should be health and safety; worthy home membership; mastery of the tools, technique, and spirit of learning; citizenship and world goodwill; vocational and economic effectiveness; wise use of leisure; and ethical character. This NEA report was destined to become one of the most influential statements on education in American history.

The National Congress, referred to as the PTA after 1924, formally adopted the NEA's *Cardinal Principles* in 1927 to "give suggestions for legislative effort and programs of work to state PTA branches and local associations."[5] Adopting *Cardinal Principles* did not mean that the National PTA would cut back on its involvement in noneducational programs; for that matter, *Cardinal Principles* was never confined to secondary education, or even to educational issues concerning kindergarten through twelfth grade.

There is no doubt that *Cardinal Principles* was very influential; the problem lies in assessing the influence of the various principles it advocated. Long before the PTA had officially adopted *Cardinal Principles,* it had supported activities and programs that embodied the principles. *Cardinal Principles* legitimized the goals that the PTA had previously encouraged local school districts to adopt.

Elsewhere, however, *Cardinal Principles* played a more substantive role, especially as the goals of secondary education became more controversial in the 1920s and thereafter. As secondary-school enrollments increased to unprecedented levels, new issues emerged. Was it fair for public schools to provide college preparatory programs for a small minority of students while ignoring the needs of the large majority of students who did not plan to seek a college education after high school graduation? Should lower-income families be required to subsidize higher education for students from higher-income groups? *Cardinal Principles* was instrumental in raising such issues, as well as in providing a respected authority for anyone who already shared the point of view it expressed.

Today, conservatives criticize the public schools for offering a cookie-cutter, one-size-fits-all curriculum. Actually, it was the public school establishment that emphasized meeting "the needs and interests" of students in the 1920s, and it was this establishment that was responsible for breaking away from the rigid secondary-school curricula that had prevailed in the early 1900s. Today, the main issue is still with us: what subjects, if any, should all students be required to study in order to preserve prosperity and cohesiveness in a highly diverse society? Unfortunately, there is no consensus on the answer to this question, and none appears to be in sight.

On other curriculum issues, also, the PTA was guided by *Cardinal Principles.* For example, *Cardinal Principles* asserted that "[t]he purpose of democracy is so to organize society that each member may develop his personality primarily through activities designed for the well-being of fellow members and of society as a whole."[6] The NEA/PTA concept of citizenship reflected this fuzzy collectivism, in which citizenship as social cooperation and working for the public good predominated, instead of citizenship as political rights and individual responsibilities.

Legislation versus Parental Concerns

Although it turned its education policy over to the guidance of professionals in the NEA, the PTA nevertheless continued its standing committee on education. However, the committee now focused its attention on issues of concern primarily to career teachers, such as teacher salaries, retirement and tenure policies, the status of teaching as a profession, and (as before) federal aid for education. Obviously, none of these items was very helpful to parents interested in improving the education of their own children, but all of these issues deeply concerned the NEA.

A report at the 1926 PTA convention reflects the NEA's strong influence on the PTA. The National PTA vice president, charged with promoting "school education," reported that "[t]he Committee on School Education receiving through its chairman all of the educational forces of the N.E.A. has concentrated on the new Education Bill."[7] As an illustration, the education chairman reported that from April 1925 to April 1926, the PTA had sent out 18,427 leaflets supporting the establishment of a federal department of education. Coordination of these activities between the PTA and the NEA was facilitated by the fact that Charl Ormond Williams, the National PTA vice president, was also the director of field service for the NEA. Several times during the year, Williams requested that PTA leaders and members write to their congressmen urging the passage of the bill. The education chairman readily acknowledged that "the aim of the school education committee is really closely related to the work of the PTA's committee on legislation."[8]

Four other areas of education were included in the PTA's agenda: humane education, illiteracy, music, and art. The PTA's humane education committee fostered benevolent attitudes toward pets and other animals. The PTA suggested that its members write articles for magazines on topics such as "Children's Attitude Toward Their Pets." The PTA also endorsed other efforts to achieve a better world for pets, including education against rodeo shows, sponsorship of poster contests, and a general observance of Be-Kind-to-Animals Week.

Alarmed over the fact that literacy rates in Denmark, Sweden, and Switzerland greatly exceeded that of the United States, the National PTA's chairman of the illiteracy committee took on the task of raising "Uncle Sam from the tenth place in the scale of literate and enlightened nations."[9] Following up on the NEA's Adult Education Conference, PTA officials worked with state superintendents and state and local PTA presidents to recruit teachers for evening classes for adult illiterates in rural school districts. When possible, the PTA cooperated with other organizations to secure home teachers to teach English to foreign-born women. Support was enlisted from the American Legion, the Daughters of the American Revolution, and the Colonial Dames. The PTA set a goal of eliminating adult illiteracy before the 1930 census, declaring it shameful that the "cross mark is still being written on court records, marriage licenses, deeds, etc."[10]

The PTA also encouraged the study of music and art in all schools. Each local PTA was urged to provide music on loan, programs on the significance of music, and even music lessons and music appreciation classes for adults. Many local affiliates sponsored a Mother's Musicale preceding Mother's Day. Local PTAs were also encouraged to survey "art conditions in the home, schools, evening art schools, libraries, museums, [and] city and community stores." Clearly, at that time, the PTA's education agenda was much less political than the NEA's, which emphasized the enactment of federal legislation, especially on funding for education.

Through the years, the National PTA and the NEA shared speakers, general programs, and award programs. As noted in a history of the PTA, "This cooperation with the National Education Association is carried down from the national to the state, district, and local levels. . . . [F]or example, the state president of the parent-teacher organization is made an ex officio member of the state education association. Similar relationships are maintained all down the line."[11] State teachers' association affiliates sometimes granted the PTA free pages in their monthly magazines.[12] In another example of cooperative relations, the state education associations often paid the expenses of National PTA officers who visited the state.

The PTA and School Administrators

At the local level, the support of school administrators was critical to both the NEA and the PTA. It was precisely because school administrators encouraged membership in the PTA and the NEA that both organizations expanded as they did. For example, in 1915, when the Cook County superintendent announced at the Illinois Teachers' Institute that his office "desires and will cooperate in the establishment of a Parent-Teacher association in every county school, and urges immediate affiliation with the Illinois Congress of Mothers and Parent-Teacher Associations," the teachers acted accordingly.[13] In 1933, PTA leaders "held regular office hours in the [McLean County, Illinois] superintendent's office on Saturday afternoons to meet with the rural teachers."[14] In certain areas, the NEA sought to require an effective PTA as a condition of school accreditation by the appropriate regional accrediting agencies, which served as a sort of "Good Housekeeping seal of approval" among educators.

The close relationship between the PTA and the NEA turned out to be invaluable after the stock market crash of 1929 resulted in severe financial problems for schools. As one of the most expensive government programs, schools were among the first public services to be cut, and the cuts were sometimes drastic. Supervisors were dismissed, the number of teachers and their salaries were reduced while class size increased, and extracurricular activities were often eliminated. Teachers in many systems went unpaid for months or were "paid in scrip or tax warrants which could be cashed only at a considerable discount."[15] As the collection of school taxes dropped drastically, the NEA appointed a Commission on the Emergency in Education to help unpaid teachers and keep schools open. In addition, the commission urged federal support to assist school systems that depended heavily on local property taxes that were often in default during the Depression years.

The National PTA supported these efforts in various ways. It flooded lawmakers' desks with letters that insisted that public education must be adequately maintained despite decreased tax revenues. Occasionally, where schools were temporarily closed, local PTAs sponsored educational programs for children. Sometimes state and local PTAs joined with teacher organizations in mass meetings to promote special measures to help school districts in dire straits. As unpaid and underpaid teachers resigned from their school districts, the National PTA urged its members who were former teachers to help alleviate the teacher shortage. In some school districts, the PTAs coordinated the emergency programs intended to ameliorate the crisis in school revenues.

Meanwhile, the PTA itself experienced the debilitating effects of the Depression. From 1932 to 1934, membership in the National PTA decreased sharply, and bank failures and widespread unemployment forced many PTAs to disband. State PTAs everywhere were forced to curtail their activities, merge committees, and reduce committee expenses.[16] Meetings were held less frequently, and some state conventions were suspended. Despite these organizational setbacks, however, the PTA continued its legislative efforts to increase state aid to public schools and raise teacher salaries. Desperation was evident in a National PTA resolution that called for an additional year of high school to ease the unemployment crisis.

After almost a decade of troublesome fluctuations, unemployment dropped appreciably in 1939 and was minimal, as the United States became "an arsenal of democracy" while fighting World War II. After the war, the PTA's new Four-Point Program resolved to strengthen school curricula, improve the health of the nation's children, promote world understanding through the United Nations, and expand lifelong education for parents. In 1946, the PTA also supported an NEA initiative relating to teacher training and certification. Efforts to attract more men to the profession of teaching were also a high PTA/NEA priority in the 1950s, but their joint efforts along this line did not have any appreciable effect on the gender composition of the teaching force, which remained almost 80 percent female.[17]

School consolidation was another PTA objective that originated with the NEA. Between 1940 and 1957, the number of school districts was reduced from 120,000 to 55,000.[18] Consolidation eventually encountered widespread opposition, but before the trend ran its course, the number of school districts had been reduced to approximately 15,000. Proponents of consolidation had argued that the result would be more effective use of public funds, improved education for millions of children, and more equitable distribution of the tax base to support poorer districts. In particular, the California PTA cited its effort to reduce the number of school districts in California as among its significant activities. The opponents of consolidation contended that it would weaken the ties between parents and schools, and that taxpayers would be more reluctant to pay for schools that they could not observe. Of course, the opponents of consolidation were sometimes motivated by more practical considerations, such as having to travel farther to school or losing control over patronage.

From 1943 to 1957, the NEA and the PTA supported federal legislation that would have provided federal aid for the education of illiterates, Americanization programs for immigrants, the partial payment of teachers' salaries, and the establishment of a federal department of education. During this period, none of these proposals was enacted.

The Federal Government and the Curriculum

All of the PTA/NEA objectives were shattered by an event that took place far from the United States—or, for that matter, from any place on earth. On October 4, 1957, the Soviet Union launched *Sputnik I*—the first man-made satellite to orbit the earth. As Americans awakened to second place in the space race, schools were subjected to a barrage of criticism from all sides. Distinguished scholars such as James Bryant Conant, a former president of Harvard University, charged that state departments of education were little more than the "willing tools" of the interests of the state NEA affiliates.[19] President Dwight D. Eisenhower urged PTAs to scrutinize school programs. Military officers like Vice Admiral Hyman Rickover argued that professional educators were bringing America to its knees before a superior Russian educational system.[20] To remedy the deficiencies in science, mathematics, foreign languages, and vocational guidance, the federal government passed the National Defense Education Act of 1958 (NDEA)—the first major step by the federal government to directly influence the curricula in America's local schools. Although the PTA and the NEA had long supported increased federal funding for education, the NEA initially opposed the passage of the NDEA because the funds it granted were earmarked for mathematics, science, and other defense-related curricula, but could not be used for teacher salaries or buildings. Subsequently, however, both the PTA and the NEA supported the NDEA.

The NDEA was just the beginning. In the five years between 1962 and 1967, Congress passed almost thirty laws that pumped vast amounts of federal support into public education. Improving occupational training and retraining the nation's labor force and jobless illiterates were targeted goals of the Manpower Development and Training Act (1962). The Vocational Education Act (1963) enlarged high school and post–high school vocational education programs. The Economic Opportunity Act (1964) was part of President Lyndon B. Johnson's declaration of "war on poverty." Among various separate programs, it authorized youth and adult work-training programs for the poor, and a domestic peace corps known as VISTA (Volunteers in Service to America). The Higher Education Act of 1965 authorized a student-loan program. Public Law 89–10, the Elementary and Secondary Education Act of 1965, also signed by President Johnson, provided $1.2 billion for public elementary and high schools during the first year of enactment. The funds were (and still are) distributed to the states based on the numbers of children in low-income families, but the efficacy of the legislation has been mired in controversy.

III. PTA/NEA Relationships: Phase II

The PTA's relationship with the NEA can best be described as a partnership with two distinct phases. In the first phase, dating from the early 1900s, the NEA was controlled by school superintendents. Because school boards were supposed to be nonpartisan agencies, they typically lacked the means of generating political support for their programs. For this reason, school boards and superintendents (who were essentially appointees of nonpartisan elected school boards) sought PTA support to legitimize their programs and actions.

With nearly twelve million members in 1965, the PTA was more than ten times larger than the combined memberships of the NEA and the American Federation of Teachers (AFT). Despite its impressive membership, however, James D. Koerner, editor-in-chief of the Education Development Center in Newton, Massachusetts, criticized the PTA after his extensive study of public education in the 1960s:

> [T]he American PTA is rarely anything more than a coffee-and-cookies organization based on vague good will and gullibility. . . .
> In a word, the local PTA does indeed have an influence on educational

policy: by failing to be more than an administrative rubber stamp, it simply sustains the existing order. . . .

Indeed the national PTA is a member in good standing of the 'Big Six,'
a sort of behind-the-scenes association of three professional groups and
three lay groups in education: The American Association of School Administrators, the National Education Association itself, the Council of
Chief State School Officers, the National School Boards Association, the
National Association of State School Boards, and the National Congress
of Parents and Teachers [the PTA]. Some people might look on the Big
Six as something of an establishment creature, as an instrument for promoting establishment policy rather than as what it is alleged to be: an instrument for hard-headed debate and bargaining among broadly based interests about what American educational policies should be. However
that may be, the three lay groups on the Big Six, the National PTA in particular, are no match for the three professional groups.[21]

Difficult as it may be to believe, Koerner's comments understated PTA sub-
ordination—hence, that of parents also—to the interests of the NEA. Although
his prediction was accurate, at the time he could not have realized how the
unionization of the NEA from 1964 to 1975 would affect NEA/PTA relations.

In the pre-unionization days, educational policy-making followed normal
political procedures. Elected school boards met as legislative bodies to adopt,
reject, or amend policies, including policies on the terms and conditions of employment for teachers. Teacher organizations and the PTA presented their
points of view along with other interested parties. For better or for worse,
school boards adopted the policies that they deemed appropriate. Insofar as the
policies were budget related, they were largely settled until the next budget cy-
cle. Granted, this is an oversimplified view; for present purposes, however, it
sets forth the policy-making structure and procedures in the pre-unionization
era accurately enough.

Despite Koerner's acerbic conclusions, local PTAs wielded considerable influence in middle- and upper-class school districts. Usually no other powerful
interest groups were active in educational affairs. Local PTAs worked closely
with school management, and for a good reason. Management had the power
to run the district on a day-to-day basis. If a local PTA became interested in a
particular program or activity, it had only to persuade the school administrators, who exercised broad discretion over the district budget and terms and conditions of teacher employment, to adopt the program or pursue the activity. Furthermore, although they lacked financial resources, local PTAs played a
significant legitimizing role; their approval was valuable even though PTAs
were not politically powerful in their own right. At the same time, the local
teacher associations were largely social organizations. Except for presentations

on school district budgets, the teacher associations welcomed new teachers at meetings and sponsored receptions for retiring teachers; typically, they were not a powerful force at the local level.

Unionization of the NEA

Teacher unionization drastically altered the political landscape. Many issues formerly resolved unilaterally by school boards after hearing anyone who wished to comment on them were resolved by collective bargaining with teacher unions—a process that excluded PTAs as well as others who wished to address the issues. Furthermore, teacher-union dues escalated to pay for union staff to negotiate contracts and process grievances. When negotiations were completed, usually for multiyear contracts, the union staff served as full-time political operatives, amply equipped with the facilities and campaign workers to be a formidable political force. Indeed, the emergence of teacher unions as a powerful political force at all levels is one of the most significant political developments in the United States since the 1960s.[22]

For practical purposes, the 1962 collective bargaining election in New York City marks the beginning of the collective bargaining movement in public education.[23] After months of rancorous negotiations, including a one-day strike by twenty thousand New York City teachers, the New York City board of education and the United Federation of Teachers (UFT, an affiliate of the AFT and the AFL-CIO) negotiated a forty-page written agreement. In addition to a substantial pay raise for teaching and pay for extracurricular activities, the striking teachers demanded and received "free lunch periods, check-off for union dues, and one hundred and forty-seven other items dealing with work-place conditions."[24]

After losing the New York City representation election to the UFT, the NEA's executive director, William G. Carr, sounded the alarm. In an address to the 1962 NEA convention, Carr expressed an apocalyptic view about the threat of unionism: "This . . . is the first time in which forces of significant scope and power are considering measures which could destroy the Association."[25]

Ironically, however, the NEA responded to the threat of unionism by becoming a union itself, albeit with nonunion terminology to maintain the pretense that it was not a union. For instance, the NEA embraced "professional negotiations," which turned out to be collective bargaining with a few cosmetic changes. Furthermore, the NEA contended that state educational boards, not state labor boards favored by the AFT, should administer the laws and regulations governing negotiations at the local level. Within a few years, however, all cosmetic differences of this sort between the NEA and the AFT positions disappeared, especially after the NEA realized that it could utilize collective bargaining to stifle the membership threat from the AFT. Both unions increased their membership dramatically under collective bargaining by enrolling teachers who had not previously been members of any union.

Prior to unionization, the NEA at the national level was not influential in political and legislative affairs because it could not provide much support for candidates for public office or for its preferred causes. Most local NEA affiliates had miniscule budgets and no full-time staff to provide grassroots support for the NEA's favored candidates and legislative agendas. These weaknesses disappeared when the NEA became a union; today, no other national organization has the power of the NEA to provide grassroots support for its candidates. According to a study by Myron Lieberman, the NEA's revenues at the local, state, and national levels exceeded $1 billion in 1996, and the association employs thousands of full-time employees who are politically active at the state and local levels.[26]

Unionization changed the NEA in three fundamental ways. First, administrators left or were excluded from the association at all levels. Second, as a result of the departure of administrators, the NEA was not restrained by any management issues. Third, the NEA became a highly influential political force.

In theory, administrators represent both public and their own welfare interests. With the administrators no longer in the NEA, local NEA affiliates faced no internal opposition to bargaining for teacher benefits that would reduce the funds available for school maintenance, textbooks, or salaries for employees not covered by union contracts. While school management would normally consider these interests, collective bargaining endangers this outcome.

Under collective bargaining, school districts and unions bargain over "terms and conditions of employment." What this phrase means varies somewhat from state to state, but it usually covers salaries, benefits and other kinds of compensation, workday, length of the school year, transfers, workload, and a host of other matters that affect a district's resources and ability to initiate or change curricula or programs. Theoretically, school boards continue to be responsible for educational policy, but as people familiar with collective bargaining can attest, "terms and conditions of employment" and "educational policy" are frequently one and the same issue regarded from two different perspectives.

For example, suppose that parents in a local PTA want the school board to adopt a policy whereby the most experienced teachers (who are invariably also the highest-paid) are assigned to inner-city schools that are presently staffed largely by new teachers or substitutes. To parents, how to utilize teachers in order to maximize learning among the disadvantaged is an educational policy issue. The teacher unions, however, regard the issue in terms of transfers and assignments, that is, as "terms or conditions of employment," subject to negotiation between the union and the school district. In such negotiations, the unions almost invariably insist that transfers be voluntary and based upon seniority—the very same policies that created the problem to begin with. Even proposing the staffing change causes problems for the local PTA—teachers predictably support their union position and a potential boycott of the PTA may result in loss of dues and leadership. Furthermore, union members may retaliate against the parents who led the effort for the change in staffing policy.

In collective bargaining, third parties are rarely allowed to be present at the bargaining tables. As a result, there is no parental representation at the bargaining table, and parental political influence is miniscule compared to that of the teacher unions. Indeed, the unions are often directly responsible for the election of school board members who establish the board's bargaining position and vote to ratify or to reject a negotiated agreement.

Consequently, instead of presenting its views at open board meetings on an equal basis with the teacher organizations and other interested parties, the PTA can only express its views at contract ratification meetings, when the contract is, in effect, a fait accompli. Theoretically, the school district could keep the PTA informed on the progress of negotiations and receive its input on union positions, but the dynamics of bargaining preclude this outcome. Both union and management prefer not to have third parties involved precisely because their objections make it more difficult to reach agreement. Furthermore, if information about negotiations is provided to third parties, there is a danger of leaks and distortions that could upset negotiations. If the PTA were entitled to information about the progress of negotiations, other groups would clamor for the same privilege, and the requisite confidentiality would disappear altogether. If bargaining were to go on until the early morning hours, or around the clock, it would not be feasible to get parental input in the climactic stages of bargaining. Collective bargaining by teacher unions is not consistent with the open manner in which public policy should be made, but unfortunately, the legislatures that enacted the teacher bargaining statutes did not know or care about this inconsistency.

At the outset of the unionization of the NEA, local PTAs frequently found themselves in opposition to union demands; when this happened, relations at the local level deteriorated rapidly. The tensions between local PTAs and local NEA affiliates came to a head during teacher strikes. Parents were inconvenienced by teacher strikes and concerned about the impact of the strikes on their children's education. Also, they were concerned about the example being set, because most teacher strikes were (and still are) illegal. Pupil safety when school was not in session was another prevalent concern. Needless to say, the teacher unions characterized teacher strikes as a benefit to pupils. Unions urged parents to keep children at home for safety reasons, thereby putting more pressure on school boards to settle on union terms.

The PTA Opts for Neutrality

To help formulate its policy on teacher strikes and bargaining issues, the National PTA appointed a task force to recommend PTA policies on these matters. The task force elicited opinions from teacher unions, school boards, school administrators, and others. At its September 1968 meeting, after receiving the task force report, the national board of directors adopted policies on the role of the PTA in teacher strikes. The board first identified several "dilemmas" that teacher strikes and negotiations posed for local PTA members.

1. If the PTA provides volunteers to man the classrooms during a work stoppage, in the interest of protecting the immediate safety and welfare of children, it is branded as a strike breaker.

2. If the PTA does not take sides in issues being negotiated, it is accused of not being interested.

3. If it supports the positions of the board of education, which is the representative of the public in negotiations, *the teacher members of the PTA have threatened to withdraw membership and boycott the local PTA activities.* (emphasis added) [27]

To resolve these dilemmas, the PTA adopted guidelines covering the prestrike period, the period during the strike, and the aftermath of the strike. Prior to the threat of a strike, PTA members are urged to keep the lines of communication open, and to seek action to remedy the causes of increased teacher complaints. If a strike occurs, PTA members may encourage action to protect children and to keep teachers involved in the PTA, but should not volunteer to help in ways that assist the administration in keeping the school open. When a strike is over, the PTA is encouraged to seek community support to ensure that implementation of the negotiated strike agreement continues. The PTA's guidelines emphasize that a local PTA should resist all activities that might be considered "taking sides" in a teacher strike; instead, it should encourage a public airing of the issues and let the school board and teacher union settle their dispute.[28]

Despite the fact that national policy called for neutrality, PTA/union conflict at the local and state levels continued to erupt. As additional states enacted teacher bargaining statutes, the conflicts emerged all over again at the legislative as well as the local level. The question of whether the PTA would represent parental or union interests surfaced in many ways; the experience in Ohio foreshadowed the eventual outcome nationally. According to an analysis of the conflict there:

[T]he state PTA and the powerful Ohio Education Association [OEA], an NEA affiliate, came to blows over three bills in the state legislature. Two of these involved teacher certification, training and dismissal; the third was a strong professional negotiations bill that included binding arbitration. The state PTA actively—and successfully—opposed several of OEA's legislative proposals in these areas, and that was when OEA apparently decided enough was enough. At its 1976 state convention, OEA adopted a resolution asking its 85,000 teachers to drop out of the PTA, to boycott all its activities, and to encourage parents to form new parent-teacher organizations that are not affiliated with the PTA. Of the 217,000 members who quit the PTA in 1976, more than 50,000 were from Ohio, where entire units disaffiliated.[29]

Robert Lucas, president of the Ohio PTA, described the change in teacher union attitudes toward PTAs after the PTA challenged the teacher unions:

> For years we did everything the teacher association wanted and we never disagreed about anything. We gave out certificates, awarded the principal a seat of honor and carried all the tax levies, and we were the nicest guys in the world. Now that we're beginning to deal with real issues, they have a different opinion of us.[30]

Although parents and the teacher unions disagreed about several issues, teacher strikes precipitated the crises that forced a resolution of the conflict. Despite the fact that strikes by public employees are prohibited by statute or judicial decision in most states, the incidence of teacher strikes increased dramatically after the teacher bargaining statutes were enacted. Actually, the number of strikes does not convey the magnitude of the problem; for every actual strike, there were scores of threatened strikes that led to turmoil in school districts. Needless to say, opinions about teacher strikes varied widely, but teachers and their unions certainly viewed them as more benign than did parents. The unions were sometimes successful in recruiting parents to their cause, but most parents were more concerned about the disruption to their own lives and their children's education than about the strike issues.

Ultimately, however, the outcome was virtually preordained. With miniscule funds, a highly transient membership, heavy dependence upon teacher support just to remain viable, and intimidation by teacher boycotts, the National PTA raised the white flag again in 1987. The board of PTA officers affirmed the 1968 board's neutrality position with only a few editorial changes. Neither the elected officers nor the PTA bureaucracy was willing to risk an organizational meltdown that might have resulted from a declaration of independence from the NEA. Neutrality marked the end of the PTA's independence because it prohibited the PTA from adopting positions that were opposed by the teacher unions.

In its defense, the PTA contends that its neutrality policy applies only to strikes. A fair reading of the policy in conjunction with its aftermath, however, demonstrates clearly that the defense is fallacious. For example, the National PTA policy advises local PTAs on what they should do in the "prestrike" period, as if PTA members could know beforehand that a strike would materialize. All the teacher union would have to do in order to neutralize the PTA would be to set a strike date, regardless of whether it actually planned to strike. Furthermore, if the PTA policy is applicable only to strikes, the PTA would have to explain why its affiliates are not involved in bargaining issues that are vital to parents and their children.

To appreciate the implications of PTA neutrality in teacher bargaining, one must consider what its guidelines recommend—and also what they do not mention. The guidelines include eighteen recommendations that either imply or suggest that strikes are justified, or ensure PTA support of union positions during a strike. The possibility that a teacher strike might be due to unreasonable union demands is never suggested, even implicitly. On the contrary, by urging PTAs to "seek action that corrects the basic cause of dissatisfaction," the resolution is clearly biased in favor of the union. "Teacher dissatisfaction" is not always justified, nor does it always merit PTA intervention. In fact, dissatisfaction is frequently fomented by the unions to cause more pressure on school boards to make concessions. The repeated support for "negotiations" implies that the school boards have not fully met their obligations to bargain in good faith before the strike. PTA guidelines do not mention the fact that when school boards do not bargain in good faith, the teacher unions have adequate remedies, such as filing unfair labor practice charges with state labor boards. The guidelines also recommend that PTAs make sure that negotiated agreements are "faithfully implemented." This ignores the fact that unions are the parties who cite contract violations, and that unions have ample legal remedies and resources to ensure that contracts are "faithfully implemented."

The omissions in PTA policy are an even more telling sign of PTA capitulation to the NEA. Significantly, PTA policy does not address parental concerns over items on which school boards are required to bargain (mandatory subjects of bargaining). One would expect several of these items to be high-priority issues in any organization dedicated to promoting parental and pupil interests:

- What are teacher responsibilities to help pupils outside of regular class hours?
- How long do teachers remain in school after class to assist pupils and/or confer with parents?
- Are there adequate procedures to resolve student/parent grievances against teachers?
- Is there any appeal from teacher grades, or negative recommendations to employers and institutions of higher education?
- Do teacher contracts provide adequate opportunities for parents to confer with teachers? For example, if parents work during regular school hours, are there opportunities to meet with parents at some other time during the day?
- Do pupil report cards convey adequate information about pupil progress?
- What is the impact of teacher seniority on continuity of instruction and teacher/pupil relationships?

- What criteria are included in teacher evaluations?
- What is the district policy on teacher tenure?
- Do district teachers have the qualifications to teach the grade(s) and subject(s) assigned?
- How does the district deal with a negative teacher evaluation?
- What is the percentage of teachers who have received unfavorable evaluations in the past 2–3 years?[31]

Surely, an organization that represents parents and students should have positions on such issues, and strive to have them adopted. Nevertheless, as a result of the PTA's "neutrality," local PTAs do not address these issues, or any others that might lead to conflict with the teacher unions. In contrast, the teacher unions aggressively bargain for their positions on all such issues. Despite the NEA's professed concern for parents and pupils, association proposals would often severely disadvantage both, to say the least. For instance, the teacher unions typically propose the following:

- No student grade may be changed without the consent of the teacher. Obviously, this assumes that teachers always recognize and agree to correct their mistakes.
- Teachers cannot be required to return in the evening or on weekends for parent conferences; if they do return voluntarily, they must be paid generously.
- Parent complaints cannot be considered as a basis for disciplinary action unless the complaint is in writing and the teacher has had time off with pay to prepare a response.
- If a parent has a complaint, the teacher has the right to have a union representative present when the complainant faces the teacher.

Parents who are not literate in English, such as many itinerant farm workers, are practically helpless in districts that accept such union proposals; even sophisticated parents are often deterred from pursuing their grievances against such union-imposed obstacles.

IV. The Aftermath of the Takeover

Although neutral on bargaining issues at the local level, the PTA is invariably supportive on other issues of importance to the NEA. It might be a stretch to assert that the NEA dictates PTA policy; it would not be a stretch, however, to assert that the NEA exercises a veto power over PTA policy on any issue that affects the NEA. PTA members often are not aware of this fact because overt coercion is no longer evident. PTA members and officials often bristle at the suggestion that the PTA is dominated by the teacher unions. If one thinks of domination only in terms of explicit union commands to the PTA, this reaction is understandable. In practice, however, NEA domination is pervasive. It shows up in the selection of speakers and convention programs, the issues that are raised and the ones shoved under the rug, the avoidance of union identification among delegates to PTA conventions, the immediate rejection at PTA conventions of any effort to reconsider union-backed positions, the similarity between PTA and union legislative agendas, and the PTA's leadership in union-funded coalitions.

Even if "shared views" explains the PTA's alignment with NEA positions, it does not explain the complete absence of attention to union policies detrimental to parental concerns at PTA meetings and conventions. Furthermore, by its own admission, the PTA has never disagreed with the NEA on any significant issue.[32]

Myron Lieberman's experience at the 1997 National PTA convention illustrates the NEA's low profile but heavy hand in PTA affairs. The PTA convention program listed workshops and showed only the name and city of each discussion leader, not his or her occupation. Lieberman, the author of several books and articles on teacher unions, attended one of the workshop sessions devoted to privatization issues. The discussion leader at the session was so skillful in presenting NEA positions without labeling them as such that Lieberman sought to identify the individual. After the session, Lieberman complimented the discussion leader and asked about his occupation. The first answer was: "I work for an educational organization." On further questioning, the discussion leader reluctantly revealed that he was a UniServ director employed by the Iowa Education Association. "UniServ director" is NEA-speak for union business agent and political operative. Lieberman was probably the only individual present at the session who realized that the discussion leader was a full-time NEA employee. The other delegates attending the session did not feel coerced, for they weren't; they were, however, exposed to only one side of highly controversial issues by someone purporting to be just an interested parent. This situation is commonplace at state and National PTA conventions; the union presence is pervasive but not usually apparent to convention delegates. Inasmuch as the divisive union/parent issues are not raised, delegates are not aware of any coercion.

The PTA has internalized its subordinate role; new members simply take for granted that the PTA is a support group for teachers. Supposedly, pupils will benefit as a result of PTA activities. Unfortunately, what the unions seek for teachers is not always good for students; hence, the PTA's neutrality is a major strategic victory for the NEA. When local PTAs do on occasion actively oppose a union position while the union is engaged in collective bargaining, the NEA does not hesitate to remind the PTA that its only option is to remain silent. For example, in April 1994, at the urging of its executive committee, NEA President Keith Geiger wrote to the president of the National PTA after the relationship between the NEA and a local PTA did not improve following settlement of a bitter contract dispute.

Geiger "emphasized the long-standing tradition of cooperation and respect between the two organizations at the national level and asked the PTA president to remind its local affiliate of the National PTA's policy of neutrality in labor/management disputes in school districts."[33]

Perhaps the strongest argument against the thesis that the union dominates the PTA is that the PTA's leadership shares the NEA's educational and political views: there is no need to dominate an organization that willingly supports your positions. Nevertheless, this convergence argument clearly is not applicable to the PTA's policies on bargaining and privatization issues. On these issues, the record is clear that the PTA's neutrality is a direct result of the NEA's threats in the 1960s to withdraw its support and launch a new parent organization unless local PTAs stopped supporting school management in bargaining disputes. Because local PTAs are bound by national policy, the PTA's neutrality in collective bargaining has removed local PTAs as players on the local school issues that matter most to parents. How the PTA's legislative agenda fills the programmatic vacuum resulting from its neutrality on bargaining issues is the subject of the next chapter.

6

The PTA and Contemporary Politics

Increasing evidence shows that the public feels a sense of helplessness, of powerlessness, about its schools. With collective bargaining now widespread, citizen participation in educational decision making is declining dramatically. . . .

The private sector trade union model that has been transplanted in school districts is a secret, bilateral, adversarial process that excludes parents, students, and other citizens from reasonable access or influence. Even school board members, administrators, and teachers are locked out of the process in the increasing number of districts where the primary responsibility has been delegated to professional negotiators hired by both the employer and employee sides.

As the scope of bargaining increases, more and more educational policy questions are settled in the process. This leaves less and less purpose for citizen participation in planning or policy making and decision making; less and less for citizens to participate about.[1]

— Don Davies, director, Institute for Responsive Education, 1976

I. Introduction

Since its inception in 1897, the PTA has adopted hundreds of resolutions, some of which have been the basis of its lobbying efforts. Over the years, the PTA board of directors has originated slightly more than one-third of the 200 resolutions classified as "current" in 2000 (about 120 others are categorized as "historic"). In short, board-generated positions form the basis for most of the National PTA's legislative program.

The scope of these issue items is staggering. Dozens of them relate to health and nutrition issues—topics here include measles, venereal diseases, AIDS, drugs, alcohol, tobacco, attention deficit disorder, mental and physical disabilities, calcium supplements, organ donation, and ingredient labeling. The PTA's current policy statements also advocate the strengthening of support for public school teachers and describe the roles of parents, teachers, and administrators. The PTA's resolutions concerning education deal with numerous specific concerns, covering topics such as communism, the dangers of nuclear technology, gender equity, homeless and migrant children, dropout prevention, and commercial advertising in instructional programs. The PTA also has positions on textbook credibility and on the selection, review, and removal of educational materials from school libraries and media centers. Decades of resolutions and position statements affirm the PTA's support for the public education system and for increased federal funding for health and education programs. Not surprisingly, the PTA has also passed a resolution in support of world peace.[2]

II. The Resolution Process

Members can participate in setting the PTA's legislative agenda through the resolution process, but member-generated resolutions are not likely to have legislative priority. Resolutions that are adopted by a local unit, council, district, or state PTA must proceed through a ten- or twelve-step process in order to meet the criteria for board approval. Even if a resolution is eventually approved by convention delegates, the National PTA board of directors can still reject it. Only those resolutions ratified by the board constitute official positions of the National PTA. Ostensibly established to guard against frivolous resolutions, the complex resolution process in practice functions to ensure leadership control over PTA policies and programs.

In addition to convention resolutions and board policy statements, PTA officials are also guided by several long-range policy statements when determining the PTA's legislative agenda. Adopted by thirty-one state PTAs prior to the late 1970s, these "specific issue items" incorporate many of the PTA's long-standing positions on various issues. Not surprisingly, child labor issues continue to concern the PTA, as do the availability of education and recreation programs for children and adults, the accessibility of health services for mothers and children, and the preservation of environmental quality. The specific issue items also touch on several more controversial issues: for instance, the PTA strongly supports various United Nations programs, statehood for the District of Columbia, and the dissemination of family planning and population control information.[3]

Eight of the seventeen specific issue items recommend increased federal appropriations or regulation; an additional seven urge expanded government spending without specifying which level of government is to do the spending. Only one of the specific issue statements would draw support across the political spectrum: the PTA opposes increases in the postal rates for educational materials.

These specific issue items are not merely matters of historical interest. Today, none of them can be deleted except by a vote of 60 percent of the state affiliates. In March 1990, the National PTA board of directors incorporated these specific issue items into its legislative policies regarding special national concerns. From these items, board-ratified resolutions, and board-generated position statements, the National PTA Legislative Program Committee crafts the annual legislative program for final approval by the board of directors.

III. Implementation of the PTA's Legislative Agenda

Once the legislative program is approved, the National PTA's government relations staff lobbies Congress to enact it. PTA lobbyists and officers testify before congressional committees and generate letters, telephone calls, and visits to elected officials in support of PTA positions. Once a bill has been enacted, the National PTA submits comments to departments and regulatory agencies on its reactions to the rules that have been proposed to implement the legislation. This is a key step for any lobbying group (albeit one little understood by the public) because much of the impact of legislation is shaped by the regulations that are adopted to implement it. In subsequent years, when a funding reauthorization is sought for programs supported by the PTA, the PTA again lobbies lawmakers for increased funding.

Despite the National PTA's extensive agenda, and the costs of its lobbying efforts, elected officials rarely cite the tax-exempt National PTA as an important player in the legislative process. In contrast, labor unions (also tax-exempt organizations), such as the NEA and the AFT, and their political action committees rank among the most influential lobbying organizations. Although PTA bylaws prohibit the organization from establishing a separate political action committee, PTA leaders have always taken great pride in their lobbying efforts, particularly within coalitions, frequently taking credit for successes that likely would have occurred without PTA support. For instance, the California PTA claimed credit for defeating Proposition 174, a 1993 California voucher initiative. However, inasmuch as Proposition 174 was defeated by a 70 to 30 margin, it would have been defeated no matter what the California PTA did to defeat it.

Although the PTA adopts the same position as the public education establishment, PTA leaders contribute very little to coalition strategy sessions. With rare exceptions, the public education coalitions do not rely upon the PTA for direct support in legislative and political battles. Instead, PTA support is featured mainly to forestall criticisms that a coalition position does not have parental support, as well as to obviate the need to gain approval from a less prestigious parent organization.

For example, the PTA is one of twelve public school organizations that formed the Learning First Alliance in September 1997.[4] The other members are the NEA, the AFT, the American Association of Colleges for Teacher Education, the American Association of School Administrators, the Association for Supervision and Curriculum Development, the Council of State School Officers, the Education Commission of the States, the National Association of Elementary School Principals, the National Association of Secondary School Principals, the National Association of State Boards of Education, and the National School Boards Association. In short, the Learning First Alliance is the public school establishment with an attractive title.

Despite its protestations to the contrary, the Learning First Alliance was established for political purposes. The NEA's executive director, Don Cameron, conceded as much when he addressed the NEA's 1997 convention. In referring to the Alliance, Cameron said that "working in isolation, we hobble ourselves and the cause of public education. NEA's future is inextricably linked to the well-being of public education. . . . [O]ur job is to continue advocating for our members, and the surest way to protect their jobs is to protect public education."[5]

Lois Jean White, PTA president from 1997 to 1999, was the chairman of the Learning First Alliance in 1998. Inasmuch as the PTA contributes little more than its name to the coalition, White's service as chairman appears to have been contrary to typical practices in coalitions. Ordinarily, the leadership of a coalition goes to a leader of the organization that provides the most support for the coalition. This is not the case in education, for a very good reason. Unions have less credibility among the public than most other special interest organizations. Poll results indicate that the "union" label is a major liability, particularly in political campaigns. While voters recognize that the AFT, which is affiliated with the AFL-CIO, is a labor union, many are unaware that the NEA is also a labor union. The NEA ranks higher in public approval than the AFT for precisely this reason.[6] Understandably, both unions prefer that PTA leaders serve as coalition leaders.

Kim Moran, director of field services for the AFT's Committee on Political Education, inadvertently confirmed this explanation at a 1995 AFT Quality Educational Standards in Teaching (QuEST) conference.[7] Moran urged AFT members to form coalitions with the PTA and other groups that need financial support to educate their own members. In emphasizing the importance of working with the PTA, Moran said that "the PTA has credibility, [and] that is why we always use the PTA as a front. They are also the most disorganized [among volunteers]. They have no money and they must be educated, so we support them in a thousand different ways."

There is really nothing new in Moran's remarks, except in their frankness.

Neither was there anything new about White, as the PTA's president, serving as chairman of the Learning First Alliance. Her predecessor as PTA president by twenty years, Grace Baisinger, served as chairman of a similar coalition that in 1978 defeated a tuition tax credit favored by parents of children attending religious and other private schools.

Coalitions are especially effective in local elections; indeed, because so few eligible voters vote in local elections, the success rate for coalitions, including school district unions, can be very high. It may be true that the PTA has never seen a school bond election it didn't like, but often PTA support is not enough. Again, coalitions come to the rescue.

IV. The PTA's Government Relations Office

In 1977, while still struggling to stop the member exodus that had resulted from the PTA's opposition to the teacher unions and its adamant opposition to government assistance to pupils in private schools, the National PTA hired thirty-seven year old Becky Schergens as its executive director. Schergens was a former deputy assistant secretary for education at the U.S. Department of Health, Education, and Welfare. Her professional background and Washington know-how were useful as the PTA and the NEA intensified their lobbying efforts on behalf of a separate U.S. department of education. To facilitate this effort, in 1977 the PTA opened a government relations office in the NEA building in Washington.[8]

After opening this office, the PTA established its Member-to-Member Federal Communications Network to assist local activists. Intended to supplement the PTA's paid lobbyists, the network urged PTA members to make telephone calls, write letters, and encourage newspaper and television editorials supporting PTA positions.[9] In 1977, the PTA staff and the network focused on the establishment of a federal department of education and the defeat of Senate Bill (S.B.) 2142. The latter was more pressing. Senators Patrick Moynihan (D–NY) and Robert Packwood (R–OR) had cosponsored S.B. 2142, legislation that would have allowed individuals to claim a tax credit of one-half of private elementary-school, secondary-school, or college tuition paid, up to a maximum of $500.

Despite the modest amount involved, the public school establishment characterized the bill as a huge threat to public education. The PTA's president, the aforementioned Baisinger, was the titular leader of the opposition to the bill, as chairman of the National Coalition to Save Public Education. The coalition included the NEA, the AFT, the National School Boards Association, the National Association for the Advancement of Colored People, the AFL-CIO, the United Auto Workers, the American Jewish Congress, the American Civil Liberties Union, and twenty-six other organizations.[10]

On April 10, 1978, more than eight hundred representatives of the National Coalition to Save Public Education came to Washington to lobby for the defeat of S.B. 2142. In urging its defeat, coalition members emphasized their determination to oppose for reelection members of Congress who voted for it. Each organization in the coalition developed its own coast-to-coast grassroots campaign to block passage of S.B. 2142. In Los Angeles, "at every high school, a teacher [was] paired with a principal and a PTA member, who as a team lobbie[d] staff members of senators' and representatives' home offices." The Indiana PTA's legislative representative appeared with teacher union executives to discredit the bill. Coalition members nationwide bombarded members of Congress with opposition messages.[11]

After the House Ways and Means Committee rejected the tuition tax credit proposal by a vote of twenty to sixteen, AFT President Albert Shanker wrote:

> There can be no question that the tide was turned because of the last-minute efforts of the National Coalition to Save Public Education, chaired by Grace Baisinger, president of the National Congress of Parents and Teachers. . . . Before these groups mounted their massive effort, the letters to members of Congress from parents of private and parochial school students were running far ahead of the opposition. But in recent days the tide turned. . . . But the fight is far from finished. . . . The campaign must remain in full swing until the issue is finally settled.[12]

As predicted at the time, the PTA lost both nonpublic and public school members as a result of its opposition to S.B. 2142. The twenty-six Republicans and twenty-four Democrats who cosponsored the proposal in the Senate enjoyed the support of constituencies in their respective states. Some in those constituencies quit the PTA, as did Catholic parents, whose children likely would have benefited from the law if it had passed. Almost 260,000 members dropped out of the PTA during Baisinger's two-year term as president of the National PTA and chairwoman of the National Coalition to Save Public Education. For better or worse, the National PTA lost its claim to being an inclusive organization that represented the parents of pupils in private as well as public schools. Twenty years later, in a striking repetition of the PTA's role as a front organization, Lois Jean White, the 1997–99 National PTA president, served as chairman of the National Coalition for Public Education, a sixty-member coalition of "education, religious freedom, and civil liberties organizations that oppose vouchers and tax subsidies."[13]

Support for the U.S. Department of Education

At the 1926 convention, the national chairman of the PTA School Education Committee announced, "It has long been acknowledged by the members of this association that the solution of many of the problems in American education lay in the creation of a federal Department of Education."[14] To promote this objective throughout several decades, the National PTA sent letters and pamphlets to urge state PTA officers to lobby for the establishment of the department, featured favorable articles in its magazine, included supportive speakers at its conventions, and joined like-minded coalitions.

Although the NEA led this effort, which succeeded in 1979, both organizations had pursued this goal since the early 1900s. Significantly, commentators for and against the establishment of the department agreed that it was a political payoff to the NEA; none mentioned it as a payoff to the PTA.

It is worth noting that the PTA's close ties to the NEA had not always extended to the AFT. Prior to the establishment of the U.S. Department of Education, the U.S. Department of Health, Education, and Welfare had administered federal programs in education. When the NEA lobbied aggressively for a federal department of education in the early 1970s, the AFT was opposed. The AFT argued (correctly, as it turned out) that the benefits of a separate federal department of education were greatly exaggerated, but AFT opposition was actually based on political factors. The AFT feared that the NEA, which was to play a critical role in President Jimmy Carter's 1976 election, would dominate the new department to the disadvantage of the AFT. Nevertheless, throughout the 1978 tuition tax credit battle, most members of the National Coalition to Save Public Education also lobbied for the establishment of a cabinet-level department of education.

V. The PTA's Contemporary Lobbying Agenda

In the 1980s and 1990s, a host of educational issues competed for public attention. School finance reform, pay equity, school dropout rates, tuition tax credits, health hazards in school buildings, vouchers, education standards, affirmative action, latchkey children, sexual harassment, and school safety were prominent issues, and most still are. These issues drove the National PTA's 2000–2001 legislative agenda.

As part of its lobbying efforts, the National PTA hosts an annual legislative conference in Washington, D.C. (due to financial considerations, no such conference was held in 2001, but the conferences were scheduled to resume in 2002). At these conferences, PTA staff and officers train state and local leaders on lobbying techniques, brief them on pending federal legislation, transport them to Capitol Hill to lobby, and then send them back to their states to activate the rank and file through the member-to-member network. Through its website, the National PTA updates members about pending legislation, provides talking points to support PTA positions, and posts action items that visitors to the website are encouraged to implement.[15]

To carry out its lobbying efforts, the PTA assigns its government relations staff to monitor legislative issues and influence lawmakers. Although no assignment breakdown has been available for several years, lobbying assignments of PTA staff members from March to June 1996 included:

> Director, Government Relations: Assault Weapons Ban, Charter Schools, Children's Television Programming/FCC Guidelines, Goals 2000 amendments, Istook Amendment [this, if passed, would have permitted student-sponsored prayer in public schools], Individuals with Disabilities Education Act (IDEA) Reauthorization, Parental Rights and Responsibilities Act, Public Money for Private Schools, including tuition tax credits, vouchers and tuition tax deductions, Tobacco FDA Regulations, TV Violence/V-Chip, Video Game Violence, Vocational Education, School-to-Work and Job Training Reauthorization, 501(c)(3) and other lobbying information
>
> Assistant Director: Child Abuse Prevention and Treatment, Child Labor, Civil Rights Protections, Early Childhood Education and Child Care, Education Reform Block Grant, Elimination of the Department of Education, Juvenile Justice/Delinquency Prevention, Local Empowerment and Flexibility Act, Public Money for Private Schools, including tuition tax credits, vouchers and tuition tax deductions, School Prayer
>
> Governmental Relations Specialist: Child Nutrition Programs, Improving America's Schools Act (IASA) programs, Funding Equity, Funding Issues, Appropriations, Balanced Budget Amendment, Block Grants, Budget Process Changes, Child-Related Tax and Entitlement Issues, Spending Cuts, Unfunded Mandates, Immigration and Public Schools, Pesticides, Public Money for Private Schools, including tuition tax credits, vouchers and tuition tax deductions, Vocational Education, School-to-Work, and Job Training Reauthorization[16]

Significantly, only opposition to "Public Money for Private Schools, including tuition tax credits, vouchers and tuition tax deductions" was assigned to all three lobbyists. Clearly, this is the highest priority for the PTA, just as it is for the NEA and the AFT. First adopted by the National PTA board of directors in 1979, the PTA position statement on school choice was reaffirmed by the board in 1991:

> The National PTA opposes education voucher proposals for public and nonpublic preschool, elementary and secondary school students.
>
> The National PTA opposes tax credits and deductions for elementary and secondary school tuition and other education-related expenses for public and nonpublic school students.
>
> The National PTA believes that these funding methods would have a detrimental effect on our public school system. Such funding would pro-

mote division without diversity, create division and separation within the community and negate the long struggle to desegregate our schools and our society. It is the opinion of the National PTA that vouchers and similar systems would violate the constitutionally mandated separation of church and state.

The National PTA recognizes that changes must be made within the public schools to provide an equitable and excellent educational opportunity for every child. Vouchers, tax credits, deductions and other such funding sources do not provide the means for bringing about improvements in our public schools.

The National PTA supports our system of public education as the major vehicle for perpetuating the basic values of a democratic system of government. This system must be strengthened and continue to be governed by public officials accountable to the public and supported by adequate public funds.[17]

As of December 2000, the Learning First Alliance had been successful in defeating most federal proposals that would have provided tax relief or school choice options for parents who enroll their children in private schools. Two of the measures passed by Congress—Education Savings Accounts and a voucher program for the District of Columbia—were vetoed by President Bill Clinton. Education Savings Accounts are intended to allow parents and others to deposit after-tax deposits into a savings account. Withdrawals of accumulated interest spent for educational expenses for children would be tax-free; withdrawals of any principal would be taxed according to tax rates in effect at the time of withdrawal.

PTA Opposition to Proposition 174

State PTAs have actively opposed school choice legislation on multiple occasions, but perhaps the most striking example of such opposition occurred in 1993 when the California PTA played an active role in defeating Proposition 174. Under this controversial initiative, California parents would have been entitled to a voucher worth $2,600 (about half of the $5,200 that the state spent at the time to educate each elementary pupil for a year) to enroll a child in any public or private school of their choice, including parochial schools.

In addition to the California PTA representatives, the anti-174 steering committee included representatives from the California Teachers Association, the California Federation of Teachers, the California School Employees Association, the Association of California School Administrators, the California State Council of Service Employees, and the California School Boards Association.[18] Nonetheless, the California PTA was not bashful about taking most of the credit for the defeat of Proposition 174. In 1994, as California PTA President Pat Dingsdale congratulated delegates on defeating the initiative, they broke into thunderous applause. Dingsdale shouted, "You were the voice of the California children! PTA volunteers defeated Proposition 174; all the California Teachers Association (CTA) did was put up the money."[19]

Indeed, the CTA spent over $13 million officially and a great deal more unofficially to defeat the measure.[20] The NEA contributed another million dollars, and other public employee unions contributed a few million dollars more. Proponents of Proposition 174 raised and spent less than $3 million, a fact conveniently ignored by the California PTA leaders who claimed that over a million PTA members worked to defeat Proposition 174. This claim is not credible; the California PTA's membership was just over one million, and it strains credulity to maintain that virtually every member worked in the campaign. Harriet Borson, the California PTA's head lobbyist, asserted that "Proposition 174 attracted PTA support much more than any other issue or project. It showed what's possible with funding, which came from the teacher unions." Grace Foster, a 36-year PTA veteran, characterized Proposition 174 as "an evil proposal to take money from public schools." Even before the vote on Proposition 174, Foster had urged members to fight the initiative "fang and claw" and ordered them not to "give our enemy the platform" by allowing debates. She and other California PTA officers tried to discourage voters from signing petitions to qualify Proposition 174 for the election. Foster also reminded local, council, and district PTA presidents that affiliates may choose not to promote actively a California State PTA position, but "they may not officially oppose a stand taken by the State Board of Managers."[21] On more than one occasion, the California PTA threatened to revoke the charter of those who disobeyed.[22] The necessity for such threats underscores the dubious nature of the claim that one million California PTA members worked to defeat Proposition 174.[23]

Charter Schools

The charter school movement began in 1991 in Minnesota. As of May 2000, there were 1,689 charter schools (serving more than 430,000 children) in thirty-four states and the District of Columbia, and the number of such schools is expected to increase.[24]

Charter schools are government-funded schools that are organized and administered without regard to some of the statutes governing public education. A charter school is an autonomous entity that operates on the basis of a charter or contract between the individual or group (for example, teachers, parents, charter school corporations, or nonprofit organizations) and a chartering authority. The chartering authority is identified in the charter school legislation and may be a local school board, university, state department of education, or charter board. The charter usually specifies the school's educational plan, its school management plan, anticipated educational outcomes, and other compliance requirements. Once granted a charter, charter schools receive local and/or state funding, usually based on a percentage of average costs per pupil in public schools, plus targeted funds that are designated for low-income children and children with special needs.

In practice, the extent to which charter schools are free from state educational statutes and the obligation to bargain collectively varies a great deal from state to state. In some states, such as New Jersey, charter schools are almost as restricted as other public schools; elsewhere, such as in Arizona, charter schools enjoy a great deal of freedom to differ from other public schools.[25]

Charter school legislation is particularly troublesome for the PTA. In 1995, when the NEA decided to sponsor and partially fund the development costs of five charter schools, the PTA had little choice but to accept charter schools in some form or other as an "experiment." According to NEA President Bob Chase, the NEA hoped that if the charter schools were successful, "they [would] become models of effective school reform for public education."[26] As we might expect, both the teacher unions and the PTA oppose waivers that would exclude charter schools from collective bargaining statutes or waive other public school restrictions. This places the PTA, along with the unions, in opposition to the principal motivation for establishing charter schools: avoiding these burdensome regulations deemed to inhibit educational excellence and experimentation.

Many delegates who attend National PTA conventions genuinely desire a discussion of the merits as well as the problems of charter schools. Instead, convention workshops over the years have been designed to arm delegates with arguments to convince state legislators to abandon or weaken charter school legislation. In fact, workshops on charter schools have been little more than pep rallies in support of NEA/AFT positions.

Perhaps the main reason for the National PTA skepticism about charter schools is that local affiliates cannot function in some charter schools without violating the charter school law, the PTA's own bylaws, or both. Laws creating charter schools often require unrestricted parental involvement. No barriers, such as individual membership dues, are allowed. A conflict arises with PTA bylaws because, in 1997, the National PTA adopted an amendment (which automatically amended all local PTA bylaws) that states: "Only members of a local PTA who have paid dues for the current membership year may participate in the business of that association." This amendment rendered charter school PTAs ineligible to affiliate with the National PTA at any level in states in which no barriers to parental involvement are permitted.

Sex Education, AIDS, and Gay and Lesbian Issues

Even before state PTA affiliates were organized, the PTA had advocated classes and conferences on health issues. In 1897, one of the first resolutions that passed supported a national training school for mothers so that they might be "taught the laws of health and heredity." By the 1920s, the PTA encouraged schools to include health education in the curriculum. In the early 1950s, the PTA and Planned Parenthood recommended that sex education be part of the health education curriculum, if not provided as a separate subject. Goals 2000, an omnibus federal education program first enacted in 1994, was the culmination of the PTA's long-time effort to achieve this objective. Goals 2000 authorizes public schools to provide various social services, health care, and related services through school-based health clinics. The school-based services include dispensing condoms and contraceptives, abortion advice, and psychological testing for mental health reasons, often without parental notification. Although the states are free to reject federal funds for these purposes, many parents regard acceptance of the funds as condoning federal intrusion into what they consider family decisions.

Supporters of sex education often endorse the guidelines proposed by the Sex Information and Education Council of the United States (SIECUS), a nonprofit organization that has promulgated national guidelines for comprehensive sex education for kindergarten through twelfth grade. SIECUS guidelines call for teaching five- to eight-year olds about sexual intercourse, masturbation, abortion, and sexually transmitted disease, as well as homosexuality, gay and lesbian relationships, divorce, and living together without marriage. SIECUS guidelines for teaching nine- to twelve-year olds assert that homosexual relationships can be as fulfilling as heterosexual relationships. This is only one of several SIECUS positions that divide proponents and opponents of sex education. Not surprisingly, many conservative parents and profamily organizations have denounced the SIECUS guidelines.

The National PTA joined SIECUS and like-minded organizations in endorsing Joycelyn Elders for U.S. surgeon general when President Clinton nominated her in 1993. As Arkansas state health director appointed by then Governor Clinton, Elders kept a "condom tree" on her desk and was characterized as the "condom queen" because of her support for condom use by sexually active youngsters. Elders advocated programs of sex education that began in kindergarten and included condom distribution through the public schools.[27]

The National PTA aggressively supported Elders's appointment as surgeon general in a news release dated July 27, 1993. In addition, the National PTA vice president for legislative activity wrote a strong letter of support to President Clinton, praising Elders's record of "expanding public health programs for children and teens" that "mirror National PTA objectives for federal health care policy."[28]

In response to inquiries from PTA members questioning the National PTA's decision to support Elders, National PTA President Kathryn Whitfill responded in August 1993. Whitfill explained in a memo to the PTA board of directors that "[t]he National PTA does not endorse all of the controversial statements made by Dr. Elders."[29] Some PTA members also expressed to their state PTA affiliates their concerns about Elders's appointment. In her August 9, 1993 response to a member troubled by the PTA's endorsement, the Texas PTA president wrote that she discussed the matter with Whitfill and Arnold Fege, National PTA director of governmental affairs. According to the letter, Fege confirmed that the PTA had conducted extensive research "on campaign stances of Dr. Eldus [sic] and . . . found no differences in her positions and the PTA's. In fact, it was found that Dr. Eldus [sic] always left final decisions of implementing plans to local control."[30]

On December 9, 1994, President Clinton fired Elders as surgeon general. A consistent advocate of health and education programs that were anathema to conservatives, Elders had become too much of a political liability as a result of her speech at the United Nations on World AIDS Day. In her presentation, Elders had expressed the view that "[i]n regard to masturbation, I think that is something that is part of human sexuality and it's part of something that perhaps should be taught."[31] Leaving aside the merits of the PTA's position on Elders's appointment, the PTA's endorsement was bound to be divisive among its own membership.

In most states, sex education and HIV/AIDS-prevention programs are extremely controversial, especially when they are perceived as outgrowths of the legislative agendas of gay and lesbian organizations. PTA members offended by this alignment often criticize PTA leaders for supporting such programs. For example, when Shirley Igo (National PTA president-elect for 2001–03) was Texas PTA president, she served on the Adolescent Pregnancy and Parenthood Advisory Council (APPAC), an organization that urged the Texas legislature to establish school clinics for confidential reproductive health care. In letters to the editors of newspapers and at PTA meetings, some Texas PTA members denounced Igo for her support of such clinics.

Controversies over sex education frequently revolve around divergent answers to this question: Is the objective of the program to teach students not to discriminate against others on the basis of sexual preferences, or does the program, in effect if not in intent, foster gay and lesbian lifestyles by its favorable treatment of them? There may not be any clear-cut resolution of the issue, since one way to foster nondiscriminatory attitudes toward gays and lesbians is to portray them in a positive way. On a deeper level, however, opposition to sex education is often based on its rejection of traditional sources of moral counsel. Opponents are troubled by videos like *Secrets,* produced by Kaiser Permanente, a health care provider. *Secrets* recommends that students who are troubled by their sexual identity should call an AIDS hotline rather than consult their parents, family doctors, or clergy.

Reaction to another highly publicized video reveals just how unlikely it is that a consensus on sex education will emerge any time soon. *It's Elementary: Talking About Gay Issues in School* was produced as a training video to show teachers how to teach elementary-school pupils as young as kindergarteners to avoid negative attitudes toward gays and lesbians. A brochure advertising the video states that "parents and PTA" are using it.[32] NEA President Chase endorsed the video, arguing that

> [s]chools cannot be neutral when we're dealing with issues of human dignity and human rights. I'm not talking about tolerance. I'm talking about acceptance. IT'S ELEMENTARY is a great resource for parents, teachers, and community leaders working to teach respect and responsibility to America's children.[33]

At the same time, conservative leaders expressed outrage over the video. Howard Hurwitz, head of the Family Defense Council and a former New York City public school principal, said of *It's Elementary,* "Never in my 50 years of experience in the schools have I seen so scandalous a plan for indoctrinating children. It is an assault on common decency and traditional family values."[34] Despite such concerns, in December 2000, National PTA President Ginny Markell represented the PTA at a White House screening of *It's Elementary*'s sequel, *That's A Family!* In this video, children talk about homosexual households as well as other families that differ from the standard, two-parent model. In her comments to representatives from gay organizations, the Girl Scouts, the NEA, and other groups, Markell said that *That's A Family!* would be among the resources that the PTA would provide to its members as it dealt with important family issues in 2001.[35] Critics, of course, greeted the PTA's intention to promote the second video by expressing concerns similar to those they had when the PTA encouraged the use of the first one.

Controversies over issues of "family values" extend beyond concerns about videos in classrooms. In September 1999, the Washington State PTA chartered the Gay Lesbian Parent Teacher Student Association (PTSA) of Greater Puget Sound, a PTA affiliate for homosexuals. The new group was formed to address issues reportedly faced in some schools by gays, lesbians, bisexuals, and transgendered students, their teachers, and parents. Unlike affiliates of the PTA that are tied to a single school, the Gay Lesbian PTSA was designed to be active in several schools and districts in the Seattle area. Not surprisingly, critics charged that since the majority of PTA affiliates function at elementary schools, the PTSA is another strategy to indoctrinate children on the gay and lesbian positions on sexual issues.[36]

Altogether, these various incidents point to a serious problem for the PTA: when PTA leaders make unilateral decisions for a membership organization with regard to controversial issues, it is difficult to see how the PTA can increase its membership. Members across the political spectrum are left frustrated when not allowed to oppose, within the organization, policies and programs that they find extremely offensive.

VI. PTA Strategy

Like the other members of the Learning First Alliance and its allies, the PTA dismisses its critics as "right-wing extremists," "the radical right," or "the religious right." To oppose "right-wing extremists," the PTA conducts training sessions for its members. In its own words, the PTA strives "to develop an awareness of the methods and strategies of extremist members or groups on school health curriculum and education reform issues."[37]

The PTA's strategy is identical to the tactics utilized by other public school organizations on the same issues. For example, when Americans United for Separation of Church and State (AUSCS) held a national conference on "Public Schools Under Assault: Why the Religious Right Must Lose!" the NEA paid the expenses of several PTA members to be trained by the group. It was an easy fit since Maribeth Oakes, director of government relations for the National PTA since 1997 and a PTA staff lobbyist before that, is a member of the AUSCS's National Advisory Council. At the November 1994 AUSCS conference, Oakes moderated the panel discussion entitled "A Report Card on the Public Schools: Combating the Religious Right's Big Lie."

NEA support for PTA delegates to attend the AUSCS conference illustrates an important point about NEA influence over the PTA. The PTA has much less discretionary funding than does the NEA, hence it is very susceptible to financial incentives to support NEA positions. PTA relationships with federal agencies also illustrate this point. When the PTA urged nationwide radon testing in schools and homes, groups critical of the Environmental Protection Agency (EPA) began to investigate the agency's political operations. The Competitive Enterprise Institute discovered from internal EPA documents that the EPA had awarded a grant to the PTA because "the PTA could become a major ally for the agency in preventing Congress from slashing [its] budget."[38] Soon thereafter, with EPA funds, the PTA began publishing an environmental awareness newsletter. This kind of cooperation with a federal agency is not an isolated incident, either for the PTA or for other politically attuned interest groups. In a similar scenario, the National PTA produced and distributed HIV/AIDS brochures as a result of a cooperative venture with the Centers for Disease Control.

Because the PTA must avoid antagonizing either school management or the unions, the organization has seemingly abdicated its original mission as advocate and protector of parent and student interests. To fill this void at the local level, local PTAs engage in activities that support local schools and teachers. The National PTA, however, would rather have its local and state affiliates fill the void with political advocacy. Then, when laws are changed, defeated, or passed, the National PTA can claim that its lobbying efforts benefited all children. It matters little that many parents neither want, nor support, nor are even aware of the legislative agenda of the National PTA. One of the findings in a 1996 poll was that "[w]hile most parents have a favorable impression of the PTA, an overwhelming majority—82 percent—are ignorant of the organization's taking a stand or having a position statement on any issues."[39]

By 2000, the PTA's reputation had apparently worsened. National PTA President Ginny Markell told the delegates at that year's annual PTA convention that according to internal and external surveys, "The rest of the world doesn't know who we are!" Furthermore, "None [see] us as the voice for children."[40]

True to its commitment to advocacy, in 2000, and again in 2001, the National PTA continued to lobby Congress for increased federal funding for public education. Also at the federal level, the PTA lobbied for increased federal funds for parent advocacy centers. If passed, the Parent Accountability, Recruitment, and Education National Training (PARENT) Act would be incorporated into the $13 billion Elementary and Secondary Education Act (ESEA), the omnibus federal law providing federal aid for schools with students in kindergarten through twelfth grade.[41] Current provisions in the ESEA already allow funds to be spent for parent involvement activities, such as family literacy programs, parent training activities, transportation, and child care so that parents can visit schools. The PARENT Act would increase federal funding for these activities.

In *Building Successful Partnerships: A Guide for Developing Parent and Family Involvement Programs,* the National PTA offers dozens of suggestions for local PTAs, parents, and teachers. One is to use the *Guide* as an "assessment tool" to evaluate the effectiveness of parent involvement activities.[42] This is a worthy goal, one that the National PTA might be well advised to adopt. To understand why, we need only review the outcomes of the parental involvement provisions of Goals 2000, the subject of the next chapter.

7

Goals 2000: Historic Victory or Educational Disaster?

By reinforcing the worst aspects of politicized schooling, and by ignoring or disparaging the principles of constitutional democracy, Goals 2000 has hastened the demise of public education at the hands of public schooling.[1]

— Stephen Arons, author, 1997

I. Goals 2000

Urging increased federal involvement and funding for a variety of welfare and education issues has always been a prominent feature of the PTA's lobbying agenda. Understandably, when the opportunity arose in the early 1990s to adopt a wide range of federal programs in the public schools, the National PTA was prepared to take advantage of it. A series of events provided the opportunity, and the PTA capitalized on it by emphasizing that federal legislation would encourage parental involvement—allegedly the key to educational achievement.

The first event drew national attention. In September 1989, President George Bush convened an education summit in Charlottesville, Virginia attended by the nation's fifty governors. At the summit, they agreed to set education goals for the nation. In 1990, when six goals were announced by the President and adopted by the state governors, the PTA moved quickly to take advantage of

the opportunity to promote its own objectives. A 1987 Harris survey for the
Metropolitan Life Insurance Company (MetLife) purported to show a wide
range of benefits from parental involvement in their children's education.[2] Parents who were more involved developed more positive attitudes toward school
personnel. Likewise, teaching improved when parental involvement was prevalent, and teachers were more satisfied with their work. The survey provided the
PTA with the kind of ammunition it needed to promote parental involvement—
one of education's fuzziest ideas.

Despite considerable publicity, the Harris survey initially had no noticeable
impact. When the Carnegie Foundation for the Advancement of Teaching surveyed 22,000 teachers in 1988, 90 percent of them cited a lack of parental support as a problem. Elementary and middle school principals agreed. They concluded that there would be significant improvement in educational achievement
if families did more to enhance children's self-esteem and work habits.

Despite the support from the MetLife survey findings, the education summit
ignored the PTA's request to treat parental involvement as a high national priority. A parental involvement provision was not included in the original proposal (H.R. 1804) to establish the six national education goals. Undeterred, the
PTA continued to strive for inclusion of a parental involvement amendment to
H.R. 1804. In April and May 1991, the National Education Goals panel held
hearings to gauge the reactions of education associations and the public to the
concept of national education goals and the criteria that would be used to measure the states' progress toward accomplishment of the goals.

Also in 1991, the PTA board of directors formally adopted a position statement on parental involvement that would provide the basis for its parent training program for years to come. The position statement was entitled "Individual
and Organizational Rights and Responsibilities in the Development of Children." The statement acknowledged that "parents are the primary influence in
children's lives," and that "parents' participation in organizations that reflect the
community's collaborative aspirations for all children" constitutes parent involvement.[3]

The PTA statement on parental involvement was the first in a series of steps
that led to national visibility for the concept and the PTA's role in publicizing it.
National PTA President Pat Henry convened a national conference on parental
involvement in April 1992. Twenty-eight education- and child-centered organizations developed a mission statement around which to rally their members. One
such statement was "to advance and ensure the highest levels of parent/family involvement." To this end, the organizations pledged to "seek legislation and the
development of policies that include parent/family involvement."[4] About half of
the organizations attended a subsequent meeting during which they sent a group
letter urging President Bill Clinton to "make parent involvement a priority."

Throughout 1993 and into 1994, opponents and proponents waged campaigns to support or change the federal legislation for national education standards, renamed the Goals 2000: Educate America Act. As parents and the public learned the details of the act, more questions were raised. To answer these questions and foster support for Goals 2000, the U.S. Department of Education provided "A Do-It-Yourself Kit for Education Renewal" on heavy, slick paper, complete with its own colorful file box, for $43. Forms, sample surveys, predesigned goals, and participant checklists were included. For activists dealing with the media, the kit provided sample news releases, feature articles, op-ed pieces, speeches, radio spots, and even tips for television appearances. Leaving very little to chance, the kit anticipated questions from community residents who might not have been completely sold on Goals 2000. Suggested responses were detailed, informative, and convincing. As might be expected, the kit suggested that the PTA be part of local leadership teams to promote the new educational reforms; the kit's Resource Guide also directed readers to three pamphlets published by the PTA.[5]

An intensive publicity campaign proclaimed PTA's message: "Goals 2000 means being an involved PTA!" and "PTA leadership is the cornerstone of this education reform." The PTA "tirelessly urged members of Congress to adopt the parent participation goal" that was not included in earlier drafts of the act.[6] Among other provisions, the PTA promoted Goals 2000 as a "public school initiative that focuses totally on improving public elementary and secondary schools," as "the first formal acknowledgment by the federal government of the central importance of parent/family involvement and decision-making in the education of children," and as "a unique opportunity for states and local communities . . . to improve their schools."[7]

To say the least, the PTA's campaign to include parental involvement as one of the national education goals was highly successful. On March 31, 1994, President Clinton signed the Goals 2000: Educate America Act, the most comprehensive statement of federal policy on K–12 education to date.[8] In its announcement of the new legislation, the U.S. Department of Education referred to Goals 2000 as "the beginning of a bold, new approach to school reform."[9]

Goals 2000, the popular name for the act, covers an extremely wide range of federal programs and policies. Services for the disadvantaged; educational technology; educational research; children with disabilities; national education goals; school prayer; gun-free schools; vocational education—the list of issues affected is virtually inexhaustible. It is a sobering experience to see the depths of trivia to which "the world's greatest deliberative body" can sink if the opportunity arises. Sections 1051–1053 of the act deal with "Midnight Basketball League Training and Partnership Programs" and read in part:

(1) Authority—the Secretary shall make grants, to the extent that amounts are approved in appropriations Acts under paragraph (113), to—(A) eligi-

ble entities to assist such entities in carrying out midnight basketball league programs meeting the requirements of paragraph (4); and (B) eligible advisory entities to provide technical assistance to eligible entities in establishing and operating such midnight basketball league programs.[10]

On almost every topic on which the act authorizes programs, there are requirements that policies be established and/or reviewed by an advisory group. In practice, the members of these advisory groups are invariably from organizations that are opposed to any basic change in our school system. Thus, the members from "teacher organizations" are from the NEA or the AFT, the members from parent organizations are from the PTA, and so on. Although the act frequently refers to the need for innovation, the forces opposed to basic changes in K–12 education positioned themselves throughout the advisory process to protect their interests.

Goals 2000 established eight national goals, all of which were to be achieved by the year 2000. Here are the first seven:

1. By the year 2000, all children in America will start school ready to learn.
2. By the year 2000, the high school graduation rate will increase to at least 90 percent.
3. By the year 2000, all students will leave grades 4, 8, and 12 having demonstrated competency over challenging subject matter including English, science, foreign languages, civics and government, economics, mathematics, arts, history, and geography, and every school in America will ensure that all students learn to use their minds well, so they may be prepared for responsible citizenship, further learning, and productive employment in our Nation's modern economy.
4. By the year 2000, the Nation's teaching force will have access to programs for the continued improvement of their professional skills and the opportunity to acquire the knowledge and skills needed to instruct and prepare all American students for the next century.
5. By the year 2000, United States students will be the first in the world in mathematics and science achievement.
6. By the year 2000, every adult American will be literate and will possess the knowledge and skills necessary to compete in a global economy and exercise the rights and responsibilities of citizenship.
7. By the year 2000, every school in the United States will be free of drugs, violence, and the unauthorized presence of firearms and alcohol and will offer a disciplined environment conducive to learning.[11]

Each of these goals was followed by a list of objectives necessary to reach the goal. Due in large part to the PTA's lobbying efforts, Congress included an eighth national goal.

II. Goal 8, the Parental Involvement Goal

The eighth goal that Congress added to Goals 2000 concerns parental involvement in education.

> 8. PARENTAL PARTICIPATION.—
>   (A) By the year 2000, every school will promote partnerships that will increase parental involvement and participation in promoting the social, emotional, and academic growth of children.
>   (B) The objectives for this Goal are that—
>   (i) every State will develop policies to assist local schools and local educational agencies to establish programs for increasing partnerships that respond to the varying needs of parents and the home, including parents of children who are disadvantaged or bilingual, or parents of children with disabilities;
>   (ii) every school will actively engage parents and families in a partnership which supports the academic work of children at home and shared educational decisonmaking at school; and
>   (iii) parents and families will help to ensure that schools are adequately supported and will hold schools and teachers to high standards of accountability.[12]

In addition to treating parental involvement as a goal, Goals 2000 was replete with references to it. In their celebratory letter to local and council PTA presidents after the enactment of Goals 2000, the PTA national officers asserted that "[r]eferences to parents and their roles in education reform at the state and local level appear approximately 50 times in this Act."

Mentions of "parent education" constitute one set of these references. Title IV of Goals 2000 defines parent education very broadly:

> The term 'parent education' includes parent support activities, the provision of resource materials on child development, parent-child learning activities and child rearing issues, private and group education guidance, individual and group learning experiences for the parent and child, and other activities that enable the parent to improve learning in the home.
>
> The term 'Parents as Teachers program' means a voluntary early childhood parent education program that is designed to provide all parents of children from birth through age 5 with the information and support such parents need to give their child a solid foundation for school success. . . .[13]

In addition, Goals 2000 provides for "regularly scheduled personal visits with families by certified parent educators; regularly scheduled developmental screenings; and linkage with other resources within the community in order to provide services that parents may want and need. . . ."

Funding to develop and implement state improvement plans to comply with the standards set in Goals 2000 was included in H.R. 6, the U.S. House of Representative's bill to reauthorize the Elementary and Secondary Education Act (ESEA). As pointed out previously, ESEA is the largest federal education program for America's elementary and secondary schools. The 980-page bill, entitled the "Improving America's Schools Act of 1994," was a five-year extension of education funding for kindergarten through twelfth grade.[14] Supporters as well as opponents of Goals 2000 lobbied intensively for their positions when the legislation came up again for reauthorization and funding in 1999 and 2000.

To encourage parental involvement, Title IV of Goals 2000 sets forth guidelines for nonprofit organizations to apply for federal funds to enable businesses, community groups, and parents to help schools achieve the goals. Grant funds may be used "to fund at least one parental information and resource center in each State before September 30, 1998."[15] The resource centers are funded from ESEA's Title I, a federal assistance program administered by the U.S. Department of Education.[16] In 1994, Title I was a $7.5 billion program for economically and educationally disadvantaged students. Up to 1 percent of a school district's Title I grant funds could be used for the benefit of parents by establishing a parent or community center, providing family literacy programs, assisting with parent training activities, purchasing materials for parents who help their children study at home, and providing transportation and child care so that parents could visit schools.

As a tax-exempt organization with a presence in all fifty states, the PTA was in a strong position to obtain federal funds for parent centers in which the PTA would play a leading role. Long a proponent of training parents, the PTA urged its members to take advantage of the revenue opportunities afforded by Goals 2000. Despite the encouragement from the National PTA, however, local PTAs have seldom availed themselves of such opportunities. However, a few local affiliates participated in coalitions with medical clinics, libraries, teacher unions, and other local agencies seeking federal funds to train parents.

To monitor trends in parental involvement after the passage of Goals 2000, the U.S. Department of Education surveyed a representative sample of nine hundred public schools enrolling kindergarten through eighth-grade students in the 1995–96 school year. At each school, the principal or the person most knowledgeable about parental involvement programs and activities at the school responded to the questionnaire. Among the highlights of the study were:

- The majority of public elementary schools (79 percent) reported having an advisory group or policy council that includes parents.
- One-quarter to one-third of all [public elementary] schools included parents to a moderate extent in most decisionmaking.

- Parent attendance at school-sponsored events varied by geographic region, poverty concentration, and minority enrollment in the school.
- Schools reported that parents were more likely to attend events that featured some interaction with students' teachers.
- Between 83 and 85 percent [of public elementary schools] provided information about the school's overall performance on standardized tests, . . . and issued interim reports on students' progress during grading periods.
- Information on community services was more available in larger schools, schools in cities, and schools with minority enrollments of 50 percent or more.[17]

Despite the accomplishments reported, a great deal of criticism of Goals 2000 was directed at the fact that federal funding was often tied to acceptance of federal policies that Congress could not impose directly on states and school districts. For example, states and school districts were required to prohibit guns within one thousand yards of schools as a condition of receiving funds for gun-free schools. When challenged, the U.S. Supreme Court held the provision to be an unconstitutional expansion of congressional power to regulate interstate commerce.[18]

There were also strong objections to the policy of tying federal funds to the "voluntary" acceptance of the Goals 2000 agenda. For example, in order to receive federal funds for Goals 2000, states were required to develop and adopt a state improvement plan. The plans were required to aim at "increasing the access of all students to social services, health care, nutrition, related services, and child care services, and locating such services in schools, cooperating service agencies, community-based centers, or other convenient sites designed to provide 'one-stop shopping' for parents and students."[19] Again, to quote the act, "The Department of Health and Human Services and the Department of Education shall ensure that all federally funded programs which provide for the distribution of contraceptive devices to unemancipated minors develop procedures to encourage, to the extent practical, family participation in such programs."[20] Unquestionably, many parents oppose these policies that intrude on or, worse yet, usurp family decision-making, regardless of the level of government that adopts them.

To no one's surprise, Goals 2000 evoked a torrent of criticism from conservative sources. Critics of Goals 2000 alleged that the federal legislation:

- Increases federal intrusion into local school affairs.
- Decreases authority of locally elected school boards.
- Substitutes a liberal social agenda for basic academics.
- Sets vague, attitudinal, and unmeasurable goals, also known as Outcome-Based Education (OBE).
- Encourages a greater role for government schools and social service agencies in family life.

- Interferes with pre-school parenting.
- Urges comprehensive health education (which includes extensive sex education and starts as early as kindergarten).
- Promotes "mandatory voluntarism," undermining the virtue of volunteering.
- Treats parents as the junior partner in the parent-school relationship.
- Creates new bureaucracies.
- Spends an exorbitant amount of program money on federal and state overhead (less than half the money reached schools in the program's first year).
- Promotes anti-American national history standards.
- Requires increased state involvement in parental training.
- Institutes a federally funded national skill certification system, known as School-to-Work.
- Interferes with curriculum creation by requiring modeling of national standards, thus overstepping the bounds set when the U.S. Department of Education was established.[21]

In editorials and a subsequent book, Robert Holland of the *Richmond-Times Dispatch* characterized Goals 2000 as an educational disaster; his unyielding opposition to the act was one of the factors that caused Virginia to be one of three states that refused to accept federal funds rather than accede to the federal requirements.[22]

Most state governors scrambled to get their share of the $91.5 million first-year appropriation of Goals 2000. In the spring of 1995, the U.S. Department of Education reported that forty-six states and the District of Columbia had qualified for their states' shares, which were allocated using a formula under the ESEA. In turn, through a competitive grant process, state education agencies awarded funds to local education agencies and individual schools.[23]

After resistance to the original act emerged, the National PTA supported an amendment which provided that "in states in which the governor has decided not to participate in Goals 2000, grants may now go to local school districts with the approval of the state education agency."[24] When the amendment was adopted in 1996, the three recalcitrant states accepted some programs and federal funds for Goals 2000.

Despite the widespread criticism of Goals 2000, its provisions on parental involvement remained unaltered as the deadline for meeting the eight goals arrived—ten years after their adoption in 1989. The PTA must have been extremely disappointed by the miniscule progress, if any, toward achieving Goal 8, parental participation. According to the most authoritative assessment, "No state had reduced the percentage of public school teachers reporting that lack of parental involvement in their schools is a serious problem." In fact, six states reported that the lack of parental involvement was a more serious problem after the adoption of Goal 8.[25] The progress report on the influence of parent associations was more favorable to the PTA and other parent organizations. Seventeen states reported that "the parent associations in their schools have influence in one or more of three areas of school policy." Thirty-three states and the District of Columbia reported "no change" on this criterion. Furthermore, of the seventeen states that reported increased parent association influence in school policy, the phenomenon occurred in less than 50 percent of the public schools in those states.[26]

Goals 2000 is the culmination of the PTA's efforts to achieve government support for its educational and social objectives. This success comes at a time when a welfare retrenchment act has been enacted and respected scholars contend that government intervention has not been the panacea that it was thought to be in the decades after World War II.[27] Critics contend that social welfare programs implemented by government agencies differ inherently from private initiatives, even when their objectives are identical. Whether the problem is feeding the hungry, sheltering the homeless, or protecting the environment, the argument is that government programs create a bureaucratic stake in perpetuating or even magnifying the problem, lest the agency lose its mission and its funding.

Much more, for and against, could be said about Goals 2000, but this much can be said about it in relation to the PTA: in its entire history, the PTA has always promoted government over private solutions to social problems. Indeed, it does not appear that the PTA's leadership has considered the possibility that government programs may have different dynamics and outcomes than do private efforts to solve the same problems. Virtually every PTA activity that started out as a private charitable activity has led to a government program that supposedly obviates the need for private action. In fact, the PTA is very concerned that its fundraising activities for the benefit of a local school not be cited to justify government unwillingness to seek increased funding. Whereas some scholars are concerned about the likelihood that government support will crowd out private support with disastrous consequences for the beneficiaries, the PTA is concerned about the possibility that private support will weaken government support for the same objective.

Undoubtedly, the failure to recognize the possible advantages of nongovernmental initiatives is one reason why PTA programs have not been as beneficial as the PTA assumed that they would be. By December 1999, the National Education Goals Panel, administered collectively by eighteen federal and state officials, declared that none of the goals set in Goals 2000 had been or would be met in the near future. Consequently, the panel changed the name of Goals 2000 to National Education Goals, dropping any mention of a deadline. Nevertheless, in its 1999 report, the goals panel stated that its "bold venture" had worked, because the goals had "helped stimulate reforms."

8

Fundraising: What PTAs Do Best

The continuing image of PTA as solely or primarily a fund-raising organization is the common perception among the American public and our members.[1]

— Kathryn Whitfill, president, National Congress
of Parents and Teachers, 1995

I. Introduction

PTA fundraising raises several practical and policy issues; the higher the level of organization, the more troublesome the issues. Local PTA affiliates are responsible for doing fundraising activities to meet their program goals. Some standardized practices which have been in place for decades have been carried forward to the present. In 1933, when it operated out of the NEA's headquarters, the PTA published *Parent-Teacher Manual: A Guidebook for Leaders of Local Congress Units.*[2] In it, the PTA set forth requirements for handling funds and guidelines to be used in developing a local budget. Unlike *PTA Money Matters,*[3] the handbook used in 2000, the 1933 guidelines were brief, specific, and uncomplicated. For example, the 1933 guidelines suggested that a local PTA allocate approximately 25 percent of its general funds for committee work, including the programs intended to educate parents on how to be better parents. The guidelines recommended that the remaining general funds be allocated as follows: 15 percent for postage, telephone, supplies, and miscellaneous; 15 percent for the pur-

111

chase of National PTA publications; 25 percent for local presidents' travel to state and national conventions; 20 percent to cover hospitality charges and other PTA expenses.

In the *Guidebook,* revenue for specific activities of a local PTA were referred to as "special funds." The National PTA encouraged local PTAs to improve the cultural atmosphere and comfort of their schools using special funds, but emphasized that the "essential material needs of the public schools should be met by a system of equitable taxation, which will provide the necessary revenue."[4] Although the line between "essential material needs" and add-ons was not clearcut, local PTAs raised and spent special funds for a wide variety of goods and services: "pictures, victrolas, senior trips, pianos, drinking fountains, playground equipment, band instruments and uniforms, furnishings for teachers' rest rooms, and even screens for the windows."[5] At times, local affiliates funded instructional services, despite a directive from the National PTA not to do so.

The 1933 *Guidebook* also encouraged local leaders to raise funds by sponsorship of amateur play productions, rummage or white elephant sales, waste paper sales, bake or food sales, art exhibits, basket suppers, book parties, community field days, picnics, fairs, cookbooks of neighborhood recipes, and flower shows.[6] The *Guidebook* also identified several fundraising activities that would damage the reputation of the PTA and were therefore to be avoided. Petty gambling, such as paddle wheels, lucky tickets, raffling, and lotteries were discouraged because the children who participated would allegedly come to believe in the doctrine of "getting something for nothing." Boxing exhibitions were also regarded as inappropriate, although the sport was immensely popular following the establishment of Golden Gloves Tournaments in 1928. Children were not to be included in amateur-night stage productions in order to avoid the implication that the PTA was exploiting children.

Not surprisingly, the 1933 *Guidebook* has been expanded in *PTA Money Matters* to include a host of tax considerations and precautions for entering into contracts, bonding, and insurance requirements, issues that were either nonexistent or not worthy of notice in 1933. At the same time, references to the PTA's role of instructing immigrant mothers to be better parents have been omitted. PTAs in mostly upper- and middle-class neighborhoods are unlikely to have many members in need of basic instruction on parenting skills. Instead, *PTA Money Matters* instructs local PTAs to budget funds to send delegates to state and national conferences and to maintain leadership development programs for officers. Likewise, funds are to be budgeted for work "such as conducting or attending conferences, participating on committees, and undertaking projects and programs . . . which can provide enrichment activities for children and families."[7]

As they have for decades, PTAs raise funds for a variety of objectives. Programs emphasizing cultural awareness and diversity are currently popular at all levels. For example, parents and children who participate in a PTA-sponsored international festival at a school might purchase ethnic desserts, with the proceeds going toward additional programs or publications celebrating diversity. The PTA's only national program is *Reflections,* a national arts competition in which several thousand children compete annually for scholarships and recognition in the visual arts, music composition, literature, and photography. Frequently, local PTAs sponsor prizes for student achievement in mathematics, reading, or another subject of interest. PTAs also help to raise funds for class travel, libraries, school equipment, and facilities—whatever the schools identify as a need that a group of parents can address effectively.

In many schools, local PTAs help teachers by providing minigrants for new programs and classroom materials. PTAs occasionally pay the salaries of teachers who cannot be paid from the regular school budget. Usually this happens when a PTA is particularly interested in retaining teachers of art, music, foreign languages, or some other subject that the regular budget cannot accommodate. In addition, schools always seem to need updated playground equipment, computers, copy machines, video equipment, and a host of other items not provided by regular school budgets.

Inadequate public school budgets, a desire to help children and the school, and interest in continuing a school project after grant money has run out are reasons cited to justify PTA fundraising. Regardless of the rationale, fundraising takes up most of the time of local PTAs. This emphasis would be obvious to even the most casual observer who strolled through the exhibit hall at state or National PTA conventions. Companies that sell fundraising merchandise or fundraising services occupy a substantial number of exhibit booths.

II. Fundraising in Operation

PTA parents and their children are armies of unpaid salespeople who sell candy, gift wrap, T-shirts, wreaths, pizza kits, cheese, sausages, cookies, magazines, and flowers. They sell to each other, coworkers, neighbors, friends, and relatives to meet PTA objectives.

Michelle Genz, a Florida PTA member who also writes a newspaper column, asks a not-so-rhetorical question: "Who needs PTA busywork these days when both parents hold jobs, and kids are in day care until dark?"[8] In one of her columns, Genz wrote about her five weeks of torture staging her childrens' school's annual PTA spaghetti dinner. After long hours of directing about forty volunteers, the dinner raised about $800. According to Genz, the amount was roughly what the volunteers would have earned at the minimum wage; Genz confessed that she would rather have contributed the cash and avoided the time and frustration associated with the fundraiser. For the PTA, however, such activity demonstrates "parent involvement," a goal that is not questioned.

The PTA's current guidelines lay down two conditions for using children as fundraisers. The guidelines state that "when children take part in fund-raising events, their role should be either a natural outgrowth of regular schoolwork or a constructive leisure-time activity. Children should never be exploited or used as fund-raisers."[9] These guidelines are contradictory: the first sentence clearly implies that children can serve as fundraisers under certain conditions, but the second sentence is a flat prohibition of the practice. In practice, the guidelines are interpreted to allow children to serve as fundraisers without much thought about whether the natural-outgrowth condition of service is actually observed. Certainly, there is reason to be concerned about this issue. Door-to-door sales, in which children take orders for a product, deliver the product, and collect the funds, may or may not be exploitative, but they are certainly potentially dangerous in some areas. In September 1997, a teenager killed eleven-year-old Edward Peter Werner as he was selling PTA gift wrap and candy in his Jackson Township, New Jersey neighborhood. The sixth-grader had been a top salesman in previous PTA fundraisers; he was trying to earn a pair of walkie-talkies as a reward for a high sales volume when he was attacked in a nearby neighborhood home.

Is selling gift wrap, coupon books, or popcorn door-to-door a constructive leisure time activity for elementary school children? It can be argued that such activities teach the importance of accounting for funds, working cooperatively to achieve shared objectives, perseverance, and other laudable objectives. However, such a loose interpretation would seriously weaken, if not eviscerate, the natural-outgrowth condition.

In some instances, the line between schoolwork and PTA work is unmistakably obliterated. This happens when school grades are based on participation in what is supposed to be a voluntary PTA-sponsored fundraiser. It is difficult to assess the frequency of such practices, but anecdotal evidence indicates that it is not unusual. It should also be noted that PTA fundraising often generates unwarranted pressure to participate. For example, if a PTA or a teacher urges "100 percent" participation in a PTA fundraiser, those students or parents who prefer not to raise funds for the PTA's agenda may feel pressured into doing so.

PTAs cannot solicit additional assessments from PTA members unless local bylaws permit such a practice. In lieu of increasing dues, PTAs necessarily turn to fundraising activities. In schools that enroll mainly affluent students, PTA fundraisers raise impressive amounts. "The Owl," a school newsletter sponsored by the Hearst Elementary School in Washington, D.C., includes updates on the school PTA's fundraising activities.[10] To raise the $227,000 budgeted for its 1997–98 fiscal year, the school's PTA leadership anticipated that dues, fees, and seven fundraising events (nearly one per month of the school year) would bring in just over $200,000. This local affiliate also expected to raise about 20 percent of its budget from one of its seven fundraising events, an evening gala and auction. Based on its gala held the previous year at the Austrian Embassy, when the event raised over $43,000, the leaders felt a similar amount could be budgeted. Parents had made all the arrangements, and along with other attendees, bid on and bought over three hundred donated items. Some of the more expensive items included a trip for two to Rio de Janeiro, a Persian rug, and a week at a beach hotel. As a final part of its fundraising schedule, the Hearst PTA sponsored a grocery scrip program in which parents purchased discounted coupons redeemable at local grocery stores.

The 1997–98 PTA membership form from the Hearst school requested the annual $10 membership fee and an additional enrichment and assessment fee of $180. The form explained that "[t]he enrichment program includes payment for an art teacher, classroom aide, Spanish teacher, science/art materials, repairs to the building, and special programs." The membership form also suggested that Hearst PTA members should check with their employers, many of whom match contributions to 501(c)(3) tax-exempt organizations. As a tax-exempt organization, contributions to the Hearst PTA, including the enrichment fee, could qualify for such a match. In fact, the form stated, "some companies can even double or triple employee gifts."[11]

About 135 children attend the Hearst school, a public school that serves pre-kindergarten to third-grade pupils. The assessment fee plus the per pupil share of the $227,000 annual PTA budget amounted to $1,376 per pupil—a sizeable amount in any school district. Similar to a magnet school, the Hearst Elementary School serves students from anywhere in the District of Columbia. The Hearst PTA demonstrates how its mostly affluent parents are able to avoid the problems associated with large urban school districts.

The Hearst PTA program is not unusual in the District of Columbia. For the 1999–2000 school year, the PTA at Horace Mann Elementary School asked parents to donate $950 per child. Although not all families contributed the requested amount, the PTA hired seven teaching assistants and a part-time vocal instructor as a result of its fundraising activities.[12] Subsequently, Arlene Ackerman, the superintendent of schools in the District of Columbia, criticized the practice, but did not take action to stop it. When Ackerman resigned her position in 2000, Paul L. Vance, her successor, expressed concerns about the fact that the PTA funded teachers not available in other district schools, but he nonetheless accepted "the largess from parents."[13]

In nearby Fairfax County, Virginia, PTAs raise anywhere from a few thousand dollars to more than $70,000 each year from sales events. The money is used for computers, field trips, playground equipment, or other items not funded in the school budget. The president of the Fairfax County Council of PTAs asserted that "some parents can't afford to make a large financial contribution and look at selling as a relatively painless way of getting funds."[14] As a result of this widespread attitude, a cottage industry has developed around PTA fundraising.

III. The Fundraising Industry

Each local PTA decides how to meet its needs, and most engage in fundraising year after year with higher and higher financial goals. In fact, a for-profit industry has emerged around fundraising for school organizations, including the PTA. Suppliers offer a wide variety of products: compact discs, bird food, popcorn, books, flower seeds, and food. Of all product fundraising, 88 percent is done through schools and school-related organizations, such as PTAs and student clubs. Gross sales from product fundraising by schools and school-related organizations exceed $3.4 billion annually. Net proceeds—proceeds remaining after payment for the merchandise—surpass $1.5 billion each year. The seller's share of the profit varies, but usually ranges from 15 to 50 percent.

The Atlanta-based Association of Fund Raisers and Direct Sellers (AFRDS), an international association devoted exclusively to the product fundraising industry, includes seven hundred of the estimated two thousand companies nationwide that specialize in products for fundraising. AFRDS members subscribe to a code of ethics that includes providing "quality products and services" and being "guided in all activities by truth, accuracy, fairness and the highest integrity."[15]

As the National PTA's executive director from 1991 to 1996, Gene Honn participated in a 1995 AFRDS meeting on "Problems and Possibilities in Product Fund Raising: An Open Forum." At the meeting, Honn discovered that some fundraising companies would not do business with some PTA affiliates because they had reason to believe that the local PTA officials were operating a personal business and pocketing the funds, using the PTA as a cover. The companies knew this was inappropriate and refused to do business with these individuals. Still other PTA affiliates were delinquent in paying their vendors, or kept such poor records that the vendors would not deal with them.

Honn and the other participants on the panel identified student safety and school liability as primary concerns of any fundraising program. All of the participants were concerned about fundraising promotion and planning interfering with educational classroom time and the financial burdens that multiple fundraisers place on single parents. Panelists reminded the companies that familiarity with federal, state, and local tax laws as well as knowledge of contractual agreements would help to assure good working relationships with local PTA officers and other fundraising groups.[16]

Fundraising often requires a considerable amount of volunteer time. Many PTAs keep track of the fundraising hours contributed by volunteers and recognize their most active members. The Buena Vista Elementary School PTA of

Greer, South Carolina recognized five hundred volunteers who provided 100,000 hours of service to school projects. Rowland PTA members in Lyndhurst, Ohio logged 1,946 volunteer hours during a recent school year. Probably no state comes close to the hours logged by California PTA activists. According to the California PTA, its "volunteers reported a total of 21,314,317 hours of service from July 1, 1993, to June 30, 1994."[17] The California PTA claimed that at $6 an hour, the volunteers' services were worth $127,885,902 in services that would have received higher wages in the marketplace. Significantly, a great deal of this volunteer time was devoted to defeating Proposition 174, the November 1993 California school-voucher initiative. California PTA leaders recognized these antivoucher volunteers at their annual convention, but it is debatable whether this activity was a service to children.

At the California state PTA convention in Long Beach in 1994, I observed delegates attending "idea exchanges." These sessions were small, informal gatherings at which local leaders shared program ideas, asked questions, and discussed their problems. Invariably, the sessions unwittingly illustrated a fundraising dilemma. On the one hand, fundraising activities are a popular form of parental involvement. Each fundraising project involves a short time-frame and presents an opportunity for new PTA members to work with veteran members. Fundraising projects are likely to be successful, and they give parents and the community a sense of accomplishment. From the local PTA's perspective, fundraising qualifies as useful parental involvement. The National PTA's problem with fundraising is that it tends to preempt parental investment of time in political action on National PTA issues, such as lobbying for smaller class sizes and increased federal funding of public schools.[18]

Because of its policy of neutrality on collective bargaining issues, most PTA members do not realize that local PTAs deliberately avoid the issues that would interest most parents at the local level. In a national poll of parents, 75 percent of those who were not active in the PTA or were not PTA members indicated that they would be more likely to attend PTA meetings if such meetings dealt with critical educational issues.[19]

IV. State and National Conventions

The national and state PTA conventions host vendors who specialize in direct selling. In between workshop sessions and business meetings, delegates head to the exhibit area to strike their deals for the upcoming season. Being good marketers, the vendors bake pizza, cookies, and turnovers. They provide sausage sticks, bread sticks, and cheese. Gift wrap, cosmetics, books, computer software, toys, bags, shirts, and jewelry displays are scattered among the food booths.

Depending upon the number of exhibitors and delegates, income from the state convention may account for up to 20 percent of a state PTA's budget. Occasionally, state education and welfare agencies exhibit materials for convention delegates. For various reasons, however, conservative policy organizations rarely occupy booth space at PTA conventions. In some cases, they are not allowed to do so. Since the early 1990s, the National PTA has refused to allow the National Rifle Association to occupy booth space at the national convention in order to promote gun safety through its "Eddie Eagle" program.

Regional, district, and council PTA affiliates are subject to the same fundraising rules as local PTAs. PTA guidelines caution that "if the council determines that membership dues are insufficient and fundraising is necessary," leaders of these area organizations should not duplicate the efforts of the local units.

At the national convention, the National PTA treasurer often conducts a session for local and state treasurers, especially those who are serving in such a capacity for the first time. The national treasurer emphasizes the necessity for maintaining a separate PTA account, keeping accurate records, and arranging for an independent audit of the books. Occasionally, examples are cited of volunteers who succumbed to the temptation to employ PTA funds for personal use.

In an association with thousands of volunteer treasurers, some cases of theft are probably unavoidable. For example, in March 1995, the former secretary/treasurer of the General Beadle Elementary School PTA in Rapid City, South Dakota was sentenced to five years in prison for stealing $9,773 from candy sales. The culprit had used the money to pay personal bills and expenses. In exchange for her guilty plea, her state penitentiary term was suspended; she was instead placed on probation for five years and was ordered to serve six months in the county jail, repay nearly $10,000, and write an apology to the victims. The theft left the school with an unpaid candy bill, as well as a $4,000 shortfall in funds for PTA programs for the students. When the candy company demanded its money, the PTA stepped up its fundraising efforts with donated products and services. In a serendipitous turn of fate, the publicity generated by the embezzlement case resulted in an outpouring of community support, and the General Beadle Elementary PTA raised more funds than it owed.[20] However, the ending is not so happy in scores of other instances, as these newspaper headlines indicate: "PTA Treasurer Pleads Guilty to Stealing"; "Records in Vancouver PTA Theft Seized in Raid"; "Probe Delays PTA Treasurer's Sentencing"; "PTA Members 'Crushed' by Theft Case"; "Frisco Police Say Leader Took at Least $10,000"; "PTA Sues, Hoping to Recover Lost Funds"; "PTA President Accused of Arson to Cover Theft."[21]

If parents are busy fundraising, they are less likely to raise tough questions about their children's education. How can students receive As and Bs and not be able to read? How do the provisions of the teacher union contract affect student performance? How can incompetent teachers be removed from their positions in the classroom? Why do school costs continue to skyrocket while no one insists upon accountability? Certainly, most state PTA leaders do not raise these questions, especially if they aspire to become National PTA leaders. Indeed, there is no better place at the National PTA convention to take your mind away from educational issues than the exhibit hall.

Convention programs urge delegates to visit with exhibitors "to discuss your needs," further advising that "exhibitors will be happy to help you determine activities and items for your PTA." The *PTA Handbook* encourages such practices, although it places some constraints on exhibitors:

> PTAs that have exhibitors at conventions or conferences should establish in advance careful procedures for soliciting and accepting exhibitors, particularly those that are commercial; have mutually agreed upon written contracts that include disclaimers of endorsement of the products, programs or services promoted by the exhibitors; limit the number of fund-raising promotions to less than one-half the exhibit space; provide for exhibits of nonprofit groups, educational organizations and federal and state agencies; include displays of educational materials and equipment beneficial to children and youth; and review all materials that will be distributed to ensure that they meet PTA standards and do not violate PTA Objects, policies or positions.[22]

Of the 173 exhibitors at the 2000 National PTA convention, approximately one-fourth identified their exhibits in the program as fundraising products or services. All of them send the same message: Get the best fundraising deal right now—take advantage of the convention specials.

Understandably, the National PTA is the major beneficiary of these exhibits. The exhibitors pay about $1,000 per booth for access to the two thousand delegates and guests at the national convention. Exhibit fees, registration fees, and payments from corporate sponsors of the national convention raised over $564,333 in 1999. Convention fees and corporate sponsorships of convention events are second only to annual membership dues as a source of National PTA income.

Concerned over its image as primarily a fundraising organization rather than an authoritative advocate for children, the National PTA appointed an eight-member Special Marketing Committee in 1994. Chaired by National PTA President Kathryn Whitfill, the committee's charge was to propose what could be done to change the PTA's image from a local fundraising group to the leading national organization working on behalf of children—while increasing membership at the same time. Part of the plan devised by the committee was to publicly discourage fundraising. In speeches, press releases, and public appearances, officers and staff were to emphasize that the National PTA would rather see parents devote more time to advocacy and less to fundraising. PTA officials and staff continue to emphasize that public school funds should come from taxpayers; parents of children in schools should not have to make up any shortfall.

Whitfill and her successor, Joan Dykstra, were members of the Special Marketing Committee, as was Lois Jean White, the 1997–99 National PTA president. Everyone recognized that conventional fundraising practices and habits would continue, but they agreed that fundraising efforts should target social change instead of support for a local school or school district. The three past presidents also supported the PTA's long-standing guidelines for fundraising to enable PTA officers to attend training and legislative conferences.

V. Fundraising Dilemmas

Prior to the 1970s, local school districts raised most of their revenue through local property taxes. Because the amount of taxable property per pupil varied enormously, there was tremendous variation in school revenue per pupil. Property-rich school districts raised more revenue on low tax rates than property-poor districts raised even with much higher tax rates. Inevitably, affluent districts spent much more per pupil than did poor districts. The inequity was the focal point in *San Antonio Independent School District v. Rodriguez,* a 1973 Texas case in which the plaintiffs alleged that large inequities in school funding violated the U.S. Constitution.[23] For better or for worse, the U.S. Supreme Court held that because education was not a fundamental federal right (education is nowhere mentioned in the U.S. Constitution), the remedy for inequitable school financing must be sought in state courts, under state constitutions and laws.

The *Rodriguez* decision led to a large number of equalization cases in state courts. Although plaintiffs seeking substantially equal funding throughout a state were not always successful, they were successful often enough to change the way schools are supported in most states. In some cases, lawsuits were unsuccessful, but the publicity associated with them led to more equitable funding patterns. In many states, the state governments assumed a larger share of the costs of public education in order to overcome the disparities in wealth between school districts. Nevertheless, substantial disparities in per pupil expenditures still exist, within as well as between school districts and states. This is the funding pattern that underlies concerns about equity.

Inasmuch as parents do not have an unlimited amount of time to devote to school affairs, PTA activists frequently face a personal dilemma. Should their time and energies be devoted to activities directly affecting only their own children in their neighborhood school? Or should they be devoted to lobbying for legislation that would, arguably at least, benefit all children?

Setting aside the question of whether "all children" in this context means "all" students in the school, school district, state, or nation, this choice facing parents reflects a genuine conflict between family and social goals. Although PTA-generated funding represents only a supplementary contribution, it can sometimes make a difference in the quality of instruction. For this reason, there is concern that students in poor areas will fall further behind students supported by affluent parents. As a result, several school districts have decided since the mid-1990s that PTA funds may not be used for district operating expenses, such as teacher salaries.

Throughout the country, policies on the issue of how to use PTA-generated funds appropriately vary among school districts. In the fall of 1994, ten days after classes began in Pleasant Hill, California, the school district decided to transfer a popular fifth-grade teacher out of a local elementary school because fewer pupils had enrolled than expected. A group of parents asked the school's PTA to pay the teacher's $33,000 salary and benefits to keep her at the school for the current year. The PTA eventually agreed, after receiving approval from a divided school board. But the decision created animosity among parents, some of whom argued that the PTA should not fund a position that helps only a small group of students. "It really only directly benefits thirty-three children out of 700," said Jessica Beerbaum, the PTA's treasurer and an opponent of the action. "I really feel that it's very inequitable."[24]

Beerbaum asserted that as many as twenty parents quit the PTA over the issue, and many parents remained angry. In contrast, although their practices came under attack in 1999, PTAs at several schools in affluent neighborhoods in Washington, D.C. routinely pay teacher salaries in whole or in part. Consequently, school administrators as well as classroom teachers frequently express concern about the equity issue. When he was superintendent of schools in Montgomery County, Maryland, Paul L. Vance concluded that PTA fundraising exacerbated inequities between schools in rich and poor neighborhoods. In 1991, the Montgomery County school board banned PTAs from paying for classroom instruction during regular school hours. This decision came after parents in East Silver Spring offered to hire a teacher for a special computer, mathematics, and science program. Vance commented that "[g]iven the disparity that exists between the economic capabilities of the differing communities in this county, I strongly support the policy decision."[25] Yet a policy that prohibits any school from a benefit until all schools can enjoy the benefit is difficult to defend.

The dilemma is this: If local PTAs are prevented from raising additional funds just for their children, or their class, or their school, then their liberty is curtailed; if they are allowed to raise funds for these smaller groups, equality of educational opportunity suffers. Undoubtedly, this conflict between liberty and equality will continue in the courts and legislatures for some time. Meanwhile, state and National PTA leaders lobby for equality in funding, while local PTA parents continue to raise funds to benefit only their own children, or their own school.

Some PTA leaders fear that districts will reduce classroom expenditures if the school board believes that the PTA will come to the rescue. Referring to this possibility, Kathryn Whitfill, a former National PTA president and strong proponent of more lobbying and less fundraising, commented that "[w]e certainly don't need to aggravate that problem";[26] her attitude is widely shared among PTA leaders.

Despite the wishes of PTA leaders, however, any restrictions on PTA fundraising to ensure equity would be difficult to justify for several reasons. Whatever the merits may be of "equity" in the distribution of government funding, they are not applicable to private decisions and private funding. It seems foolish to prohibit parents from spending more for the education of their children through the PTA, while they can spend all they wish on liquor, tobacco, gambling, and pornographic videos, to cite just a few possibilities. The fact that the amount that parents will spend on their children's food or shelter varies is rarely a source of concern. The idea that parents should be able to help their children only by helping all children (assuming that we know how to do this) is a drastic departure from traditional principles of individual liberty. It means that state-mandated equality prohibits private, collective action to improve government services.

The equity dilemma, if we can call it that, is closely related to the PTA's organizational dilemma related to fundraising. On the one hand, National PTA leaders would like members to devote more time to lobbying on behalf of all children, less to fundraising on behalf of children in their neighborhood school. As we have seen, however, the local PTAs depend on fundraising for most of their revenue.

Here again, the context may help to clarify the dilemma. An argument for "equalization" in school finance is invariably an argument to increase expenditures for students receiving less than an average share. Nobody advocates that we achieve "equalization" by reducing expenditures for pupils receiving more than an average share.

Education is unusual in the emphasis that is placed on "equality" by those in the education establishment. With the possible exception of health care, we do not encounter arguments for equality in other services (transportation, housing, safety) as frequently as we do in education. We do encounter arguments for achieving *adequacy* with respect to other services, but it is rare indeed to encounter an argument that they should be "equalized."

The explanation for the discrepancy is simple enough. In other services, no group of producers stands to benefit very much from the appeal to equality. Even if equality of nutritional opportunity were somehow a viable ideal, no particular food producer would benefit enough to justify the cost of an all-out effort to achieve it. Not so in public education, where the entire education establishment benefits from the increased expenditures resulting from equalization.

Prior to the equalization movement, local property taxes accounted for more than half of school revenue. As support for equalization of expenditures per pupil increased, the solution was to shift some of the property tax revenue from affluent districts to poor districts. The anticipated benefits of such a shift for the poor districts are often offset by costs in the form of increased resistance in the affluent districts to higher taxes. Naturally, the fact that the benefits often do not outweigh the costs is a disincentive to raising property taxes for public education.

To be sure, PTA leaders themselves are not usually members of the lower socioeconomic strata whose children would benefit from equalization. PTA leaders' stake in the issue lies in the fact that their leadership positions and their organization are dependent upon adherence to equalization programs. We may wish, as most parents do, that what PTA fundraisers provide for their own children could also be made available to all children. We may want to support legislation that is intended to facilitate this objective. But to discourage assistance to one's own children or the school they attend because such assistance is not available to all children is a dubious strategy. Needless to say, merely pointing this out frequently evokes the charge that the critic favors inequality. Anyone who points out the problems of changing the status quo is usually accused of approving of it, if not supporting it. What ought to be done about the inequities in government spending that are present in American education is a legitimate issue, but discouraging parents from helping their children and their neighbors' children is not the solution. Parents should feel free to help their children, or those in their children's school, without feeling guilty about not wanting to lobby for the PTA's legislative agenda.

The PTA's support for "equity" is really a backdoor way of generating support for whatever services the PTA is trying to expand. The PTA's egalitarian ideology is not encumbered by any doubts about the expansion of government services; whatever the service is, the PTA believes that if some children do not have it, government should provide it. It is small wonder, then, that the PTA's social and welfare agenda is as broad as it is. This broad agenda, and the PTA's efforts to implement it, are the subject of the next chapter.

9

Conflicting Approaches to
Parental Involvement

*It is axiomatic that for education to be a successful enterprise, parents
and teachers have to work together and relations have to be comfort-
able—not marred by distrust, fear, and recrimination.*

*Yet teachers—and parents themselves—are far from being satisfied
with the state of parental involvement in education today. Moreover, discussions on how to improve parental involvement are complicated – even
bedeviled—by conflicting, overlapping, and even confused definitions
about just what it should be.[1]*

— Public Agenda, survey finding, 1999

I. Introduction

Most citizens assume that parental involvement in education is a good thing.
Membership in the PTA is widely regarded as evidence of such involvement.
PTA membership supposedly reflects parents' commitments to work with
teachers in order to enhance the education of their children.

Unfortunately, matters are not so simple. What is regarded by some parents
as parental involvement is often perceived by others as parental meddling, as a
violation of academic freedom, or in some other negative way. For example, in
1994, the National PTA's officers and staff conducted convention workshops

on how to deal with individuals and groups whose activities are contrary to the PTA's positions. In its "Extremism" workshop, PTA leaders identified the Christian Coalition, the Free Congress Foundation, the Family Research Council, Concerned Women for America, the Eagle Forum, Christians for Excellence in Education, the American Family Association, and the Traditional Values Coalition as extremist organizations. Arnold Fege, the PTA's director of government relations, said that these organizations were run by "religious and cultural extremists." He warned the convention delegates that these groups were growing in membership, becoming more organized, and involving themselves in a wider array of educational issues than ever before.

Fege's comments are similar to those frequently made by individuals defending public education from criticism. If anything is clear, however, it is that Fege's objection is to greater involvement in public education by "religious and cultural extremists." His objection illustrates the widespread tendency to apply the phrase "parental involvement" only to the kinds of involvement that the person applying the phrase deems desirable. This tendency underlies most of the literature on parental involvement.

In any case, characterizing unwanted parental involvement as "right wing extremism" confuses the real issue, which is how to distinguish between appropriate and inappropriate parental involvement. Is objecting to instructional materials parental involvement? Is challenging teacher union contract provisions deemed detrimental to students parental involvement? "Parental involvement" is not always constructive, but not necessarily because the PTA objects to it. Parents may become involved over racial or religious slurs, student grades, school safety, bus transportation, a student's failure to be on an athletic team, and so on—the list is almost endless, as many publications have pointed out.[2]

Despite its long-time efforts to foster parental involvement, the PTA has never defined or clarified the term, even though it adopted position statements on parental involvement in 1991 and again in 1999. In the absence of a clarifying definition, "parental involvement" is just another confusing buzzword. It must be said, however, that educators generally, not just the PTA, bear some of the responsibility for the confusion.

Building Successful Partnerships: A Guide for Developing Parental and Family Involvement Programs is the National PTA's most detailed statement on parental involvement.[3] The *Guide* includes dozens of suggestions to facilitate parental involvement as the PTA understands the concept. Intended as a blueprint for action, the *Guide* is also intended to serve as an "assessment tool" to evaluate the effectiveness of parental involvement activities.

Some of the recommendations in the *Guide* are sensible ideas that schools and parents have practiced for decades. Others, however, are unrealistic and suggest that the National PTA is out of touch with the realities of school operations. The following examples illustrate this point.

Under "Ideas for PTAs and the School Community Working Together," the *Guide* suggests:

> Making Contact: When and How. Publicize the hours when administrators and teachers are available for parental visits along with any procedures for contacting teachers by telephone or in writing. Send home a teacher directory that lists each teacher's name and provide the phone number of the school and/or each teacher's extension, along with the times they are available for contact.[4]

This proposal is problematic. The contracts between NEA and AFT local affiliates and school boards typically relieve teachers from classroom duties for one class period per day in secondary schools, and a somewhat shorter period in elementary schools. The contracts ordinarily characterize this time away from the classroom as a "preparation period," but there are usually strict restrictions on administrative discretion to require teachers to work during their preparation periods. For example, teachers can be required to cover someone else's class only in case of an "emergency," which does not include telephone calls from concerned parents. Furthermore, another common contract provision is the requirement that the school district pay an additional amount if it preempts a teacher's preparation period by assigning work.

Would teachers voluntarily take calls on an ongoing basis from parents during their preparation periods? Most probably would occasionally, but the vast majority would not take calls on a daily basis if they could avoid it. Teacher collective bargaining contracts demonstrate conclusively that most teachers would not allow their preparation period to be used routinely for discussions with interested parents. There are several reasons for this conclusion.

First, the unions negotiated for the preparation period on the basis that teachers needed a rest to offset the grueling demands of classroom teaching. Teachers' willingness to use their preparation periods for discussions with parents would seriously weaken the argument for preparation periods, especially since discussions with parents can be as difficult as classroom teaching.

Second, NEA and AFT affiliates are in the business of reducing, not increasing, the work that teachers do. Discussions with parents are regarded as work. This is why teachers are paid to confer with parents on school days or evenings set aside for this purpose. In fact, teachers who perform certain duties without compensation are apt to be criticized by teachers who believe that the duties should be compensated.

Finally, there would be substantial differences in the time required of teachers of different grade levels and subjects. A high school teacher may teach 125 pupils every day, an elementary school teacher only 25. If the school districts cannot pay for the time required for telephone conferences with parents, major inequities in the time required of teachers would be inevitable. For the sake of internal harmony, the unions are very reluctant to tolerate these differences.

The foregoing comments do not include all of the problems with the proposed increase in parent access to teachers from the teachers' perspective, but let us consider just one difficulty from the parents' side. The time available to teachers to confer by telephone with parents will depend on the teachers' schedules, a matter over which teachers exercise limited control, if any. Suppose, however, that the teacher is free to take calls from parents from 2:30 to 3:00 in the afternoon on Mondays, Wednesdays, and Fridays. How many parents will be free to call the teacher during these windows of opportunity? And of those who can call during these times, how many will get through to the teacher, and for what period of time? The answers to these questions underscore the naivete about school operations that pervades the *Guide*.

At the risk of belaboring the point, consider the following passages in the *Guide*:

- Plan three parent/teacher conferences — one at the beginning of the school year, one in the middle, and one at the end — to establish mutual expectations and understand family/child strengths, needs, and progress. Educators should schedule home visits when appropriate.[5]

- Hold a Saturday "parents' breakfast" where teachers and school administrators prepare the meal and serve parents. After breakfast, initiate round-table discussions on important parenting issues.[6]

First of all, bear in mind that the work of most public school teachers is regulated by collective bargaining contracts between the teacher union and the school board. In negotiating these contracts, the unions try to limit the teachers' working hours as much as possible. The contracts typically prohibit the school board from requiring teachers to work on weekends, allow teachers to leave shortly after the pupil workday, and strictly limit the number of evening meetings teachers are required to attend. The contracts also limit parental conferences after the regular school day or render all such conferences voluntary on the teacher's part.[7]

In this light, how realistic is the suggestion to "plan three parental conferences" that are apparently not tied directly to discussions of report cards? To put the issue in a favorable light, assume an average of five high school classes per day, and twenty pupils per class. We are now looking at 300 conferences per teacher, per school year of 180 days.

Inasmuch as the *Guide* suggests that teachers use newsletters, telephone calls, web pages, and other means to inform parents about parent/teacher conferences beforehand so that those conferences are productive, some preparatory work before each conference would be necessary. If each conference required thirty minutes for preparation, conferencing, and follow-up, then a teacher with the schedule noted above would have to spend 150 hours implementing the PTA's suggestion. This is twenty-three workdays for most teachers, inasmuch as most work no more than six and a half hours during a regular workday. Obviously, holding the conferences during the teacher workday would severely disrupt the educational program. Furthermore, many parents would not be able to accommodate such a schedule because they work outside the home, have more than one child in school, or must travel long distances between work and the school. In short, the PTA's "practical" idea is clearly impractical, whether or not the school boards are willing to absorb the costs involved. Most teachers would not devote this much time to parental conferences after their regular workday was complete unless they were paid for doing so. If the conferences were held during the school day, the disruption of regular classes and the costs of substitute teachers — if substitute teachers were available — would be prohibitive.

The "Saturday breakfast" is another dubious suggestion. Finding teachers who would volunteer to serve (and pay for?) a Saturday breakfast for parents could require quite a search, especially if the parents had expressed any criticisms of the teachers beforehand. I do not doubt that somewhere, sometime, teachers and school staff have sponsored such breakfasts, but it is a highly impractical suggestion for teachers who might commute long distances to school, are employed or attend graduate courses on Saturdays, or would prefer to avoid rather than meet with parents on a weekend. Businesses and professionals often host events of this sort for their clients, but the reason for this is that clients can take their business elsewhere. This is not the case in public education: in most situations, students are assigned to their schools and to their teachers, and the PTA accepts this practice.

II. A Framework for Analyzing Parental Involvement

The confusion over parental involvement results partly from failure to recognize the different contexts in which parental involvement is an issue. Generally speaking, parental involvement arises in three contexts:

- Activities at home involving interaction between parents and children
- Activities at school or the board of education involving parents as volunteers, or as participants in the school or district policy-making process
- Activities outside of the school environment involving parents in political activities

Let us analyze parental involvement in these different settings.

Parental Involvement in the Home

In the *Guide,* the PTA provides recommendations on parental involvement in the home for each stage of child development: infants, toddlers, preschoolers, elementary-school-aged children, middle-school-aged children, and teenagers. While recognizing the importance of all of these stages, the PTA provides specific recommendations for the three stages in which children are normally in school. In these recommendations, the PTA proposes, among other things, that parents of children of elementary-school age "[u]nderstand the importance of peer acceptance to children" and "[p]rovide opportunities for children to practice making choices." When children reach middle-school age, parents are to "[u]nderstand and support children's growing need for independence"; "[t]alk to children about sex, and help them develop healthy and safe relationships"; and "[a]ccept, rather than approve of, children's odd and antagonistic behaviors that may challenge [parental] authority." Finally, once children become teens, the PTA recommends that parents "[a]ccept and help them establish independence and an identity separate from their family and their peers," and "[h]elp them establish their own set of values to guide the many choices and decisions they will face."[8] Although this is only a partial list of the PTA's recommendations, it is suitable for showing the PTA's perspective on appropriate parent-child interaction.

Notwithstanding some overlap, the PTA's recommendations contrast sharply with most other efforts to spell out what parents can do at home to help their children achieve more in school. In 1994, after reviewing and consolidating decades of research on effective parental involvement programs, the U.S. Department of Education published *Strong Families, Strong Schools.*[9] Let us compare the suggestions for effective parental involvement from that publication with the PTA's advice on the subject. *Strong Families, Strong Schools* advises parents to:

- Read [with their children]
- Use TV wisely
- Establish a daily family routine
- Schedule daily homework times
- Monitor out-of-school activities
- Talk with children and teenagers
- Communicate positive behaviors, values, and character traits
- Expect achievement and offer praise[10]

These recommendations have been discussed in countless media programs and commercial and nonprofit publications. There is no reason to believe that these activities would be curtailed if the PTA did not exist. Actually, the PTA's recommendations for parents are remarkable for their lack of specificity. For instance, the *Guide* states that parents of elementary-school-aged children should "[d]evelop a home environment that supports learning."[11] This is obvious—surely more explicit guidance should be expected of the organization that claims to be the leading advocate of parental involvement.

What is even more peculiar about the PTA's recommendations is their dubious psychosocial objectives. The PTA's recommendations are not so much about what parents can do to help their children learn; they are largely a list of psychosocial objectives for children worded as recommendations to parents. Parents who question these recommendations are not to worry: schools should provide "effective and meaningful parent education classes and programs."[12]

The foregoing PTA recommendations, as well as several others, are open to serious challenge on their merits. One can only speculate why the PTA emphasizes the importance of talking to middle school children about sex, but does not mention the need to do so with teenagers. Many parents will challenge the idea that their children need to develop "safe" sexual relationships. Of course, nobody is a proponent of unhealthy or unsafe sexual relationships, but the PTA recommendation implies that "healthy and safe" relationships should be emphasized. In view of the huge numbers of teenage parents who are unable or unwilling to provide a positive environment for their children, the failure to emphasize the procreative and family aspects of sexual relations should be a concern. The message concerning sex is like that concerning skate-boarding: "It's okay, but be careful or you will hurt yourself." Similarly, the recommendation that parents should "accept children's . . . antagonistic behaviors that may challenge the parents' authority" is simply indefensible. Children might experiment with drugs to challenge parental authority, but the idea that parents must "accept" this behavior hardly merits discussion.

Parental Involvement in Schools

The PTA's approach to parental involvement in schools emphasizes the role of parents as volunteers. However, the activities that the PTA suggests exemplify how parents should be used as volunteers give parents little real responsibility. For instance, PTA recommendations for using parents as volunteers suggest that parents can help schools by, among other things, performing various secretarial duties in school offices, assisting in the physical maintenance of school grounds, or serving as bus monitors.[13] Though all of these things may well be useful from the school's point of view, they—and most of the other tasks the PTA proposes as being suitable for parent volunteers—imply that parents should have little, if any, decision-making power when they are involved in school activities. In most of the PTA's proposed volunteer roles, parents are managed from the time they set foot in the schools until they leave. It should be noted here that, as a matter of fact, schools and teachers frequently regard parents as intruders and are not very receptive to parental volunteers. Unions of school district employees, including teachers, sometimes prefer that students go without services rather than have them performed by competent parental volunteers. The union concern is that parental volunteers pose a threat to union jobs.[14]

The PTA's emphasis on the sort of volunteer activities that make teachers' work easier for them illustrates the pervasive NEA domination of the PTA. Most of the activities cited by the PTA are menial tasks with no stake in the educational outcome, and only a few of the activities bear directly on educational matters. It is a list of involvement activities merely for involvement's sake rather than involvement in ways that contribute to student achievement. The basic objection to the PTA's concept of parental involvement in the schools, however, is its complete dependence upon what teachers and school administrators are willing to accept. For example, parents might be deeply concerned about the grading practices in their school. Nevertheless, they would be precluded from conducting their own research on the practice unless the teachers and administrators approved the PTA inquiry. In view of the fact that the school authorities, including the teachers, are the parties who might be embarrassed by such an inquiry, they probably would not allow the PTA to conduct it.

In a 1999 survey of public school parents and teachers, Public Agenda reported that "volunteering in the schools is seen by both parents and teachers as a supplemental role parents can play in their children's education, but not the fundamental one." In fact, 65 percent of the teachers surveyed said they had academically successful students whose parents they had never met.[15]

The preceding comments should not be construed as a criticism of parents who volunteer to perform any of the activities cited above or any other involvement activities. These activities are usually helpful, sometimes invaluable. Furthermore, there is certainly a symbolic value in volunteer efforts, just as there is when highly educated adults lick stamps and seal envelopes in political campaigns; their willingness to do these things sends a message that can be more valuable than the dollar value of their work. More importantly, in the schools, valuable educational opportunities may be lost unless parents are willing to help in some way.

In most schools, only a minority of parents is likely to be interested in challenging a school practice or activity. The fact remains, however, that what a dissident minority does is sometimes of great benefit to everyone in the organization. Unfortunately, the PTA sees no value in any challenges to school authority, and does not treat such challenges, justified or not, as a mode of parental involvement.

There are more effective ways for parents to contribute to their child's success in school than by volunteering at school. Under the direction of Joyce L. Epstein, the Center on School, Family, and Community Partnerships at Johns Hopkins University has conducted extensive research on parental involvement. In a 1991 study by the Center, Epstein and coauthor Susan Dauber show that attitudes and practices of teachers are the most important variables for involving parents effectively.[16] In subsequent findings, Epstein and researcher Henry Becker found that because of their attitudes toward parents, teachers may discourage home-based parental involvement activities.[17] Some literature suggests that activities at home by parents may have the greatest impact on the achievement of students from low-income homes, where parents are generally not as involved as parents with higher incomes.

When at-school activities are reinforced by at-home activities and vice versa, positive results are likely. To test the effects of parents' at-home activities on improving proficiency in mathematics, researchers at the University of Pennsylvania conducted an experimental study of at-risk black students in the fourth and fifth grades. In a tutoring program previously determined to be an effective instructional strategy, tutors and students set team goals as they worked together. When goals were attained, students were rewarded. In addition, a parental involvement component had school personnel communicating with parents who, in turn, celebrated and reinforced the academic achievement of their children. Parents then rewarded their children with activities such as going to movies, shopping, and playing games. Parents adapted the program to their particular situations, including how they would communicate with the school and how they would reward their children's achievements. Parents did not supplement teaching activities, but they did reinforce positive school experiences. Students in the tutorial group enjoyed a statistically significant improvement over the achievement scores of a control group.[18]

Such long-term involvement by teachers beginning in the elementary grades usually has positive effects on students. Students who have succeeded academically in the past will tend to do so in the future. Because parents' expectations for their children's success are positively correlated with student achievement, parents have higher aspirations for children when they have succeeded in the past. Not surprisingly, parents who regularly communicate with the school tend to have higher aspirations for their children's success, but schools must reciprocate with activities that parents can repeatedly reinforce.

Schools can benefit from collaborating with parents, but progress is based upon agreement about educational goals. Parents often agree on instructional matters, but often disagree about the objectives. Most parents identify the acquisition of basic skills and knowledge as the most important objective of schooling. In contrast, the PTA *Guide* often emphasizes social harmony and social skills. Differences such as these help to explain why teachers and administrators are reluctant to encourage parents to become involved in school governance.

Nonetheless, in the *Leader's Guide to Parental and Family Involvement,* the National PTA suggests that "[y]our PTA *can* make a significant difference in the lives of children."[19] Accordingly, the PTA urges its members to serve on advisory bodies for schools and school districts. These bodies may be school- or district-based, hence their titles vary: school improvement council, parental advisory council, site-based council, and local school council are some of the most common titles. Council members may be volunteers, appointed, or elected to serve by their peers. Although some parents volunteer, others cannot afford the loss of time or wages that volunteering requires. Class, race, and language barriers also inhibit some parents from participating.

The size of school councils varies, but the councils often include parents, business leaders, community representatives, classified staff, students, administrators, teachers, and union representatives. Typically, parents are outnumbered in such a group by school district staff. Furthermore, school administrators can ignore the recommendations of the councils or committees, and teachers may resent the councils as intrusive. In its effusive praise for parental involvement and parental participation, the PTA simply does not acknowledge these drawbacks, or the fact that individuals who have a career stake in the schools typically dominate parental members of school councils.

In 1988, the Illinois PTA promoted participation in school councils when it testified at legislative hearings in support of site-based management of the Chicago school system, even though the PTAs had been involved in the school advisory councils which interviewed and recommended candidates for principals since the 1970s.[20] However, by 1987 the business community and others in Chicago were concerned: too many graduates were unemployable, student achievement was declining, and teacher strikes were too frequent. In addition, the system was financially bankrupt, the result of an ineffective city government and its "spoils" system.[21] As a result, in 1988 the Illinois legislature changed the way Chicago's 450,000 students would be governed. Each of Chicago's 542 schools would be governed by a local school council composed of six parents, two community representatives, two teachers, and the principal. The rhetoric of reform asserted that the "local leaders would have the interests of their students at heart, rather than being focused upon maintaining the status quo of the bureaucracy and its stable employment opportunities."[22]

As we might expect, the teachers and the Chicago Teachers Union were concerned about the potential for confrontations with empowered parents. Teachers felt a sense of "powerlessness" and "did not like the council's being composed of parents and community representatives, who, in their view, were least equipped to make crucial decisions."[23] Furthermore, principals were reluctant to give up power, and members of the local school councils were reluctant to assume the power previously unavailable to them. At first, the mandated top-down change did not include either a fiscal plan or support personnel to sustain the actors in the local school councils, but training and support was included in subsequent changes in the system.

To bring further accountability to the school system, Chicago mayor Richard J. Daley took control of the Chicago school system in 1996 by appointing the school board members and the president of the board. As a result, the top layers of the school administration have been consolidated into six administrative regions of about one hundred schools each. The local school council system remained intact.

In 1989, nearly seventeen thousand people entered the contest for the first election for positions on the local school councils. In recent elections, no more than about half of the fifty-seven hundred seats on the Chicago local school councils were contested in the elections held every four years. But in March 2000, when fewer than four thousand candidates filed for the election, Chicago school district officials extended the filing deadline by two weeks. After the Chicago School Leadership Development Cooperative, a group paid by foundations, finished recruiting candidates and publicizing the election, another thirty-two hundred people were in the race.

While the opportunities for parental involvement have increased in the Chicago schools, James Deanes, a former local school council member who currently oversees the councils and other community partnerships for the school district, said that the "councils [still] need more and better training . . . to avoid power struggles or influence by Chicago's many competing school advocacy groups."[24] Neither the Illinois PTA nor its Chicago region PTA office had statistics on how many of its members serve on the local school councils.

The Illinois experience with local school councils illustrates an important point about parental representation on school councils. Quite frequently, the statutes or regulations establishing the school councils mandate "parental representation" on the body. When some authority appoints a parent or two, it is assumed that parents are "represented," even though the other parents in the school or district play no role in the election of the "representatives," and may even oppose their views.

Practically speaking, most parents do not know the other parents in their schools very well, if at all, and the logistics of a parental vote in a large school or school district would be very difficult. Regardless, parental involvement on school councils or advisory bodies often amounts to the involvement of one or two parents who are somehow expected to represent the views and interests of all parents.

Lack of time and lack of real representation are not the only factors that discourage parental involvement on advisory bodies. In 1992, the National PTA conducted a survey of its local presidents asking them what barriers they faced when trying to get parents involved in the PTA or school activities and committees. The respondents revealed that almost one-third of parents "feel they have nothing to contribute."[25]

Parental Involvement in Politics

In the final analysis, the PTA treats political activism as the main mode of parental involvement. At first glance, this is surprising, because PTA publications studiously avoid terms such as "politics," "Democrat," "Republican," "lobbying," and "campaign contributions," to cite just a few. Readers should bear in mind, however, that the PTA is a 501(c)(3) organization and that the political activities of such organizations are ostensibly strictly limited by IRS regulations. To be sure, the PTA is not the only 501(c)(3) that disguises its political activities in various ways, but the fact that other organizations do so is a weak justification for the PTA's doing so.

From 1921 to 1979, the PTA lobbied intensively for a federal department of education, and the establishment of the department in 1979 was characterized by the PTA as a major achievement. In 1978, the PTA opposed a bill to establish a federal tuition tax credit (S.B. 2142) despite the fact that it would suffer huge membership losses as a result of its opposition. For decades the PTA lobbied for federally funded health care, and in 1992 it lobbied for Goals 2000, which expanded health services provided through public schools. In 1993, its lobbying efforts led to the adoption of the aforementioned Goal 8 on parental involvement. In 1998, the PTA's president was also the chairperson of an alliance of public school organizations dedicated to increasing federal funds for education and defeating legislation that would have strengthened parental school choice. The PTA's 1993 role in defeating Proposition 174, a school voucher proposal in California, was another example of PTA political activity at the state level. In 1997, after Senator Carol Moseley-Braun (D–IL) opposed vouchers in a congressional hearing, the Illinois PTA encouraged its nine hundred local leaders to "include an article about vouchers in your newsletter or other communique."[26] In its newsletter, the California PTA reported that during the 1999–2000 legislative session, it had positions on approximately four hundred bills. In 2000, the PTA continued its opposition to state voucher initiatives on the ballots in Michigan and California. Whether at the state or national level, the PTA's governance documents affirm that "state PTAs are subject to National PTA Bylaws and policies."[27] As we have seen, very often those policies call for political activism.

The early years of the new millenium are as good a time as any to reconsider the PTA's approach to parental involvement. Under one title or another, the PTA has been a presence on the American scene since 1897. The 1996 National PTA convention launched the centennial celebration in impressive fashion in Washington, D.C. Government officials and videos praised the PTA's past and present state and federal lobbying efforts before 2,166 delegates and guests. Hillary Clinton lauded the PTA's support of Goals 2000. Donna Shalala, the U.S. secretary of health and human services, thanked the PTA for being a "wonderful partner." Richard Riley, the U.S. secretary of education, saluted the PTA's "tremendous help" in fighting for President Clinton's budget, remarking that "[w]hen the Cabinet meets, you are there." This is perhaps harmless hyperbole, but is symbolic nevertheless.

Despite the failure of Goals 2000 to improve parental involvement, the National

PTA again promoted new federal legislation in February 2000 to encourage and fund parental involvement programs. The proposed legislation, the "Parent Accountability, Recruitment and Education National Training (PARENT) Act," was stalled in Congress as the 106th Congress ended. On March 8, 2001, Congresswoman Lynn C. Woolsey (D–CA), who had sponsored it previously, introduced the PARENT Act of 2001, H.R. 972. As proposed, the funding provisions would be incorporated into the $13 billion Elementary and Secondary Education Act, the omnibus federal law affecting K–12 schools. As envisioned by the PTA, the PARENT Act would allow schools to use federal funds to increase parental involvement, no doubt as outlined in the PTA's guidelines on the subject. As I previously pointed out, the PTA's guidelines treat parents primarily as closely supervised aides who make life easier for teachers.

Another weakness in the PARENT Act is that there is no basis for assuming that it would have any effect upon parental involvement. Presumably, parents are not involved in their children's education for different reasons. To be effective, legislation should address the reasons for this lack of involvement; to propose a remedy without understanding the problem is not likely to improve matters, even if there were agreement that federal legislation could remedy the lack of parental involvement. In any event, there is no such agreement among parents.

Federal programs already in place are also a part of the problem. Critics argue that many of the 760 federal education programs, such as breakfast and lunch programs as well as before-school and after-school programs, already take over parents' responsibilities. The result is that the need for parental involvement is discouraged or diminished. Federal funding that subsidizes child care is another example. In 1997, "[l]ocal, state, and federal governments paid about 40 percent of the total annual estimated expenditures for child care in the United States."[28] Instead of making it easier for parents to take care of their children at home, government-subsidized child care makes it easier for parents to be away from their children. Furthermore, as noted in the previous chapter, survey results suggest that parents would be more likely to become involved in their children's education if PTA meetings dealt with substantive issues, such as teacher evaluation procedures and criteria. Of course, teachers, administrators, and teacher unions are opposed to parental involvement in such issues.

Finally, there is reason to question whether the PARENT Act is really needed. The Elementary and Secondary Education Act already includes provisions that allow funds to be spent to:

- Provide after-school, weekend, or summer school programs
- Train teachers and other staff
- Buy equipment and learning materials
- Support parental involvement activities, including family literacy programs, parental meetings, and training activities

- Provide transportation and child care so that parents can come to school
- Purchase materials that parents can use to work with their children at home, and at parental resource centers

Furthermore, federal programs for low-income children, such as Head Start, have required parental participation since the 1970s. Special education legislation has also required parental involvement in the development of children's individual education programs. However, it is unlikely that the PARENT Act will affect the parental involvement of parents whose children have not been identified for special services any more than did Goals 2000. Nor is the PARENT Act likely to change teachers' and administrators' attitudes toward parental involvement.

Although the PTA characterizes its lobbying efforts as services to children, several of its efforts are substantively dubious and highly divisive among both parents and society generally. Even by its own standards, the PTA's greatest achievement, the addition of Goal 8 to Goals 2000, has not affected parental participation. In the most recent report of the National Goals Panel, forty-four states and the District of Columbia reported no change in parental involvement from 1991–1994; six states reported that parental involvement dropped.[29] This outcome raises the issue of whether lobbying should be the main focus of the PTA. Political advocacy runs a substantial risk of divisiveness and does not appeal to parents who are more interested in helping their children than in implementing the PTA's agenda.

Inasmuch as home schooling is the ultimate in parental involvement, one might expect the PTA to be supportive of it, but this is not the case. Advocating family and freedom, the Home School Legal Defense Association (HSLDA) was established in March 1983. At the time, home schooling was "just a tiny blip on the education radar screen."[30] In fact, many school officials considered home schooling to be illegal, as indeed it was in many states in 1983. By 1998, all states had legalized home education, albeit with regulations that varied widely from state to state. As the 2000–2001 school year began, approximately 1.7 million students were being educated at home and, on average, were scoring above the national average on standardized tests, including college-entrance examinations.[31] In 2000, home-educated students outperformed their counterparts at the Scripps Howard National Spelling Bee and the National Geography Bee, winning first place in each competition.[32] Despite the fact that home-educated students consistently rank higher than public school students in nationally standardized tests, the National PTA has not changed the position it adopted in 1987. The PTA resolution on "Minimum Education Standards for Home Schools," which is still in effect, states:

> Whereas, the National PTA believes that all children should have access to equal educational opportunities; and

Whereas, the National PTA has consistently supported a quality education for all students; and

Whereas, the number of home schools and other non-approved schools has increased significantly in the last five years; and

Whereas, there are no uniform standards that home schools and other non-approved schools must meet, such as hours and days of instruction, curriculum, teacher certification and reporting; now therefore be it

Resolved, that the National PTA encourage state PTAs to urge State Boards of Education and/or state legislatures to require home and other non-approved schools to meet the same minimum educational standards as public schools.[33]

This PTA resolution must be seen as being opposed to home schooling. Most state efforts to regulate home schooling along the lines suggested by the PTA are intended to weaken home schooling. It is interesting that the "Whereas" clauses in the PTA resolution do not cite any negative evidence about home schooling.

III. The National Coalition of Parent Involvement in Education

The PTA is not the only organization interested in parental involvement. On the contrary, there are scores of independent organizations; the PTA is only one member of the National Coalition of Parent Involvement in Education (NCPIE), a coalition of approximately sixty-one "major education associations and advocacy groups" that support public education.[34] Coalition representatives meet monthly at the NEA building to share information, work together on projects, and serve as an advisory group on parental involvement. The meetings frequently include guest speakers who have conducted research on parental involvement, directed a successful program, or recently authored a relevant publication. NCPIE's major activity is an annual information fair that provides each member organization with an opportunity to exhibit its programs and products.

NCPIE works with the Partnership for Family Involvement in Education, an initiative launched by the U.S. Department of Education in September 1994 after Goals 2000 was enacted. The Partnership promotes family-school-community partnerships as a means of improving educational achievement; partners include families, schools, communities, religious organizations, and employers who work together to support high standards. NCPIE is also a member of the Families and Advocates Partnership for Education (FAPE), an entity intended to promote better understanding of legislation on special education, such as the Individuals with Disabilities Education Act (IDEA).

IV. Concluding Observations

Despite the current attention to it, parental involvement is not a new concept in American education. From the time of colonization in the early 1600s through the 1850s, education was primarily a family responsibility and was essentially religious in purpose. The idea that a system of education should be available to the masses — at least for white children — gave rise to the common-school movement that began in the 1830s.[35] Common or public schools supported by taxation grew rapidly as states enacted compulsory education laws; by 1918, all forty-eight states then in the union had done so. Supporters of public education, including the National Congress of Mothers (the forerunner, recall, of the National PTA), argued that public schools were essential for Americanizing immigrants and that private schools did not foster that goal. As state governments passed laws about the subjects to be taught, the length of the school term, the kinds of schoolhouses to be built, and the training requirements for teachers, the American public education system became more and more bureaucratized. As intended, the state solidified its monopoly status in providing education services: parents were increasingly shut out of the educational process as education was taken over by the professionals.

The current push to involve the family in education began in the 1960s, when President Lyndon Johnson's "war on poverty" called for more citizen involvement generally. Programs for low-income individuals, such as Head Start, included parental involvement. Special education legislation required parental involvement in developing a child's individual education program. Throughout the 1980s, more parents demanded involvement in their children's education. In the 1990s, parental dissatisfaction with public education, especially in the inner cities, has been a major factor underlying increased home education and charter schools.

In one way or another, the PTA has been a part of the history of parental involvement for one hundred years. While advocacy has always been a part of its agenda, the PTA's increased emphasis on lobbying at the federal level is a costly diversion to parents whose interests are focused on the achievement of their children and the success of their local school. Changes to help students achieve and schools succeed will happen at the local level, school by school. As long as the PTA accepts the education establishment's concept of parental involvement, its lobbying for federal legislation that would mandate parental involvement is an exercise in futility. Furthermore, there are dozens of other special interest groups that are far more powerful and influential lobbyists for public education than the PTA is. What, then, is the future of the PTA?

10

The Future of the PTA

In case after case where a group that's been important in the past now finds itself losing ground, or at least struggling to maintain its place, investigation shows that the main cause is simply strong competition. The PTA has been getting beat by local entrepreneurs who are more concerned with "hometown" than with Chicago headquarters.[1]

— Everett Carll Ladd, author, 1999

I. Introduction

The preceding chapters suggest that the National PTA is a figurehead organization that does not conduct itself in an open and straightforward manner, either with the public at large or with its members. Most members would be much more involved if the PTA were primarily interested in meeting the needs of members' children in their local schools. Instead, the National PTA devotes its energies to lobbying for welfare and educational legislation, and tries to persuade parents to do so also.

Everyone has heard the advice, "If it isn't broken, don't fix it." Nonetheless, if "it" is broken, "fixing it" may not be the answer. Reforming the PTA to become more responsive to parent needs would require making basic changes in the National PTA, especially its governance structure and its neutrality with regard to collective bargaining issues.

A new organization—or a multitude of new organizations—rather than modifications to the old one may be the solution. There is a third alternative. Perhaps the National PTA is an organization that has outlived its usefulness, and should be left to wither away. Choosing among these options is difficult, but let us consider some factors that will affect the choice.

II. Factors Affecting Reform of the National PTA

To be realistic, any discussion of the future of the PTA must take into account the basic social and demographic factors that will not only directly affect its future, but the future of public education as well. The close ties between the PTA and public schools suggest a difficult future for the PTA. For one thing, birth rates are declining in the socioeconomic classes that historically have provided the PTA with most of its members and leadership. For example, Jewish communities have always been strong supporters of public education, and provide more active PTA supporters, proportionally speaking, than do other ethnic groups. Nonetheless, the low birth rate among Jewish women is leading to steep declines in the number of Jewish children in public schools.[2]

Demographic and Diversity Issues

Furthermore, even if birth rates were relatively stable among groups likely to join the PTA, changes in the labor force indicate that participation in the PTA would nevertheless continue to decline. A 1990 study by the Bureau of the Census found that 55 percent of all new mothers returned to the work force within one year—up from 31 percent in 1976, and from even lower percentages before then.[3]

While membership that includes different socioeconomic groups is desirable, the interests among those groups can be divisive. Consider the following subgroups of parents:

- Upper-middle-class parents in the suburbs
- Single, unmarried mothers in the inner cities with two to three children
- Yuppie parents previously divorced
- Working mothers who regard day care as their highest priority

All of these groups may support the "child welfare" mission of the PTA, but what concrete program can they agree upon? If the issue is higher taxes for public schools, the upper-middle-class parents may be more concerned about the higher taxes than the need for increased school revenue. Parents interested in college admission for their children have little in common with parents of teenage children who can barely read or write. In public schools, parental interest during their childrens' years of schooling tends to focus on a particular school for a limited period of time. There is a shared interest among parents in a particular school, but this shared interest does not ordinarily survive the time after their children leave school. This is not the case with many private schools, especially if they operate under the auspices of an organization, such as the Catholic Church, that has independent ties to the parents. In such cases, the school is part of an organization that the parents supported before their children were in school, and which they will continue to support after their children move on. These sorts of ties are lacking in public schools.

As we have seen, the PTA is and has always been dominated by upper- and middle-class white females. The rising percentages of married mothers who enter the labor market, and therefore have less time and energy for the PTA, is a major demographic negative in the PTA's future. The tremendous increase in pregnancies by unmarried mothers, especially teenagers, is even more problematic. Whether such mothers work or stay at home, it is impossible for the majority of them to participate in local, state, and National PTA affairs. PTA leadership inevitably becomes the prerogative of grandmothers and married mothers who do not work outside the home—a declining proportion of all mothers and grandmothers. Of course, one need not be a single mother to be sensitive to their needs and interests, but it is difficult to see how the PTA can recruit single and working mothers into its membership, let alone its leadership ranks.

The graying of our population will also have a negative effect on public education, and hence on the PTA. As our society ages, young children constitute a declining percentage of the population. Out of the American population of 281,421,906 in April 2001, fewer than 25 percent had school-age children. Americans already spend more to take care of their parents than to take care of their children, and this trend will continue indefinitely.[4] Furthermore, senior citizens are the demographic group least supportive of increased funding for public education. The PTA's efforts to enroll grandparents of school children to join PTAs are not very successful. Grandparents frequently do not live near their grandchildren, and voluntary age segregation is becoming a more prominent feature of American society. An estimated three million grandparents are rearing their grandchildren, but many went through the PTA routine when their children were in school and are not likely to be interested in PTA activities this time around.

The increased diversity of the population poses several problems for the PTA. In addition to age and economic status, race, religion, color, cultural orientation, and lifestyle are some of the most prominent ways in which our society is becoming more diverse. Although praising diversity is de rigeur in the PTA, its lack of ethnic diversity constitutes a major obstacle to the PTA's effectiveness in helping America's neediest children.

The Internet

Perhaps no other development will impact the future of the PTA more than the Internet. Whereas the National PTA brings fundraising businesses together with state affiliates at the annual convention for the purpose of sharing information, that information is now available directly through websites on the Internet. When the National PTA sent a copy of its magazine to state and local leaders, the information in it was intended to be shared with local leaders and used in training sessions. Now, members and nonmembers alike can access the information from the PTA website. Furthermore, thousands of companies, organizations, and government agencies publish information that the PTA provided in the past on such topics such as juvenile justice, HIV/AIDS prevention, and the dangers of teenage smoking. The information and, often, the publications are available on-line twenty-four hours a day. Determining what legislation to support or to oppose was once a complicated, time-consuming process developed by the PTA to keep its most active members in the loop. Now, dozens of websites provide instant access to state legislators, members of Congress, and other elected officials, bypassing the need for the PTA. Parent training and educational opportunities are also available through the Internet. Furthermore, schools are abandoning the monthly-meeting format of PTAs and communicating regularly, even daily, with parents through the Internet.

To be sure, Internet technology could transform the way the National PTA does business. In fact, however, the National PTA shut down the discussion group section of its website and threatened to reduce other technology-related services in 2000. In her on-line letter of explanation for closing the only member-to-member communication available for sharing information in the PTA, President Ginny Markell said that "closing this group was a business decision—not one based on the topics discussed or intended to undermine your abilities to network as members." (Prior to the closing, a number of PTA members had posted comments critical of the National PTA's refusal to provide copies of its annual budget at a time when its board was calling for an increase in dues.) As the PTA reduced expenses in other areas, Markell said that better use could be made of the "10 hours/week of staff time and the dollars allocated to technology."[5] Even if the National PTA did take advantage of technological innovations, however, its governance structure, its policies and programs, and even its organizational structure would impede reform of the organization.

The PTA's Governance Structure

Teacher and teacher union opposition are probably an insuperable obstacle to any fundamental reform of the PTA. The beneficiaries of the status quo are not going to stand by idly in a struggle to convert a docile ally into an independent force with its own agenda. Even if this obstacle did not exist, or were somehow overcome, the PTA's governance structure may also be an insurmountable obstacle to reform. Despite the fact that revised bylaws, intended to change the PTA's governance structure, were adopted by delegates at the PTA's 2001 national convention, it is unlikely that the provisions will significantly change the PTA's operations.[6] As we have seen, the PTA's structure enables a small group at the top to exercise extraordinary power over the organization. For example, the PTA's board of directors even has the power to nullify actions taken by delegates to the national convention. The problem, however, is not simply top-down control. The problem is that the conditions of eligibility for national office render it virtually impossible for supporters of basic change to challenge the entrenched leadership. Even if a cadre of reformers were willing to commit a tremendous amount of time and resources over many years to effectuating change, and were able to somehow overcome the problems of turnover, networking, and having to use their own resources, the outlook for reform from within still would not be very promising.

One might suppose that an organization devoted to promoting policies of one kind or another would foster robust discussions of policy issues, but this is not the case in the PTA. As previously noted, candidates for PTA office run on the basis of their service to the PTA, never on the basis of policy differences. No one knows how the PTA would react to a campaign based on policies instead of popularity in the old-girls network, but such a campaign would be a drastic change from the PTA culture; what the rank-and-file reaction to it would be is anyone's guess. A major problem would be that challengers to the status quo do not have any cost-effective way to send their message to the rank and file. With the exception of its Internet site, most National PTA communications are to state and local leaders, not rank-and-file membership. Inasmuch as national communications are controlled by staff and officers, the chances that opposition forces could use them are slim to zero.

Granted, most critics of the PTA could easily become members and elected delegates to PTA state and national conventions. Anyone who can afford the expenses can probably become a delegate to both. In fact, inasmuch as local affiliates need not be connected to a school, it is possible for PTA critics to establish free-standing PTAs that send delegates to state and national conventions. The problem facing reform-oriented parents is not, however, getting elected as delegates to state and national conventions, but forming and maintaining an effective caucus within the PTA. This problem is compounded by the high turnover among convention delegates: approximately one in three delegates to the national convention is a first-time delegate.

If there is any hope for reform from within, it lies in the possibility of a conflict at the leadership level, such that a leadership faction appeals to the rank and file in order to form a winning coalition. Realistically, however, the president has very limited powers within the PTA. In addition to presiding over meetings and representing the organization at social and political functions, the president appoints the chairman of five of the PTA's seven committees and makes the other committee appointments, subject to approval by the National PTA board of directors. The president has virtually no authority to act unilaterally on policy matters because the board of directors has the sole authority to manage the organization's affairs, except in instances when convention delegates or the executive committee are required to act. In short, the president's influence depends much more on her ability to persuade than upon the powers of the office.

Aspirants for PTA leadership positions or jobs may conclude that the only way to achieve their objectives is to conduct a grassroots reform campaign. Reform is not likely to happen this way, but the slight chance that it might is greater than the chance of a grassroots uprising. For reform-minded parents and PTA members, this is a grim diagnosis, but I believe that it is a realistic one.

The PTA's Policy on Collective Bargaining

In collective bargaining, the teacher unions and school management are supposed to protect the interests of parents and pupils, but this is not the way the process actually works. In the real world, the responsibility for protecting parental rights and interests falls on school management. Because the PTA uses a policy of neutrality concerning collective bargaining issues, however, school management lacks the support that it needs to effectively protect parental interests.

What if PTAs abandoned their policy of neutrality in collective bargaining? How could they play a constructive role in the process? One way would be to present the data needed to clarify issues that affect parents. For example, bargaining on teachers' hours of employment raises these issues:

- How much time before and after the regular pupil day should teachers be available to help students or meet with parents?
- For how many evening and/or Saturday meetings should teachers be available to meet the needs of parents who cannot meet during the regular school day?
- Can school management assign teachers on the basis of student needs?

Ideally, PTAs should conduct their own research on such issues. They could find out how many parents do not confer with teachers because of teachers' unavailability and what options would be most helpful to remedy the problem. An active parent organization could find out how well parents understand report cards and how the report cards might be made more informative. On several issues such as these, the PTA might try to be an independent force, subservient to neither the teacher unions nor to school management.

Realistically, it is doubtful that local PTAs could act this way with teacher union members and principals posted at every step of the PTA's governance structure. Parents are usually very reluctant to challenge teachers, especially if teachers can retaliate against the parents' children. Although teacher retaliation may not happen very often, the fear that it might is quite common. In any case, PTAs are not likely to exclude teachers from membership, or even to try to do so.

The PTA's Policy on School Choice

In recent years, public opinion polls consistently show that a majority of parents support school choice in one form or another.[7] A press release by the National Congress of Black Conservatives (NCBC) at the 1998 National Association for the Advancement of Colored People (NAACP) convention asserted that "[b]lack parents overwhelmingly support School Choice in all major surveys and polls, and every private scholarship program in the nation . . . is over enrolled."[8]

Clearly, the PTA's all-out opposition to school choice weakens its claim to represent parental interests. In the first place, the PTA's opposition cannot obscure one overriding fact: providing parents with a choice of schools would empower them as nothing else would or can. In contrast, requiring parents to become involved in establishing charter schools, or in time-consuming, arduous, and expensive political activities that have little prospect of affecting their children's education, is an ineffective strategy. Under a policy of school choice, parents would have the power—or, at least, much more power—to effectuate their educational preferences.

Although the PTA supports public education as a unifying institution, it is actually one of the most divisive. Curriculum issues, teacher tenure, textbook adoptions, student dress codes (or lack thereof), and safety in school create conflicts that are having a negative impact on public education and, consequently, on the PTA. As economist and Nobel Prize winner Milton Friedman (among others) has pointed out, our political system cannot deal effectively with growing conflict over school issues.[9] As special interest groups increasingly demand more attention to their interests in the schools, public education will become even more contentious in the future.[10] This is bound to strengthen the school choice movement despite the education establishment's opposition to it.

The PTA's objections to school choice reveal a basic contradiction. On the one hand, the organization is constantly glorifying the wisdom and concern that parents have for their children. On the other hand, its opposition to school choice is based on the assumption that large numbers of parents will choose schools that are economically exclusive, racially divisive, ideologically antidemocratic—the list of potential evils goes on and on. The PTA's position is that parents must be prevented from making the wrong choices by limiting their options to public schools alone. Just how the parents who would make poor school choices are nevertheless able to make sound choices for all other facets of their children's lives, and to vote constructively for multiple candidates for multiple public offices, is never discussed.

The PTA's Policy on Public Schools

The PTA's title refers to parents and teachers, but its programs and policies are clearly antagonistic toward teachers and parents in private schools, especially denominational schools. In the past, religion was the main factor driving enrollment in private schools. In the 1950s, Catholic schools accounted for about 80 percent of all private school enrollment. In 1950, 10,800 Catholic schools served over three million students; other denominations accounted for an additional 10 percent of total private school enrollment.[11] Enrollment in Catholic schools was made possible by the financial contributions of Catholic religious communities. As membership in these religious communities dwindled sharply over the decades, so has Catholic school enrollment. Today, Catholic school enrollment accounts for only about half of private school enrollments. Furthermore, many parents enroll their children in denominational schools for secular reasons, and do not even observe the religion associated with the school.

PTA opposition to private schooling was a major factor in its membership decline in the late 1970s and 1980s. Parents of children in private schools understandably did not wish to be members of an organization that supported policies contrary to their interests. If (or, more likely, when) school choice comes to pass, however, PTA membership is likely to drop substantially. More parents will enroll their children in private schools of one sort or another, and parent loyalties will be to parent organizations in particular schools, not to a state or national organization such as the PTA.

Home schooling is the ultimate expression of parental involvement, but the PTA only grudgingly tolerates it.[12] In a 1997 book, Michael P. Farris, president of the Home School Legal Defense Association, predicted that "40 percent of all children will receive at least some material portion of their education at home in the next ten to twenty years."[13] Whatever the increase may be, as sophisticated communications technology enables more parents to work at home, and also to utilize educational resources that were formerly limited to schools, home schooling will attract more parents who might otherwise have been active in the PTA.

The PTA's Organizational Status

Although my criticisms of the PTA may seem unduly harsh, many of them are shared by the PTA itself. In the past few years, the PTA has been concerned by the fact that although student enrollments are up, PTA membership is down. These trends are leaving the PTA in an extremely vulnerable financial condition. Eighty percent of its income comes from member dues, and only 20 percent from all other sources. Obviously, continued erosion of its membership base will endanger the PTA's financial stability. As noted previously, the PTA was advised by outside consultants to begin a concerted effort to increase non-dues revenue to 50 percent of total revenue, with half of that amount to come from corporate sponsors.[14]

Potential corporate sponsors, however, raise their own issues when approached by the PTA for support. As reported by PTA leaders, sponsors and foundations will not "invest" in the PTA unless the organization can show that members have made a serious commitment to the PTA. Corporate sponsors also want demographic information about PTA members, but the PTA cannot provide such information. Without member names and demographic data, the PTA cannot attract member benefit programs such as credit cards, travel discounts, and other services that attract major corporate sponsors, such as airlines and carmakers.

To effect the changes suggested by potential corporate sponsors, PTA leaders urged delegates to the PTA's 2000 convention to approve a dues increase—from $1.00 to $2.00. Delegates balked, but approved a $.25 increase. Assuming that the membership remained at 6.5 million, the new rate generated $8,125,000 in annual national dues revenue. It is unlikely, however, that corporate sponsors viewed the $1.25 dues with any less concern than they viewed the $1.00 commitment from PTA members. (Nor will the recent increase of dues to $1.75 encourage sponsors to invest in the PTA.)

The PTA committed most of the year-2000 dues increase to a public relations and marketing campaign, citing a survey of its members indicating that they wanted an "identity awareness campaign" to show that the PTA is "the authority on parent/family involvement."[15] (The concern about the visibility of the National PTA that inspired the campaign was foreshadowed by a Wirthlin Worldwide survey conducted in 1996 for this project.)[16] While "PTA" is a household word, many people are not familiar with its current programs, initiatives, and activities. Indeed, of those who were surveyed by the PTA, "[N]one saw us as the voice for children," a dismayed National PTA President Ginny Markell told convention delegates in 2000.

In an almost complete reversal of its commitment to *all* children and to the gamut of issues concerning all children, Markell announced in 2000 the decision of PTA leaders to focus in the future on three areas only. As it enters the new millenium, the PTA will promote parental involvement, call for a safe environment for children, and vocalize the PTA's support of public education through a "massive" advertising campaign. (The new focus is remarkably similar to the legislative and public relations agenda of the NEA.)

To continue its commitment to advocacy, PTA leaders in 2000 also increased support for legislation identified as PTA priorities and for increased dissemination of information about key PTA issue positions to its grassroots lobbyists. The PTA intends to train its volunteer and staff leaders to use "consistent messages" when speaking on behalf of the association.[17]

What new or different services does the PTA propose to offer its members? The astonishing answer is: "None." In fact, Markell made it clear in her remarks to convention delegates in 2000 that "state PTAs will be the National PTA's primary customer." The National PTA intends to devote more time and effort to train state leaders to speak with authority and effectiveness on PTA issues, including the three areas mentioned above. Whether the National PTA's advertising campaign results in increased public awareness of the organization, generates additional members, or attracts more corporate sponsors, remains to be seen.

Furthermore, the 2000 convention's rejection of a $1.00 dues increase necessitated cutbacks in PTA services and programs. In its deliberations during the preparation of the operating budget for 2001, the National PTA board of directors pointed out that "[r]ising costs of operations . . . make it difficult to maintain the standards of programs and services at the current dues level."[18] Therefore, some services and programs will be reduced or eliminated, and fees for other services will increase. There was no legislative conference in Washington, D.C. in 2001. Training programs may be reduced for regional PTA conferences. The staff time spent on updating the National PTA's website may be reduced. The PTA's technology help-desk and toll-free number may be discontinued. Registration fees for the national convention may be increased, and the number of workshops reduced.

The National PTA dues level and the PTA's inability to generate demographic data continue to weaken the PTA's appeal to potential corporate sponsors. Compared to most membership organizations, it is surprising that the National PTA has not raised its dues to at least $5.00 a year. With such higher dues, even if it lost 20 percent of its members, the organization would be in much better financial condition than it is now. Annual dues in the American Association of Retired Persons are $8.00, yet it still has a membership of about thirty-two million.

Actually, as low as the national and state PTA dues are, perhaps they should be abolished altogether. With a substantial increase in membership, the PTA could sell advertising space in its publications and increase the fees for exhibit space at its conventions; it might also be a more attractive recipient of foundation grants.

Does the dues level serve to insulate the PTA from scrutiny by its members? Would higher dues lead to higher expectations for PTA performance, expectations that PTA leaders prefer to avoid? Undoubtedly, both factors are present. Another advantage of low dues is that competing parent organizations will not be able to offer membership dues lower than the PTA's. In addition, higher dues would likely lead to fewer members and weaken the PTA's claim to represent all parents.

III. Who Is Competing with the PTA?

The PTA is not the only parent game in town; on the contrary, parent organizations thrive or struggle to survive in every region of the country. A brief review of their status will be helpful in assessing the prospects for the PTA.

My estimate is that 90 percent of parents of K–12 children in the United States are not members of the National PTA and its affiliates; of this group, perhaps half are involved in local school organizations. Many parents do not participate in school associations. Although a few parent organizations aspire to become national, and include the word "national" in their title, none has a significant national membership. Like the PTA, these organizations either develop new local and state affiliates or convert existing associations to their network. Realistic estimates indicate that over eighty thousand schools have parent organizations that operate at the local school level without any affiliation with a state or national hierarchy. Such independent parent groups existed even before our nation was founded. Today, although known individually by a variety of names, they are most often referred to as parent-teacher organizations (PTOs). Other organizations, however, have been established for specific purposes, such as supporting or opposing legislation or generating support for new schools. In such cases, the organizations are generally not associated with individual schools.

Parent-Teacher Organizations (PTOs)

Because PTOs are not affiliated with a state and national organization, estimates of their membership are rather speculative. My guess is that they enroll about half of the parents of K–12 students, but the number could be much higher or lower.

Despite many similarities between PTOs and local PTAs, the differences are significant. One difference is that the PTA is legally independent of any governmental agency, such as the school district, while many PTOs are not. Some school districts include the school PTO in the district's liability insurance policy, an acknowledgment that the PTO and its activities are part of the school. The cost and availability of liability insurance is frequently a factor in whether the PTO is independent from the school district. In our litigious society, parents are understandably reluctant to become involved in activities without assurance of some insurance protection. Where state laws permit the practice, some state affiliates of the PTA assist its local affiliates with group liability insurance coverage. This practice is made easier because all PTA local and state affiliates must join the PTA's unified membership structure; PTOs are not subject to any such requirements.

As discussed previously, unified membership also requires that National PTA policies be incorporated by reference in state and local PTA bylaws, a requirement not applicable to PTOs. Therefore, PTOs are usually governed through simple bylaws adopted by parents who attend the meetings, not just those who have paid dues, as is the case in the PTA. In fact, sometimes there are no PTO dues at all. Even if PTOs have a dues structure, all funds generated remain with the local organization, whereas the "average PTA forwards $750 to its state and national leadership in dues alone."[19]

PTOs do not emphasize lobbying, which is why some parents prefer them to complying with the PTA's strong emphasis on supporting (or opposing) state and federal legislative positions endorsed by the organization. The vast majority of the reported 6.5 million members of the PTA consider themselves members of their school group and nothing more, whereas virtually all National Rifle Association (NRA) members or Sierra Club members join to support "the cause." As a special interest organization, the PTA's cause of "advocating for all children" at the state and national levels is a broad agenda that appeals to very few PTA parents. In contrast, PTOs encourage parents to work within the political party structure and through other special interest organizations to engage in state and national political activities. At the local level, however, PTO (and PTA) parents are likely to be involved in issues that affect their school and community.

Although PTOs are not likely to challenge teacher unions or school administrators, they are not subject to the PTA's requirement of neutrality on collective bargaining issues. In general, PTOs function as school support organizations without getting involved in state or national agendas.

In early 1999, Tim Sullivan, a Franklin, Massachusetts entrepreneur, established PTO Today, Inc. to help PTOs help their schools become more effective "communities of caring and learning." Company services include *PTO Today,* a bimonthly publication delivered free of charge to every K–8 parent group in the United States, including PTAs. Individual subscriptions are available as well. Because the publication is intended to help independent parent organizations share ideas, *PTO Today* is posted on-line and includes a variety of features and articles as well as advertisements for fundraising projects. Sullivan makes extensive use of the Internet. He invites parents to log on to the PTO Today website and to join on-line discussions among PTO (and PTA) members who share issues of concern and practical advice to parents and teachers. An on-line archive provides users with easy access to issues previously discussed. In addition, the website features nationwide news items concerning parental involvement and links to other appropriate websites.[20] Given discussions posted on the PTO Today website, inquiries from PTA parents, and even discussions on the PTA website (before the PTA closed those discussions down), it seems that many PTA-affiliated groups remain so only because of group services they receive by virtue of affiliation. If PTO Today can continue to develop services (competitive group liability insurance, for example), the PTA may well see significant attrition.

Other Parent Organizations

In recent years, other organizations designed to help parents have emerged in several states. Some, such as the Kansas-based Parents in Control and the Black Alliance for Education Options, support school choice. Parents in Charge, an organization launched in April 2001 by entrepreneur and philanthropist Theodore J. Forstmann, encourages parents to support a version of school choice that will result in a competitive education industry. To achieve this objective, Parents in Charge will conduct an extensive media campaign to convince the public that parents and students should have the right to choose their schools instead of being required to attend a government-assigned school.[21] The Parents' National Network in California works closely with parent groups throughout the state to keep them advised about pending legislation that weakens traditional family values. In addition to analyzing proposed legislation in California, the group has successfully staged rallies and opposed legislative proposals to liberalize sex education, especially when the proposals have a gay and lesbian orientation. The organization serves as a clearinghouse for parents who seek information on proposed legislation.

Other conservative organizations, including Concerned Women for America, the Eagle Forum, and the Family Research Council, have organizational components that offer advice to parents. Focus on the Family publishes numerous publications for parents and teachers as well as pupils. Through *The Home School Court Report,* the Home School Legal Defense Association keeps its parent-educators informed about legal and legislative matters while at the same time giving them practical advice on matters involving home-school resources.

Some programs provide parents with the skills they need to become more knowledgeable about school and community issues, and thus prepare them to participate more effectively in parent organizations. The Parent Leadership Training Institute (PLTI), founded in Hartford, Connecticut in 1994, conducts an intensive parent training program. The PLTI now operates in several cities in Connecticut as well as in Minnesota and California. The PLTI's curriculum provides twenty-week training sessions, which PLTI describes as "lessons in democracy for parents who otherwise might feel powerless."[22] Parents from large cities are trained to develop such skills as writing letters to editors and participating at public and school meetings. Trainees are also taught how to initiate cooperative projects, such as child care cooperatives, neighborhood crime watches, and school safety patrols. Public and private support is used to fund the training program.

In its literature, PLTI maintains that "parents, across race and class lines, are able to describe the needs of children and the obstacles to address them. Yet, they do not see themselves as capable of effecting change. The majority of parents do not know how to work within the city, school, or state system, nor do they believe they are entitled to do so."[23] The PLTI's training program, then, is intended to empower parents who feel disenfranchised.

Though much less intensive than PLTI, the Parent University program, adopted by a number of school districts, also helps parents understand school and student issues. For example, Parent University in Savannah, Georgia educates parents about the school district's goals by offering weekend classes with motivational speakers and parent testimonials. In classes I observed in February 2000, instructors showed parents how to access the Georgia Department of Education website; there the parents learned about the state's sequence of requirements for students and were given helpful advice about talking to kids about drugs and about setting goals. Furthermore, the program encouraged parental involvement in education by mandating that parents attend their local school's PTO or PTA meetings as a prerequisite for completion of the course. The Parent University concept could have widespread appeal as another way to help parents help their children succeed in and out of school.

These are only a few of the more than two hundred organizations that exist to help parents and schools interact more effectively. Competition among them often provides opportunities for parents to help their children in school.

The United Parents Associations

The model for a parent organization that limits teacher participation exists in New York, where the first state affiliate of the National Congress of Mothers was established in 1897. The United Parents Associations of New York City (UPA) has represented public school parents in New York City since 1921.

In April 1921, Robert Simon, a parent whose child attended the Horace Mann School of Teachers College, Columbia University, chaired a committee to bring public and private school parents into a federation of parent associations. From its inception, the UPA emphasized that it would be an association of, by, and for parents whose children were enrolled in school. Local parent associations joined the UPA, which vowed "to study the educational problems of the school" and to improve the schools in greater New York. Thus, the UPA's mission and membership requirements differed from the noneducational, social welfare concerns of the early PTA. The PTA allowed membership to parents whose children were no longer enrolled in K–12 classes; the UPA did not. In 1932, the UPA required all associations to hold some evening meetings to accommodate the schedules of working parents, especially fathers. In fact, the UPA refused to permit association with any other groups, particularly mothers' clubs, that limited membership to one gender. Through the years, other conflicts of policy between the two groups effectively eliminated any UPA affiliation with the National PTA.[24] Throughout its history as a federation of local-school parent associations, the UPA encountered organizational and financial hardships, but it also worked to revise school policies regarding report cards, to develop a school conflict resolution project, to produce a comprehensive leadership manual, to prepare school safety plans, and to implement a myriad of other projects on behalf of parents in New York City schools.

In 1967, the New York City Board of Education codified the regulations that had previously governed parental involvement in the schools. The board issued the *Blue Book,* an official publication that set forth the rights and responsibilities of all parent associations in the city.[25] With periodic revisions, the *Blue Book* remains the New York City Board of Education's policy statement on parent associations and the schools. Every school is required to have a parent association (PA) that represents all (and only) parents whose children currently attend the school. Payment of dues cannot be a condition for PA membership or the right to run for office in the PA, although contributions to the PA can be solicited. Fundraising activities are restricted to one or two per year, and house-to-house solicitations are strictly forbidden. Only parents can decide if teachers or other school employees will be eligible for membership in a local association. If they were granted eligibility for membership, the group would be known as a P.T.A. (not to be confused with local affiliates of the National PTA). Principals, assistant principals, and supervisors may not be members of a PA or a P.T.A., or intrude in PA or P.T.A. affairs. No school employee can serve as an officer, committee member, or executive board member of a PA or P.T.A. in the school at which he or she is employed. Governance of the PA or P.T.A. is implemented through locally adopted bylaws that comply with the policies set forth in the *Blue Book*. In 1998, the New York City Board of Education updated the *Blue Book* to expand the definition of parents to include grandparents.

The UPA is poorly funded, understaffed, and lacks clout in the citywide system. It operates as a federation of approximately two hundred local PAs and P.T.A.s that includes over two hundred thousand parents in the thirty-two separate school districts in New York City. Thus, in the 1,189 public schools in New York City, about 16 percent of the local parent associations have joined the UPA network as of 2000.

The UPA has always operated as an independent entity with its own agenda, and the *Blue Book* continues to require this independence from teacher unions and administrators. Even so, in 1999, the United Federation of Teachers (UFT) challenged the board of education's prohibition on school employees serving on a local PA. After strong lobbying by the UFT, the New York City Board of Education relented; educators can now serve on PA leadership teams at the schools their children attend, provided they do not work at the same school.

Despite its independence, however, the UPA is not a powerful influence in the New York City schools. Indeed, one wonders how it could be. UPA revenues are miniscule compared to the UFT's budget, which was $79 million in 1999. The UPA lacks full-time staff and other capabilities essential for an influential organization; the UFT has hundreds of full-time staff. The UPA is not an effective counterweight to UFT influence in district affairs; the most that the UPA can hope to do is to raise public awareness of issues that concern parents. And if two hundred thousand parents in New York City cannot establish a credible counterweight to teacher union influence in New York City, there is even less likelihood of establishing such an organization where the demographics and geographical concentration are much less favorable.

Independent National Parent Organizations

What are the prospects for a new national parent organization? Presumably, the organization's raison d'être would be that it would represent parents more democratically and more effectively than the PTA does. To achieve this goal, teachers would have to be barred from membership or restricted in some less drastic way, but as previously noted, it is difficult to see how this could be done. Furthermore, the teacher unions would do everything within their power to prevent the emergence of an independent national parent organization. Since the NEA and the AFT dominate the National PTA, they have every reason to prevent the emergence of a less compliant parent organization.

There is one organization that has national pretensions, but its ineffectiveness is symptomatic of the difficulties facing any potential competitor to the PTA. Founded in 1991, Parents for Public Schools (PPS) is a national organization of grassroots chapters "recruiting families to stay in or come back to public schools."[26] PPS is a nonprofit organization headquartered in Jackson, Mississippi. Its local affiliates are organized on a community basis, not affiliated with individual schools. As of March 2001, PPS had one hundred chapters in fifteen states; those chapters work to "build both strong public schools and healthier, more vital communities."[27] Like the PTA, PPS opposes school vouchers and tax credits, and is careful not to get into controversies with the NEA and the AFT. PPS is not a major organizational threat to the PTA, nor has it avoided the subservience to teacher unions that has undermined the National PTA's claims to independence.

In obvious contrast to the National PTA's approach to increased parent involvement through federal funding and mandates, the National Network of Partnership Schools (NNPS) operates on the basis that successful programs "will not come from Washington; [instead,] parents at the local level must be motivated and activated." In 1995, after many years of conducting research on effective programs featuring school, family, and community partnership, Joyce L. Epstein established the NNPS. This organization focuses on improving schools through research, policy, and practice.

As director of the Center on School, Family, and Community Partnerships at Johns Hopkins University, Epstein developed a framework for involvement that guides the work of the NNPS. Epstein's six types of involvement are parenting, communicating, volunteering, learning at home, decision making, and collaborating with community.

The NNPS emphasizes training for school personnel because leadership changes frequently at the local school level. After training school staff, the NNPS challenges the school to engage parents and involve community members to help the school achieve its goals. It also works with state education agencies and school districts to help them set appropriate goals for school, family, and community partnership. Finally, the NNPS assists school districts in designing appropriate assessment mechanisms to measure progress.

To track the success of parent involvement, the participating schools provide data to Johns Hopkins University for analysis. Distribution of the results and other NNPS news is provided through publications and on the website of the NNPS.[28] As of February 2001, eighteen state departments of education and 142 school districts—with more than 1,415 schools in nine states—were participating in the NNPS. Its programs are in private schools, charter schools, and public schools. In some public schools, the local PTA affiliate participates in NNPS programs, but schools dominated by the NEA and the AFT refuse to cooperate. The NNPS is what the National PTA might have become with professional staff, a clearly defined mission, and a singular focus.

IV. Will the PTA Wither Away?

In 1994, *Education Week,* a weekly newspaper covering K–12 education, conducted a survey of education committees in state legislatures, asking which education organizations were most influential in shaping education policy.[29] The PTA ranked last among the major organizations that lobby on education issues. This result raises hard questions about the time, expense, and attention that the National PTA and its state affiliates devote to lobbying. In view of their ineffectiveness, is it worth the time and trouble to try to remedy their weakness in this respect? The reflexive answer to this question is "Yes, of course," but a more judicious response might be more uncertain.

Consider the answer to this question: What would be different about teaching and learning in American schools if there were no National PTA? I believe that the answer is "Nothing," at least in recent decades. The National PTA was responsible for adding a parent involvement goal to Goals 2000, but there is no evidence that this addition has had any positive effect on schools or, for that matter, on parental involvement. The PTA may have had a marginal influence on other federal legislation, but it is difficult to be certain of this because so many other organizations with more political clout supported the same positions as the PTA did. Of course, local PTAs provide assistance to pupils and schools through fundraising, and some of their activities are very beneficial at the school and district level. Nevertheless, it is difficult to discern any widespread improvement in schools from PTA programs or legislative activities. If there had been no National PTA, Goals 2000 would have been enacted anyway, and produced the same results.

Of course, the impact of the PTA on education is only part of the picture. As the PTA itself emphasizes, it does not focus primarily on formal schooling. It stands to reason, however, that if the National PTA's influence on schooling is marginal at most, its impact in other venues would be even less significant. Again, I wish to emphasize that some state and some local affiliates undertake valuable projects from time-to-time, but the National PTA is not a factor in these projects.

Perhaps the most that can be said about the National PTA is that it plays a legitimizing role to organizations and government officials who accept the premise that the PTA represents the views of millions of parents. When the National PTA adopts a position, the erroneous but widespread assumption is that the organization represents *most* parents. The reason for this is that most citizens apply the term "PTA" to all parent organizations, regardless of whether they are affiliated with the National PTA. Seeing "PTAs" everywhere, people understandably conclude that the National PTA's positions enjoy strong grassroots support. Most parents may be opposed to, indifferent to, or unaware of PTA positions, but to the public, the PTA's endorsement carries disproportionate weight. Smaller parent groups, such as those in denominational organizations that are ignored by the media, may strongly oppose the PTA's policies.

Most parents in the United States take the PTA for granted, but it is an anomaly. In most western democracies, there is no national organization of parents. To be sure, schools hold meetings of parents, especially in the elementary grades, but nowhere in Western Europe outside of Great Britain do we find an organization comparable to the National PTA. This fact does not prove that a national parent organization should not exist in the United States. It does suggest, however, that parents are not a natural basis for a national organization.

Essentially, the PTA is a policy organization that utilizes a school connection to recruit its members, the vast majority of whom are either unaware of or indifferent to its welfare-state agenda. This cozy arrangement is unlikely to continue for much longer. As we have seen, the PTA faces an uncertain future as the self-appointed guardian of children's interests. Rather than dwelling any further on reasons for the PTA's slow demise, let me conclude by speculating on the features that might make for a successful national parent organization. I remain skeptical that such an organization is likely to emerge in the current public school environment, but it might be worth the effort. Such an organization would:

- Help all parents of children in school, not just the parents of pupils in public schools.
- Recognize that parental interests sometimes conflict with the interests of teacher unions and/or school administrators, and be prepared to uphold parental interests in such conflicts.
- Present all sides of controversial issues, leaving it to members to pursue their legislative objectives and lobbying through other organizations.
- Sponsor or support research on issues that affect parents directly. For example, how much useful information is conveyed by report cards? Are parents receiving a realistic assessment of their children's educational progress? How often do parents confer with teachers? How much time do teachers devote to helping pupils exclusive of regular class time? Research on issues such as these would enable parents to play a constructive role at the local level in school district negotiations with teacher unions.
- Recognize that all family structures and lifestyles are not equally conducive to children's welfare, and hold to this position even when facing the organization's need for members and revenue.
- Assist local parent organizations in locating services, train officers, develop communications, use technology efficiently, and plan conferences.

In any event, the PTA is a reality. It would not be the first organization to survive long beyond its utility. Today's PTA is largely a political arm of the teacher unions, a force that did not exist when the PTA was founded at the end of the nineteenth century. Perhaps this shows that the PTA has alertly adjusted to social change, but I believe that this evaluation would be far too generous. What I see instead is an organization that has lost its rationale for existence along with its independence. It can neither stand up to teacher union interests nor fairly represent parental interests in improving their children's local schools. On the most fundamental of its tasks, the National PTA has proven itself irrelevant.

Notes

Introduction

1. Myron Lieberman, Charlene K. Haar, and Leo Troy, *The NEA and AFT: Teacher Unions in Power and Politics* (Rockport, MA: Pro>Active Publications, 1994). This book is out of print, but a much expanded and more up-to-date analysis may be found in Myron Lieberman, *The Teacher Unions* (San Francisco: Encounter Books, 2000).

Chapter 1. About the PTA

1. Ginny Markell, "President's Report" (speech given to delegates at National PTA's annual convention, Chicago, IL, June 26, 2000), available on-line at http://www.pta.org/aconvent/virtconv/00/president.htm.
2. According to the American Society of Association Executives, the top five individual-member organizations in 1998 were the American Automobile Association, the American Association of Retired Persons, the Young Men's Christian Association of the United States, the National Geographic Society, and the National Congress of Parents and Teachers. American Society of Association Executives, "Why Are Associations So Important?" available on-line at http://www.asaenet. org/newsroom/faq2/0,2412,showarticle=yes^articleId=261,00.html.
3. The fall in membership has been precipitous: in 1958 the PTA had over 11 million members, but now has fewer than 6.5 million. See National PTA, *PTA Handbook: 1979–81* (Chicago: National PTA, 1979), 283; and National PTA, "Convention Program" (distributed at the 2000 National PTA convention, Chicago, IL, June 24–26, 2000), 34.

4. National PTA, *PTA Handbook: 1993–95* (Chicago: National PTA, 1993), 5.
5. Ibid.
6. U.S. Department of Education, National Center for Education Statistics, *Projections of Education Statistics to 2010* (Washington, DC: U.S. Department of Education, 2000), 12. The complete text of the *Projections* is available on-line at http://www.nces.ed.gov/pubsearch/pubsinfo.asp?pubid=2000071. In a telephone interview I conducted on March 5, 2001, Debra E. Gerald, one of the coauthors of the *Projections,* stated that the ratio of public schools (including charter schools) to private schools in the 1999–2000 school year was 90,874 to 27,402.
7. According to the U.S. Census Bureau, *Current Population Survey—March 1998 Update,* "Table A. Household and Family Characteristics," available online at http://www.census.gov/population/socdemo/hh-fam/98ppla.txt, there were 34,740,000 families with children younger than 18 living at home in 1998. Absent any data to the contrary, I estimate one PTA membership per family; using Census data, I further estimate that 28,346,500 families had children in kindergarten through twelfth grade. According to the PTA's Auditor's Report for the year ending December 31, 1999, 6,250,000 members paid $1.00 dues to the National PTA (thus, the PTA does not have the 6,500,000 members that it claims). Using these figures, if all of the PTA's paid members were parents, then the PTA would enroll members of about 22 percent of families with school-age children. If we allow for the U.S. Census Bureau's calculation that each family has 1.65 children and assume that each family has a like amount of duplicate PTA memberships, then the PTA has approximately 3,788,000 (6,250,000/1.65) individual members. However, this membership may include teachers and individuals who are not parents of K–12 students. If we assume that each of the 25,000 local PTA affiliates has 30 teacher members and 10 members who are not parents of K–12 children, then the PTA's membership rolls include 750,000 teachers and 250,000 people without K–12 children. This yields a figure of 2,788,000 individual PTA members with a child in grades K–12, representing about only 10 percent (2,788,000/28,346,500) of all families with school-age children at the end of 1999.
8. National Center for Education Statistics, *Digest of Educational Statistics: 1999* (Washington, DC: U.S. Government Printing Office, 2000), 14. The *Digest* is available on-line at http://nces.ed.gov/pubsearch/pubsinfo.asp?pubid=2000031.
9. Providing a broadly similar estimate, Everett Carll Ladd has written that in 1995, only 26,152 of the nation's 112,314 public and private schools (23 percent) had a parent-teacher association affiliated with the National PTA. See Everett Carll Ladd, *The Ladd Report* (New York: Free Press, 1999), 34–35.
    The figure attributed to an internal PTA document appears in item 4 on a page of that document entitled "Demographic Study of PTA Schools." A copy of this document is on file with the author.
10. National PTA, "PTA in the New Millenium" (handout distributed at the 1999 National PTA convention, Portland, OR, June 26–29, 1999), 11.
11. This was confirmed in a focus group conducted by Wirthlin Worldwide (McLean, VA) during its "National Benchmark Survey among Parents of Children in K–12," a national survey on the PTA conducted in 1996 and sponsored as part of the research for this book. Within the assembled group were local PTA members and

individuals who did not belong to the PTA; neither group was aware of the existence of the National PTA.

The National PTA's own statements also support the claim that many individual members of state and local PTAs are unaware of the National PTA. In 2001, in its rationale for proposing another $1.00 annual increase in National PTA dues, part of which was to be spent to improve the PTA's image, the National PTA board of directors stated that "during the last 10 years, National PTA has conducted a variety of research with our state PTA organizations, local members, and non-PTA parents. Our research told us that many of our own members are unaware they're part of a 6.5-million member group with a national voice for children." National PTA, "Proposed Dues Increase to $2.25 (Total) in 2002," available on-line at http://www.pta.org/aconvent/01/dues/how_used.htm.

12. National PTA, "National PTA Fact Sheets, Dues and Membership History" (document dated June 2000), 6.
13. National PTA, "National PTA Bylaws" (1994 version), VII.9.
14. National PTA, "Auditors' Report, Financials for January 1, 1999 through December 31, 1999," published in the program for the 2000 National PTA convention, Chicago, IL, June 24–26, 2000, 33–38.
15. These facts are from PTA data provided confidentially to the author.
16. Victoria Benning, "Fairfax Virginia Debates PTA Flier Rules," *Washington Post,* January 25, 2000, B1; Stephen Dinan and Jabeen Bhatti, "Virginia Schools Warned Against Advocacy," *Washington Times,* January 26, 2000, C1.
17. Governmental Accounting Standards Board, "Summary of Statement No. 14: The Financial Reporting Entity" (issued June 1991), available on-line at http://accounting.rutgers.edu/rawlgasb/pub/index.html.
18. Edward Jay Beckwith (National PTA legal counsel) to James Davis (project manager, Governmental Accounting Standards Board), May 4, 1995, 3.
19. Charlene K. Haar, "'P' Is for Politics, Not Parents: National PTA Looks to Expand Federal Lobbying Efforts," *Organization Trends,* May 2000, 1–7.
20. Patty Yoxall, National PTA director of public relations, quoted in Tim Sullivan, "PTO vs. PTA," *PTO Today,* August/September 2000, 1–7. The article is a discussion of the differences and similarities between nonaffiliated parent groups and those affiliated with the National PTA.
21. National PTA, "Auditors' Report, Financials for January 1, 1999 through December 31, 1999."
22. National PTA, "The 'Why' of Sponsorship" (flyer distributed as part of workshop on corporate sponsorship at the 1998 National PTA convention, Nashville, TN, June 27–30, 1998), 1–3.
23. National PTA, "Corporate Sponsorship, State-Level Membership Focus Group" (handout distributed at the 1998 National PTA convention, Nashville, TN, June 27–30, 1998), 1.
24. Constance L. Hays, "PTA under Fire for Letting Advertiser Use Its Name," *New York Times,* September 1, 1998, A18. Other headlines about the issue included Tamara Henry, "PTA Getting Lectured about Office Depot Deal," *USA Today,* September 2, 1998, A1; and Paul Farhi, "Office Depot–PTA Deal Comes under Attack," *Washington Post,* September 10, 1998, C1.

25. Office Depot representatives at the 1999 National PTA convention in Portland, OR, conversations with author, June 26–29, 1999.

26. Office Depot, "Back to School" flyer (distributed at the 1999 National PTA convention, Portland, OR, June 26–29, 1999).

27. Nancy Schlemmer, report delivered to delegates at the 1999 National PTA convention, Portland, OR, June 26–29, 1999. Schlemmer served at the time as the National PTA's vice president for organizational services and as chairman of the National PTA's convention management committee.

28. Corporate sponsors for the National PTA in 2000 were Office Depot, Dannon Natural Spring Water, Hefty ElegantWare, Archway/Mother's Cookies, Family Education Network, SchoolCash.com, and Betty Crocker/General Mills. See "Sponsorship Update from National PTA," *Our Children*, September 2000, 29.

29. See "National PTA Bylaws Amendments Approved at the 1997 National PTA Convention," *Our Children*, December 1997/January 1998, 28.

30. Ginny Markell, "My Vision for Our Future" (brochure used in Markell's campaign for the presidency of the National PTA, distributed at the 1997 National PTA convention, Kansas City, MO, June 18–21, 1997.

31. National PTA, "National PTA Bylaws" (2000 version), XVI.3.

32. Myron Lieberman, *The Teacher Unions* (San Francisco: Encounter Books, 2000), 32–57.

33. National PTA, *PTA Handbook: 1993–95*, 11.

34. Arizona, California, Colorado, Nevada, New Mexico, and Utah are the states whose congresses are assigned to Region 8; the Pacific Congress, which represents various PTAs in Pacific-region schools serving American dependents (i.e., schools associated with military bases or the Department of Defense), is also included in the region.

35. The address of the National PTA website is http://www.pta.org.

36. National PTA, program distributed at 1998 National PTA Awards Ceremony, Nashville, TN, June 28, 1998, 16.

37. National PTA, *PTA Handbook: 1993–95*, 5.

38. See National PTA, "National PTA 1995–1997 Biannual Report" (National PTA publication available upon request from the National PTA), 17.

39. National Congress of Parents and Teachers, Internal Revenue Service Form 990 — Return of Organization Exempt from Income Tax (1996–97 filing), pt. III, line a: Statement of Program Service Accomplishments.

Chapter 2. The Founding Mothers and Their World

1. Organizers for the first Congress of Mothers sent this invitation to all leading women's clubs and societies in the country, in the "hope of interesting at least fifty women sufficiently to make them come to Washington." National Congress of Parents and Teachers, *Through the Years: From the Scrapbook of Mrs. Mears, The Beloved Originator of Founders Day* (Washington, DC: National Congress of Parents and Teachers, n.d.), 13.

2. Jeanne Madeline Weimann, *The Fair Women* (Chicago: Academy Chicago, 1981), 15.
3. For an analysis of the impact of changes in the countries of origin, see George J. Borjas, *Heaven's Door: Immigration Policy and the American Economy* (Princeton, NJ: Princeton University Press, 1999).
4. Nancy F. Cott, *The Grounding of Modern Feminism* (New Haven, CT: Yale University Press, 1987), 21.
5. Time-Life Books, *This Fabulous Century: Prelude, 1870–1900* (New York: Time-Life Books, 1970), 124.
6. Weimann, *The Fair Women,* 5–6.
7. Cott, *The Grounding of Modern Feminism,* 16–17.
8. Karen J. Blair, *The Clubwoman as Feminist: True Womanhood Redefined, 1868–1914* (New York: Holmes and Meier, 1980), 8.
9. Hester M. Poole, "History of Sorosis," Sorosis papers, Smith College Library, 25, quoted in Blair, *The Clubwoman as Feminist,* 20. For a comprehensive history of Sorosis and the General Federation of Women's Clubs, see Mary Jean Houde, *Reaching Out: A Story of the General Federation of Women's Clubs* (Chicago: Mobium Press, 1989), 483.
10. Theda Skocpol, *Protecting Soldiers and Mothers: The Political Origins of Social Policy in the United States* (Cambridge, MA: Harvard University Press, 1992), 337.
11. Cott, *The Grounding of Modern Feminism,* 20.
12. National Congress of Parents and Teachers, *Golden Jubilee History, 1897–1947* (Chicago: National Congress of Parents and Teachers, 1947), 15–16.
13. Ibid., 29.
14. National Congress of Parents and Teachers, *Through the Years,* 12.
15. Harry Overstreet and Bonaro Overstreet, *Where Children Come First: A Study of the PTA Idea* (Chicago: National Congress of Parents and Teachers, 1949), 44.
16. Ellen M. Henrotin to Phoebe Apperson Hearst, November 2, 1896, Phoebe Apperson Hearst Papers, Bancroft Library, University of California, Berkeley, quoted in Skocpol, *Protecting Soldiers and Mothers,* 645–46 n. 60.
17. Overstreet and Overstreet, *Where Children Come First,* 45.
18. "A Thousand Mothers," *Washington Post,* February 18, 1897, 3.
19. National Education Association, *The National Education Association: A Special Mission* (Washington, DC: National Education Association, 1987), 9.
20. Weimann, *The Fair Women,* 533.
21. "A Thousand Mothers," 3.
22. "Training the Young," *Washington Post,* February 19, 1897, 1.
23. "Mothers' Last Words," *Washington Post,* February 20, 1897, 3.
24. Ibid.
25. Ibid.
26. "A Thousand Mothers," 1.
27. Viviana A. Zelizer, *Pricing the Priceless Child: The Changing Social Value of Children* (New York: Basic Books, 1985), 24.
28. Ibid., 9.
29. Ibid., 28.
30. Rheta Childe Dorr, *What Eight Million Women Want* (1910; reprint, New York: Kraus Reprint, 1971), 327.

Chapter 3. From Mothers Only to Parents and Teachers

1. Mrs. G. H. Robertson, "The State's Duty to Fatherless Children" (address to the National Congress of Mothers, Washington, DC, April 25, 1911), published as an article in *Child-Welfare Magazine,* January 1912, 160.
2. National Congress of Parents and Teachers, *Golden Jubilee History, 1897–1947* (Chicago: National Congress of Parents and Teachers, 1947), 44.
3. Ibid., 36.
4. Ibid., 43.
5. Dorothy Sparks, *Strong Is the Current: History of the Illinois Congress of Parents and Teachers, 1900–1947* (Chicago: Lakeside Press, 1948), 27.
6. Ibid., 36.
7. Ibid., 143.
8. Ibid., 49.
9. National Congress of Parents and Teachers, *Proceedings of the Thirtieth Annual Convention of the National Congress of Parents and Teachers* (Washington, DC: National Congress of Parents and Teachers, 1927), 74.
10. Theda Skocpol, *Protecting Soldiers and Mothers: The Political Origins of Social Policy in the United States* (Cambridge, MA: Harvard University Press, 1992), 426–28.
11. Ibid., 448.
12. Illinois Congress of Mothers, Illinois report in "State News," *Child-Welfare Magazine,* March 1916, 256–57.
13. Elizabeth Hayhurst, "How Pensions for Widows Were Won in Oregon," *Child-Welfare Magazine,* March 1913, 248–49.
14. Skocpol, *Protecting Soldiers and Mothers,* 536.
15. Sparks, *Strong Is the Current,* 46.
16. Linda Gordon, "Putting Children First: Women, Maternalism, and Welfare in the Early Twentieth Century," in Linda K. Kerber, Alice Kessler-Harris, and Kathryn Kish Sklar, eds., *U.S. History as Women's History: New Feminist Essays* (Chapel Hill: University of North Carolina Press, 1995), 66.
17. The text of the enabling act originally appears in U.S. Children's Bureau, *First Annual Report of the Chief of the Children's Bureau to the Secretary of Labor* (Washington, DC: U.S. Government Printing Office, 1914), 2, quoted in Skocpol, *Protecting Soldiers and Mothers,* 481.
18. Lawrence A. Cremin, *American Education: The Metropolitan Experience, 1876–1980* (New York: Harper and Row, 1988), 283.
19. Advertisement in *Child-Welfare Magazine,* February 1920, 165.
20. Linda Gordon, *Pitied But Not Entitled: Single Mothers and the History of Welfare, 1890–1935* (Cambridge, MA: Harvard University Press, 1994), 69, 93.
21. See National PTA, "Parents, Join the Campaign" (handbill announcing the first Summer Round-Up of the Children), in Maryland Congress of Parents and Teachers, *A History of the Maryland Congress of Parents and Teachers, 1915–1965* (Baltimore: Maryland Congress of Parents and Teachers, 1965), 35.
22. National Congress of Parents and Teachers, *Proceedings of the Thirtieth Annual Convention,* 19.

23. Ibid., 3.
24. *Congressional Record,* 67th Cong., 1st sess., 1921, 61, pt. 8:76945–46, quoted in Skocpol, *Protecting Soldiers and Mothers,* 501. Skocpol herself found the quotation in Joseph Benedict Chepaitis, "The First Federal Social Measure: The Sheppard-Towner Maternity and Infancy Act, 1918–1932" (Ph.D. diss., Georgetown University, 1968), 144.
25. In 1946, the Children's Bureau was permanently removed from the U.S. Department of Labor; it is now located within the U.S. Department of Health and Human Services' Administration for Children and Families. With an annual budget of over $4 billion in 2001, the Children's Bureau works with state and local agencies to develop programs that focus on preventing the abuse of children in troubled families.
26. Nancy F. Cott, *The Grounding of Modern Feminism* (New Haven, CT: Yale University Press, 1987), 87.
27. Sparks, *Strong Is the Current,* 102–3.
28. Unpublished letter from past president of Mississippi PTA to Harry Overstreet and Bonaro Overstreet, cited in Harry Overstreet and Bonaro Overstreet, *Where Children Come First: A Study of the PTA Idea* (Chicago: National Congress of Parents and Teachers, 1949), 268–72.
29. Ibid., 271.
30. Maryland Congress of Parents and Teachers, *A History of the Maryland Congress of Parents and Teachers,* 68.

Chapter 4. The PTA's Extensive Agenda

1. Margaretta Willis Reeve, "President's Report," in National Congress of Parents and Teachers, *Proceedings of the Thirtieth Annual Convention of the National Congress of Parents and Teachers* (Washington, DC: National Congress of Parents and Teachers, 1927), 16–17, 30.
2. Maryland Congress of Parents and Teachers, *A History of the Maryland Congress of Parents and Teachers, 1915–1965* (Baltimore: Maryland Congress of Parents and Teachers, 1965), 20–22.
3. National Congress of Parents and Teachers, *Proceedings of the Thirtieth Annual Convention,* 157–64.
4. See Maryland Congress of Parents and Teachers, *A History of the Maryland Congress of Parents and Teachers,* 159.
5. Campaign for Tobacco-Free Kids, "Teen TV Actors Appointed Ambassadors for Anti-Tobacco Crusade" (press release distributed on June 3, 1996).
6. The resolution is National PTA, "Second Hand Tobacco Smoke," in National PTA, *National PTA Resolutions and Positions* (Chicago, IL: National PTA, 1995), XI.2I. The EPA publication quoted in the resolution (and upon which the resolution is based) is Jennifer Jinot and Stephen P. Bayard, eds., *Respiratory Health Effects of Passive Smoking: Lung Cancer and Other Disorders* (Washington, DC: Environmental Protection Agency, 1993).
7. On the research disputing the EPA's findings, see Damaris Christensen, "Child-

hood Smoke Exposure Not Linked to Lung Cancer," *Medical Tribune: Internist and Cardiologist Edition* 39, no. 19 (1998): 25, available on-line at http://www.medscape.com/jobson/MedTrib/interncard/1998/v39.n19/Childhood SmokeExposureNotL.html. See also Joseph Perkins, "Has EPA Been Promoting One Big Secondhand Smoke Screen?" *Ventura County Star,* July 29, 1998; and "Sound Science Up in Smoke," *Washington Times,* July 21, 1998.

8. Children's Partnership, "The Parents' Guide to the Information Superhighway" (pamphlet distributed by Children's Partnership, May 1998), 29.

9. Maryland Congress of Parents and Teachers, *A History of the Maryland Congress of Parents and Teachers,* 10–16.

10. National PTA, "Teaching about Religion in the Public Schools," in National PTA, *National PTA Resolutions and Positions,* XVII.1.

11. National Congress of Parents and Teachers, *Policies and Procedures of the National Congress of Parents and Teachers,* rev. ed. (Chicago: National Congress of Parents and Teachers, 1967), 48.

12. Freedom Forum First Amendment Center, "A Parent's Guide to Religion in the Public Schools" (pamphlet released in 1995), 14.

13. Maryland Congress of Parents and Teachers, *A History of the Maryland Congress of Parents and Teachers,* 10–16.

14. Dorothy Sparks, *Strong Is the Current: History of the Illinois Congress of Parents and Teachers, 1900–1947* (Chicago: Illinois Congress of Parents and Teachers, 1948), 40–42.

15. Quoted in ibid., 41.

16. Ibid., 40–42.

17. Nancy F. Cott, *The Grounding of Modern Feminism* (New Haven, CT: Yale University Press, 1987), 248.

18. Quoted in Sparks, *Strong Is the Current,* 58.

19. Quoted in National Congress of Parents and Teachers, *Proceedings of the Thirty-First Annual Convention of the National Congress of Parents and Teachers* (Chicago: National Congress of Parents and Teachers, 1927), 313.

20. National PTA, "PTA Milestones: 1897–1979," in National PTA, *The National PTA Handbook: 1979–1981* (Chicago: National PTA, 1979), 288.

21. National Congress of Parents and Teachers, "Peacetime Military Training and Postwar International Planning," *National Congress Bulletin,* December 1944, 5, quoted in Harry Overstreet and Bonaro Overstreet, *Where Children Come First: A Study of the PTA Idea* (Chicago: National Congress of Parents and Teachers, 1949), 171.

22. Minetta A. Hastings, "Informal Report of the San Francisco Conference" (distributed by National Congress of Parents and Teachers in 1943), 1, quoted in Overstreet and Overstreet, *Where Children Come First,* 175.

23. Hastings, "Informal Report," 7, quoted in Overstreet and Overstreet, *Where Children Come First,* 176.

24. Hastings, "Informal Report," 7, quoted in Overstreet and Overstreet, *Where Children Come First,* 176–77.

25. Overstreet and Overstreet, *Where Children Come First,* 219.

26. Maggie Black, *The Children and the Nations: The Story of UNICEF* (New York: UNICEF, 1986), 83.

27. In January 2000, the United States Committee for UNICEF changed its name to the United States Fund for UNICEF "to more accurately reflect its fundraising mission," according to its office in Washington, D.C.
28. Lawrence A. Cremin, *American Education: The Metropolitan Experience, 1876–1980* (New York: Harper and Row, 1988), 372.
29. "A Letter in Support of U.S. Ratification of the United Nations Convention on the Rights of the Child," letter from United States Committee for UNICEF to all U.S. Senators, July 10, 1997.

Chapter 5. The PTA, the NEA, and Education

1. Grace Baisinger, "The National PTA: New Power on the Block," *National Elementary Principal,* March 1979, 76.
2. Lawrence A. Cremin, *American Education: The Metropolitan Experience, 1876–1980* (New York: Harper and Row, 1988), 311.
3. Allan M. West, *The National Education Association: The Power Base for Education* (New York: Free Press, 1980), 7.
4. Commission on the Reorganization of Secondary Education of the NEA, *Cardinal Principles of Secondary Education* (Washington, DC: U.S. Bureau of Education, 1918).
5. National Congress of Parents and Teachers, *Proceedings of the Thirty-First Annual Convention of the National Congress of Parents and Teachers* (Washington, DC: National Congress of Parents and Teachers, 1927), 311.
6. Commission on the Reorganization of Secondary Education of the PTA, *Cardinal Principles of Secondary Education,* 35.
7. National Congress of Parents and Teachers, *Proceedings of the Thirtieth Annual Convention of the National Congress of Parents and Teachers* (Washington, DC: National Congress of Parents and Teachers, 1926), 96.
8. Ibid., 113.
9. Ibid., 99.
10. Ibid., 102.
11. National Congress of Parents and Teachers, *The Parent-Teacher Organization* (Chicago: National Congress of Parents and Teachers, 1947), 51.
12. See, for example, the list of accomplishments in G. G. Koenig, "State President Reports—South Dakota," in National Congress of Parents and Teachers, *Proceedings of the Thirtieth Annual Convention,* 293. See also Alabama Branch of the National Congress of Parents and Teachers, *Year Book 1928–1929* (Birmingham, AL: State Board of Education, 1929), 17; Naomi Adams Whitesell and Louise Eleanor Ross Kleinhenz, *The First Fifty Years of the Indiana Congress of Parents and Teachers, Inc.* (Indianapolis, IN: Indiana Congress of Parents and Teachers, 1962), 44, 81, 83–85, 88; Thad Stem, Jr., *PTA Impact: 50 Years in North Carolina, 1919–1969* (Raleigh, NC: North Carolina Congress of Parents and Teachers, 1969), 63, 67; and Dorothy Sparks, *Strong Is the Current: History of the Illinois Congress of Parents and Teachers, 1900–1947* (Chicago: Illinois Congress of Parents and Teachers, 1948), 11, 37–40, 58–59, 131–32, 139, 235–36.

13. Sparks, *Strong Is the Current,* 37.
14. Ibid., 38.
15. Ibid., 136.
16. Ibid., 126.
17. Cremin, *American Education,* 554.
18. West, *The National Education Association,* 29–30.
19. James Bryant Conant, *Shaping Educational Policy* (New York: McGraw-Hill, 1964), 37–38.
20. Joel Spring, "The Evolving Political Structure of American Schooling," in Robert B. Everhart, ed., *The Public School Monopoly: A Critical Analysis of Education and the State in American Society* (Cambridge, MA: Ballinger, 1982), 97.
21. James D. Koerner, *Who Controls American Education? A Guide for Laymen* (Boston: Beacon, 1968), 147–49.
22. Clive S. Thomas, "Understanding Interest Groups in Midwestern Politics," in Ronald J. Hrebenar and Clive S. Thomas, eds., *Interest Group Politics in the Midwestern States* (Ames: Iowa State University Press, 1993), 13–14.
23. For a detailed account of the emergence of teacher bargaining, see Myron Lieberman and Michael H. Moskow, *Collective Negotiations for Teachers* (Chicago: Rand McNally, 1966).
24. Ibid., 35.
25. West, *The National Education Association,* 64.
26. Myron Lieberman, *The Teacher Unions* (New York: Free Press, 1997), 124–46, 170.
27. National PTA, "Teacher Negotiations, Sanctions, and Strikes," in National PTA, *National PTA Resolutions and Positions* (Chicago: National PTA, 1995), IV.3B.
28. See ibid. for the text of the PTA's guidelines. The National PTA Board reaffirmed its position statement on "Teacher Negotiations, Sanctions, and Strikes" in 1987.
29. Rose Marie Scott-Blair, "The Changing PTA: No More Tea & Cookies and—Maybe—No More 'T,'" *Learning Magazine,* January 1978, 68.
30. Ibid., 69.
31. Charlene K. Haar, "The Teachers' Unions," *Crisis in Education,* February 1998, 39–40.
32. Lieberman, *The Teacher Unions,* 225.
33. See National Education Association, *Reports on Implementation of Actions of the 1993 Representative Assembly of the National Education Association* (Washington, DC: National Education Association, 1994), 52.

Chapter 6. The PTA and Contemporary Politics

1. Don Davies, "Are Citizens Being Left Out of Educational Planning: Making Citizen Participation Work," *National Elementary Principal,* March/April 1976, 27.
2. For the full list of PTA resolutions, see National PTA, *National PTA Resolutions and Positions* (Chicago: National PTA, 1995).
3. For the full list of these issue items, see National PTA, "Legislative Program: Leg-

islative Specific Items," in National PTA, *National PTA Resolutions and Positions,* XIX.5–6.

4. Learning First Alliance, press release distributed on September 29, 1997.
5. Don Cameron, "NEA Executive Director Address," *RA Today,* July 7, 1997, 9.
6. National Institute for Labor Relations, "The National Education Association's 'Reality Gap,' According to Nationwide Poll" (research brief based on a national poll conducted by Research 2000 [formerly Mason-Dixon] in August 2000). Among other issues, respondents were asked a series of questions measuring the NEA's favorability among registered voters. At first, 55 percent of voters nationwide had a "very favorable" or "favorable" opinion of the NEA, while 32 percent held an unfavorable view. Of those polled, 56 percent also said they would vote for a legislative candidate endorsed by the NEA, in contrast to just 39 percent who would vote for a "labor union"-endorsed candidate. That about 17 percent of the nation's voters apparently do not realize that the NEA is a teacher union is a reality gap from which the NEA hierarchy still benefits.
7. Kim Moran, remarks made during a workshop session at the Quality Educational Standards in Teaching (QuEST) conference (a biennial conference organized by the American Federation of Teachers and the AFL-CIO), Washington, DC, July 29, 1995.
8. See Peter Brimlow and Leslie Spencer, "Comeuppance," *Forbes,* February 13, 1995, 125.
9. Grace Baisinger, "The National PTA: New Power on the Block," *National Elementary Principal,* March 1979, 77.
10. See Albert Shanker, "Jobs Are at Stake, Massive Action Needed to Stop Tuition Tax Credit Bill," *American Teacher,* April 1978, 3.
11. "Grassroots Lobbying Effort Grows, Coalitions Mushroom from Coast to Coast," *American Teacher,* May 1978, 13, 27.
12. Albert Shanker, "Where We Stand—Tax Credits: The Battle Goes On," *American Teacher,* May 1978, 11.
13. National PTA, *1997–1998 Annual Report* (Chicago: National Congress of Parents and Teachers, 1998), 8.
14. National Congress of Parents and Teachers, *Proceedings of the Thirtieth Annual Convention of the National Congress of Parents and Teachers* (Washington, DC: National Congress of Parents and Teachers, 1927), 112.
15. The website at which it does this is http://www.pta.org/programs/legini.asp.
16. National PTA, "Staff Issue Assignments, March 1996–June 1996" (handout [dated May 1996] distributed at the 1997 National PTA convention, Kansas City, MO, June 18–21, 1997).
17. National PTA, "Opposing Vouchers, Tuition Tax Credits and Deductions as Systems of Education Aid," in National PTA, *National PTA Resolutions and Positions,* XVIII.4.
18. Myron Lieberman, Charlene K. Haar, and Leo Troy, *The NEA and AFT: Teacher Unions in Power and Politics* (Rockport, MA: Pro>Active Publications, 1994), 71–82.
19. Charlene K. Haar, "PTA: It's Not 'Parents Taking Action,' " *Organization Trends,* November 1994, 2.

20. Ibid.
21. California State PTA, "Legislation Policies," in California State PTA, *Guidebook of the California State PTA, 1993–1994* (Los Angeles: California State PTA, 1993), 39.
22. David Harmer, *School Choice: Why We Need It, How We Get It* (Salt Lake City, UT: Northwest Publishing, 1993), 146–48.
23. In November 2000, voters in California again rejected (70.7 percent to 29.3 percent) a voucher proposal; Proposition 38 would have provided at least $4,000 per student for children anywhere in the state to attend private or religious schools. Though the proposal was backed by a $23 million campaign, opponents of Proposition 38 spent more than $30 million to defeat it. Similarly, another voucher proposal, Michigan's Proposal 1, was also defeated in November 2000, by a margin of 69 percent to 31 percent. Jessica Sandham, "Voters Deliver Verdict on Host of State Ballot Questions," *Education Week,* November 8, 2000, 1.
24. The source of these numbers is Center for Education Reform, "CER National Charter School Directory 2000 Now Available," available on-line at http://www.edreform.com/press/ncsd2000.htm.
25. Andrew J. Coulson, *Market Education: The Unknown History* (New Brunswick, NJ: Transaction Publishers, 1999), 17; subsequent chapters include a thorough analysis of school choice as well as other education reform issues.
26. Although the NEA and the AFT view charter schools as a threat to their hard-won job protections, in 1995 the NEA pledged $1.5 million over five years to start five of its own charter schools. The NEA provides support to its charter schools with budgeting, staff training, and public relations. Critics perceived the NEA's decision as a public relations ploy. The NEA claims that the charter project is part of the union's effort to emphasize its education reform efforts. However, the NEA's charter school teachers are not relieved of collective bargaining restrictions, and in keeping with the NEA's other rules, its charter schools are to hire only traditionally certified teachers.

    As of mid-1998, only the CIVA (Character, Integrity, Vision, and the Arts) Charter School in Colorado Springs and the Integrated Day Charter School in Norwich, Connecticut had been newly created. Internal conflicts among members and other problems delayed the opening of the Ixcalli Charter School in San Diego, California. A proposed school in Phoenix, Arizona was abandoned. The 360-student, K–6 Lanikai school in Hawaii converted to charter status in 1996.
27. Donald Lambro, "Clinton Fires Elders as Surgeon General," *Washington Times,* December 10, 1994, A1.
28. National PTA (signed by Catherine A. Belter, vice president for legislative activity) to President Clinton, July 13, 1993.
29. Kathryn Whitfill to PTA board of directors, memorandum in regard to PTA support of Joycelyn Elders for U.S. Surgeon General, dated August 1993.
30. Dixie Surratt (Texas PTA president) to Christine Redding (Texas PTA member), August 9, 1993.
31. Ruth Marcus, "President Clinton Fires Elders," *Washington Post,* December 10, 1994, A1.
32. "Shortened Film Version Available," *NEA Gay/Lesbian Caucus Connection,* March 1998, 7.

33. Bob Chase, comments in "About *It's Elementary*" (advertising brochure in *Women's Educational Media,* n.d.), inside page.
34. Howard Hurwitz, quoted in Ray Kerrison, "Gay Flick Sickens Kids' Minds," *New York Post,* September 21, 1997, 6. Beverly LaHaye, chairman of the Concerned Women for America, characterized *It's Elementary* as "an abomination [that] shows just how low homosexual extremists will stoop to ensnare children." Concerned Women for America, fundraising letter, August 1997.
35. Women's Educational Media, "Women's Educational Media Showcases Powerful New Film on Family Diversity at the White House" (press release sent out December 20, 2000).
36. See Andrea Billups, "Homosexual PTA Awaits Charter from State Group," *Washington Times,* September 5, 1999, C2.
37. National PTA, "Convention Program" (program for the 1994 National PTA convention, Las Vegas, NV, June 12–15, 1994), 20.
38. Competitive Enterprise Institute, "More Than Just Your PTA," *CEI Update,* June 1997, 12.
39. This was a finding of the "National Benchmark Survey among Parents of Children in K–12," which was conducted by Wirthlin Worldwide (McLean, VA) as part of the research for this book. The participants surveyed included PTA members and individuals who did not belong to the PTA. The finding noted in the text can be found on page 17 of the survey.
40. Ginny Markell, comments to Region 8 delegates at the 2000 National PTA convention, Chicago, IL, June 24, 2000.
41. The Parent Accountability, Recruitment, and Education National Training (PARENT) Act, S. 1556, 106th Cong., 1st Sess. (1999), and H.R. 2801, 106th Cong., 1st Sess. (1999).
42. See Charlene K. Haar, "'P' is for Politics, Not Parents: National PTA Looks to Expand Federal Lobbying Efforts," *Organization Trends,* May 2000, 1–3.

Chapter 7. Goals 2000: Historic Victory or Educational Disaster?

1. Stephen Arons, *Short Route to Chaos: Conscience, Community, and the Reconstitution of American Schooling* (Amherst: University of Massachusetts Press, 1997), 140.
2. Louis Harris and Associates, Inc., *Metropolitan Life Survey of the American Teacher, 1987: Strengthening Links between Home and School* (New York: Metropolitan Life Insurance Co., 1987).
3. National PTA, "Parent Involvement: Individual and Organizational Rights and Responsibilities in the Development of Children," in National PTA, *National PTA Resolutions and Positions* (Chicago: National PTA, 1995), IV.2.
4. National PTA, *The PTA Story: A Century of Commitment to Children* (Chicago: National PTA, 1997), 151.
5. U.S. Department of Education, *Community Action Toolkit—Resource Guide* (Washington, DC: U.S. Department of Education, 1994), 9.
6. Kathryn Whitfill (National PTA president), Ja net' Crouse (National PTA Education Commission chair), and Catherine Belter (National PTA vice president for

legislative activity), letter to local PTA presidents and council presidents, May 2, 1994.

7. National PTA, "Goals 2000 Fact Sheet" (distributed to PTA leaders and members after Goals 2000 was signed into law in 1994).

8. Goals 2000: Educate America Act, Pub. L. No. 103–227, 108 Stat. 125 (codified in scattered sections of 20 U.S.C.). According to its prefatory materials, Goals 2000 was an act "[t]o improve learning and teaching by providing a national framework for education reform; to promote the research, consensus building, and systemic changes needed to ensure equitable educational opportunities and high levels of educational achievement for all students; to provide a framework for reauthorization of all Federal education programs; to promote the development and adoption of a voluntary national system of skill standards and certifications; and for other purposes."

9. U.S. Department of Education, *Goals 2000: Educate America Act, Guidance* (Washington, DC: U.S. Department of Education, 1994).

10. Goals 2000: Educate America Act § 1052, 108 Stat. at 275.

11. These goals are found interspersed in id. § 102, 108 Stat. at 130 (codified at 20 U.S.C.S. § 5812 [2001]).

12. Id. § 102(8), 108 Stat. at 133 (codified at 20 U.S.C.S. § 5812(8) [2001]).

13. Id. § 405, 108 Stat. at 189 (codified at 20 U.S.C.S. § 5915 [2001]).

14. Improving America's Schools Act of 1994, Pub. L. No. 103–382, 108 Stat. 3518 (codified in scattered sections of 20 U.S.C.).

15. Goals 2000: Educate America Act § 401(a)(4), 108 Stat. at 187 (codified at 20 U.S.C.S. § 5911(a)(4) [2001]).

16. Title I is the best-known program in ESEA (it was called Chapter I in the original ESEA enacted in 1965). Title I grants are awarded to state education agencies, local education agencies, and Indian tribal schools to improve the educational opportunities of educationally disadvantaged children. Title I services are intended to help students succeed in the regular school program, attain grade-level proficiency, and improve achievement in basic and advanced skills; the services are supposed to supplement, not replace, the regular school services. Title I funds reach 90 percent of the nation's school districts. Note that the Improving America's Schools Act included over thirty other programs aside from Title I.

17. U.S. Department of Education, National Center for Education Statistics, *Parent Involvement in Children's Education: Efforts by Public Elementary Schools* (Washington, DC: National Center for Education Statistics, 1998).

18. *U.S. v. Lopez,* 514 U.S. 549 (1995).

19. Goals 2000: Educate America Act § 306(f)(2), 108 Stat. at 164 (codified at 20 U.S.C.S. § 5886(f)(2) [2001]).

20. Id. § 1018, 108 Stat. at 268–69 (codified at 20 U.S.C.S. § 6064 [2001]).

21. Information packet distributed by Representative Lindsay O. Graham (R–SC) to support his proposed legislation to repeal Goals 2000, September 3, 1996.

22. Robert Holland, *Not With My Child You Don't: A Citizens' Guide to Eradicating OBE and Restoring Education* (Richmond, VA: Chesapeake Capital Services, 1995).

23. U.S. Department of Education, *Goals 2000: A Progress Report* (Washington, DC: U.S. Department of Education, 1995).

24. National PTA, *What's Happening in Washington* (newsletter), May 1996, 2.
25. National Education Goals Panel, *The National Education Goals Report: Building a Nation of Learners, 1999* (Washington, DC: U.S. Department of Education, 1999), 65.
26. Ibid., 67.
27. For an excellent summary of these developments, see James L. Payne, *Overcoming Welfare* (New York: Basic Books, 1998).

Chapter 8. Fundraising: What PTAs Do Best

1. Kathryn Whitfill, "Today's PTA: A National Action Plan (Draft #10) in Regard to the National PTA Marketing Plan," March 3, 1995.
2. National Congress of Parents and Teachers, *Parent-Teacher Manual: A Guidebook for Leaders of Local Congress Units* (Washington, DC: National Congress of Parents and Teachers, 1933).
3. National PTA, *PTA Money Matters* (Chicago: National PTA, 1996), 24.
4. Whitfill, "Today's PTA," 5.
5. National Congress of Parents and Teachers, *The Parent-Teacher Organization: Its Origins and Development* (Chicago: National Congress of Parents and Teachers, 1944), 167.
6. Ibid., 102.
7. National PTA, "Fund-Raising," in National PTA, *PTA Money Matters,* 6.
8. Michelle Genz, "The Spaghetti Conspiracy," *Miami Herald,* February 26, 1995, C2.
9. National PTA, "Standards for PTA Fund-Raising," in National PTA, *The National PTA Handbook, 1993–95* (Chicago: National PTA, 1993), 28–29. See also National PTA, "School District Policies," in National PTA, *PTA Money Matters,* 6.
10. See "Fund-Raising Update," *The Owl* (newsletter of the Hearst Elementary School, Washington, DC), February/March 1995, 8.
11. Hearst Elementary School (Washington, DC) PTA, "PTA Membership Form" (distributed to parents of children at the school during the 1997–98 school year).
12. Justin Blum, "PTAs Give Some D.C. Schools an Edge," *Washington Post,* April 17, 2000, B1.
13. "Chief Won't Tamper with PTA Practices," *Northwest (D.C.) Current,* August 2, 2000, 9.
14. Sandra Evans, "Parents Pay Price in School Fund-Raising," *Washington Post,* May 8, 1995, A1.
15. Association of Fund Raisers and Direct Sellers, "How Do More Than 500 Suppliers and Distributors Stay Ahead of the Pack in Product Fund Raising and Direct Selling?" (brochure printed in 1995).
16. See Association of Fund Raisers and Direct Sellers, "Problems and Possibilities in Product Fund Raising: An Open Forum—Executive Summary and Transcript" (report distributed after AFDRS meeting, Orlando, FL, January 7, 1995).
17. Ann Desmond (vice president for communication, California State PTA), letter to author, August 17, 1994.

18. National PTA leaders and staff lobbyists reiterated this point at the 2001 National PTA convention (held June 23–26, 2001 in Baltimore, MD), in workshops such as "Hot Topics in Legislation" and "PTAs to Action: Programs That Work!"

19. Wirthlin Worldwide (McLean, VA), "National Benchmark Survey among Parents of Children in K–12." This survey, conducted in May 1996 as a part of the research for this book, polled both PTA members and non-PTA members.

20. See Hugh O'Gara, "Former Treasurer Accused of Stealing PTA Candy Money," *Rapid City (S.D.) Journal,* January 31, 1995, A1; Erin Andersen, "Donations Pour in for School Fund," *Rapid City Journal,* February 8, 1995, C1; and Hugh O'Gara, "Woman Sentenced in Candy Case," *Rapid City Journal,* March 1, 1995, B1.

21. These headlines were found during an Internet search by the author on September 1, 2000. The same search also turned up reported cases of theft by PTA officials in Crofton, MD; Huntsville, AL; Tempe, AZ; Deltona, FL; and Elyria, OH. Undoubtedly, many thefts are never reported.

22. National PTA, "Basic Policies," in National PTA, *National PTA Handbook, 1993–95,* 7.

23. *San Antonio Independent School District v. Rodriguez,* 411 U.S. 1 (1973).

24. Steve Stecklow, "Parents' Largesse to Schools Splits Communities," *Wall Street Journal,* January 26, 1995, B1.

25. Ibid.

26. Ibid.

Chapter 9. Conflicting Approaches to Parental Involvement

1. Steve Farkas et al., *Playing Their Parts: Parents and Teachers Talk about Parental Involvement in Public Schools* (New York: Public Agenda, 1999), 9.

2. See William J. Bennett, Chester E. Finn, Jr., and John T. E. Cribb, Jr., *The Educated Child: A Parent's Guide from Preschool through Eighth Grade* (New York: Free Press, 1999). Dozens of references to effective parental involvement are included in this 666-page book.

3. National PTA, *Building Successful Partnerships: A Guide for Developing Parental and Family Involvement Programs* (Bloomington, IN: National Educational Service, 2000).

4. Ibid., 37.

5. Ibid., 37–38.

6. Ibid., 61.

7. George W. Liebmann, "The Agreement: How Federal, State and Union Regulations Are Destroying Public Education in Maryland," *Calvert Issue Brief* 2, no. 2 (1998): 11–14.

8. National PTA, *Building Successful Partnerships,* 54–55.

9. U.S. Department of Education, *Strong Families, Strong Schools: A Research Base for Family Involvement in Learning from the U.S. Department of Education* (Washington, DC: U.S. Department of Education, 1994). Other excellent publications include *Phi Delta Kappan* 72, no. 5 (1991): 344–97 (a special issue focusing on parental involvement); *Contemporary Education* 70, no. 3 (1999): 4–43 (issue

on parental involvement); and Melanie R. Scott Stein and Ron J. Thorkildsen, *Parent Involvement in Education: Insights and Applications from the Research* (Bloomington, IN: Phi Delta Kappa International, 1999).

10. This list is taken from a summary of *Strong Families, Strong Schools* that is available on-line at http://eric-web.tc.columbia.edu/families/strong/.

11. National PTA, *Building Successful Partnerships,* 54–55.

12. Ibid., 55.

13. Ibid., 92–93.

14. Charlene K. Haar, *Teacher Unions and Parental Involvement* (Washington, DC: Education Policy Institute, 1999), 12–25.

15. Farkas et al., *Playing Their Parts,* 19.

16. Joyce L. Epstein and Susan L. Dauber, "School Programs and Teacher Practices of Parental Involvement in Inner-City Elementary and Middle Schools," *Elementary School Journal* 91, no. 3 (1991): 289–305.

17. Joyce L. Epstein and Henry J. Becker, "Parent Involvement: A Survey of Teacher Practices," *Elementary School Journal* 83, no. 2 (1982): 86–102.

18. John W. Fantuzzo, Gwendolyn Y. Davis, and Marika D. Ginsburg, "Effects of Parental Involvement in Isolation or in Combination with Peer Tutoring on Student Self-Concept and Mathematics Achievement," *Journal of Educational Psychology* 87, no. 2 (1995): 272–81.

19. National PTA, *A Leader's Guide to Parental and Family Involvement,* rev. ed. (Chicago: National PTA, 1996), 3.

20. See G. Alfred Hess, Jr., and John Q. Easton, "Monitoring the Implementation of Radical Reform: Restructuring the Chicago Public Schools," in Kathryn M. Borman and Nancy P. Greenman, eds., *Changing American Education* (Albany: State University of New York Press, 1994).

21. Andrew J. Coulson, *Market Education: The Unknown History* (New Brunswick, NJ: Transaction Publishers, 1999), 213.

22. Hess and Easton, "Monitoring the Implementation of Radical Reform," 226–27.

23. Ibid., 237.

24. Alan Richard, "Elections for Chicago's School Councils Draw 7,200 Candidates," *Education Week,* March 15, 2000, 10.

25. National PTA, *A Leader's Guide to Parental and Family Involvement* (Chicago: National PTA, 1992), 3.

26. Sharon Voliva (Illinois PTA legislation chairman), "Calls to Action" (flyer sent to PTA leaders in Illinois, n.d.).

27. National PTA, "State PTAs," in National PTA, *National PTA Handbook, 1993–95* (Chicago: National PTA, 1993), 19.

28. Darcy Olsen, *The Advancing Nanny State: Why the Government Should Stay Out of Child Care* (Washington, DC: CATO Institute, 1997), 3.

29. National Education Goals Panel, *The National Education Goals Report* (Washington, DC: U.S. Government Printing Office, 1999), 65–67.

30. Home School Legal Defense Association, *Marking the Milestones* (Purcellville, VA: Home School Legal Defense Association, 1998), 2.

31. Andrea Billups, "Home Schoolers No. 1 on College-Entrance Test," *Washington Times,* August 22, 2000.

32. Andrea Billups, "HSLDA Puts 27 Students in National Spelling Bee," *Washington Times,* May 31, 2000.
33. National PTA, "Minimum Education Standards for Home Schools," in National PTA, *National PTA Resolutions and Positions* (Chicago: National PTA, 1995), VI.7.
34. For a list of the members of the National Coalition of Parent Involvement in Education, see the NCPIE's website at http://www.ncpie.org.
35. Lloyd P. Jorgenson, *The State and the Non-Public School, 1825–1925* (Columbia: University of Missouri Press, 1987).

Chapter 10. The Future of the PTA

1. Everett Carll Ladd, *The Ladd Report* (New York: Free Press, 1999), 52.
2. Charles Krauthammer, "At Last, Zion: Israel and the Fate of the Jews," *Weekly Standard,* May 11, 1998, 23–29.
3. Martin O'Connell, "Maternity Leave Arrangement: 1961–85," in U.S. Census Bureau, *Work and Family Patterns of American Women* (Washington, DC: U.S. Government Printing Office, 1990).
4. See Ken Dychtwald, *Age Power: How the Twenty-First Century Will Be Ruled by the New Old* (New York: Jeremy P. Tarcher/Putnam, 1999).
5. Ginny Markell, "President's Response" (posted to the ChildrenFirst@list.pta.org website, accessed May 9, 2000).
6. The provisions before the 2001 convention included the following changes, many of which were noted in Chapter 1:

- Reducing the prior-service commitment required of a president from ten years to eight years.
- Eliminating the requirement that the past-president serve on the National PTA board of directors.
- Reducing the National PTA's executive committee from ten elected officers to three—the president, the president-elect, and the secretary-treasurer.
- Reducing the size of the National PTA board of directors from eighty-seven members to twenty-six.
- Creating a sixty-six-member National Council of States in lieu of having each state president serve on the National PTA board of directors.
- Revamping the vice-president and committee positions into seven committees, and giving the president more power to appoint committee members based on diversity, PTA knowledge, and professional expertise.
- Removing the uniform bylaw requirements for all levels of the PTA, while still forbidding any state or local affiliates to have bylaws conflicting with those of the National PTA. (Allowing such conflicts could give each state PTA more direct authority over its local affiliates, and give more discretion to National PTA leaders.)
- Granting authority to the National PTA to organize affiliates.

- Eliminating from PTA literature all references to procedures for withdrawing PTA charters, disaffiliating from the PTA, and disassociating state- and local-level PTAs.

7. See Steve Farkas et al., *On Thin Ice: How Advocates and Opponents Could Misread the Public's Views on Vouchers and Charter Schools* (New York: Public Agenda, 1999).

8. National Congress of Black Conservatives, press release distributed at the 1998 NAACP convention in Atlanta, GA, June 30, 1998.

9. See Milton Friedman, *Capitalism and Freedom* (Chicago: University of Chicago Press, 1962); John E. Chubb and Terry M. Moe, *Politics, Markets, and America's Schools* (Washington, DC: Brookings Institution, 1990); and Myron Lieberman, *Public Education: An Autopsy* (Cambridge, MA: Harvard University Press, 1993).

10. Lieberman, *Public Education,* 36–38.

11. Rhonda Goldstein, "Enrollment: Facts and Forecast," *Momentum: Journal of the National Catholic Educational Association* 8, no. 2 (1997): 4.

12. See Isabel Lyman, *Homeschooling: Back to the Future?* (Washington, DC: CATO Institute, 1998); and Charles S. Clark, "Home Schooling," *CQ Researcher* 4, no. 33 (1994): 769–92.

13. Michael Farris, *The Future of Home Schooling: A New Direction for Christian Home Education* (Washington, DC: Regnery, 1997), 81.

14. National PTA, "Corporate Sponsorship" (handout distributed at a workshop held at the 1998 National PTA convention in Nashville, TN, June 27, 1998).

15. National PTA, "What Would We Get for the Extra $1 in Dues?" (fact sheet prepared for the National PTA board of directors and distributed at the 2000 National PTA convention, Chicago, IL, June 24–26, 2000).

16. See Wirthlin Worldwide (McLean, VA), "National Benchmark Survey among Parents of Children in K–12" (survey conducted in May 1996). Furthermore, as noted in Chapter 1, note 11 above, in its rationale for proposing another $1.00 increase in dues at the 2001 National PTA convention, the National PTA board of directors stated that research done by the National PTA itself indicated that "many of [its] own members are unaware they're part of a 6.5 million member group with a national voice for children." National PTA, "Proposed Dues Increase to $2.25 (Total) in 2002: How Will the Additional Money Be Used?" available on-line at http://www.pta.org/aconvent/01/ dues/how_used.htm.

17. National PTA, "What Would We Get for the Extra $1 in Dues?"

18. National PTA, "What If the Proposed Increase Does Not Pass?" (fact sheet prepared for the National PTA board of directors and distributed at the 2000 National PTA convention, Chicago, IL, June 24–26, 2000).

19. Tim Sullivan, "PTO vs. PTA: National PTA Faces Key Decisions as Local Groups Increasingly Turn to PTO," *PTO Today* 2, no. 1 (2000): 4.

20. The website's address is http://www.ptotoday.com.

21. Theodore J. Forstmann, "Make Education Look More Like America: Put Parents in Charge" (speech delivered at the National Press Club, Washington, DC, April 3, 2001).

22. See Robert A. Frahm, "Parents Learn to be Community Activists," *Hartford Courant,* June 29, 1999, B7.
23. Connecticut Commission on Children, Parent Leadership Training Institute materials, 10.
24. See United Parents Associations of New York City, Inc., "60th Anniversary" (commemorative document, n.d.), 8.
25. New York City Board of Education, *Parent Associations and the Schools: The Blue Book* (Brooklyn, NY: New York City Board of Education, 1993), 1–11.
26. Parents for Public Schools, "About PPS," available on-line at http://www.parents4publicschools.com.
27. Ibid.
28. The website's address is http://www.partnershipschools.org.
29. Lonnie Harp, "Who's Minding the Children?" *Education Week,* September 28, 1994, 28–33.

Index

About the Author

Charlene K. Haar is President of the Education Policy Institute, a Washington, D.C.-based policy organization that promotes competition in education. She is also a Research Associate of the Social Philosophy and Policy Center. She has written numerous articles on parent organizations and the teacher unions, and is coauthor of *The NEA and AFT: Teacher Unions in Power and Politics* (with Myron Lieberman and Leo Troy, 1994). In 1992, Haar was South Dakota's Republican candidate for the U.S. Senate.